Global Faulkner
FAULKNER AND YOKNAPATAWPHA
2006

Global Faulkner

FAULKNER AND YOKNAPATAWPHA, 2006

EDITED BY
ANNETTE TREFZER
AND
ANN J. ABADIE

UNIVERSITY PRESS OF MISSISSIPPI
JACKSON

www.upress.state.ms.us

The University Press of Mississippi is a member of the Association of
American University Presses.

First printing 2009

Library of Congress Cataloging-in-Publication Data

Faulkner and Yoknapatawpha Conference (33rd : 2006 : University of Mississippi)
    Global Faulkner : Faulkner and Yoknapatawpha, 2006 / edited by Annette Trefzer
and Ann J. Abadie.
       p. cm.
    Includes bibliographical references and index.
    ISBN 978-1-60473-211-5 (cloth : alk. paper) 1. Faulkner, William, 1897–
1962—Political and social views—Congresses. 2. Literature and globalization—
Congresses. 3. Regionalism in literature—Congresses. 4. Literature, Comparative—
Congresses. 5. Modernism (Literature)—Congresses. I. Trefzer, Annette, 1960–
II. Abadie, Ann J. III. Title.
    PS3511.A86Z489 2006
    813'.52—dc22   2008033338

British Library Cataloging-in-Publication Data available

In Memoriam
William Boozer
February 18, 1927–June 22, 2006

Dorothy Hagert Crosby
September 6, 1908–April 5, 2006

Frances Gregory Patterson
August 11, 1916–October 3, 2006

Contents

Introduction

In our globally interconnected world, William Faulkner's "postage stamp of native soil" can be read as a local landscape in a global network. But what precisely are the effects of such a reading? What are the social, cultural, and literary implications of a global worldview for the study of Faulkner? This volume attempts to initiate a dialogue about the global dimensions in and of Faulkner's work.

Twenty-five years ago, at the 1982 Faulkner and Yoknapatawpha Conference devoted to "International Perspectives," scholars from nine nations gathered in Oxford, Mississippi, to discuss Faulkner's global reception and status in different parts of the world, including South America, particularly Chile; Europe, especially France, Italy, Britain, and Germany; and Asia, specifically China and Japan. They came together to ask "what accounts for Faulkner's appeal to people of every nationality?" And they concluded that "because Faulkner writes about man in history, about eternal questions, or as Faulkner put it, about 'the same griefs grieving on universal bones,' the Mississippi author's voice transcends ephemeral, manmade boundaries and is heard by people all over the world."[1] Faulkner scholars then emphasized the cultural universality of his regional texts that carried their signification across national borders.

A quarter century later, at the 2006 Faulkner and Yoknapatawpha Conference, the discussion of the "Global Faulkner" emerging in the following essays differs significantly from the earlier one in three ways: First, scholars in this present volume seem more cautious of a narrative of human universality to which Faulkner's fame was largely attributed then. The vocabulary of universal humanism has given way to a new critical language inspired by postcolonialism, economic theory, and theoretical approaches to transnationalism and globalization. Second, the question of Faulkner's international reception, translation, and influence remains central. However, scholars in this collection are more interested in exploring this question as a study of mutual influence or confluence, as many take their cue from the Martinican writer and critic Édouard Glissant, who invites us to "abolish the arrow like trajectory of influence" and "enter into the equivalencies of relation."[2] And third, Faulkner's global dimensions reach well beyond the international circulation of his books and his own world travels as a cultural ambassador for the U.S. Studying the global Faulkner means not only linking his texts to those of other authors around the world, but understanding his settings as part of global geographies and excavating the historical deep space of globalization embedded in his texts and contexts. New studies that focus on diasporas, international labor migrations, border crossings, and cultural hybridity have helped critics rewrite regional culture within a global context. Such a global context is helpful for recognizing "the broader meanings of regional and national particulars" and for understanding the global traffic of local cultures.[3] Today, debates about globalization raise both hopes and anxieties. But during Faulkner's time? Was Faulkner aware of global capitalist development? And if so, to what degree was he interested in modernization and its relation to class consciousness, mass production, gender, industrial and cultural modes of exchange and domination? In brief, just how interested was Faulkner in the global scheme of things?

For the first three contributors to this volume, the global Faulkner is a writer aware of changing geopolitical maps of the world, debates about modernity and colonialism, territory and imperialism, regional culture and the role of the state. The post–Cold War period is often seen as a starting point for the current era of globalization. With the disintegration of the three world system—what was during Faulkner's time called the First, Second, and Third World—we now witness the latest incarnation of an era of global capitalism. John T. Matthews's examination of Faulkner begins at this historical threshold to contemporary globalization. Matthews argues that in the twenty-year span between the publication of *The Hamlet* (1940) and *The Mansion* (1959), Faulkner "globalizes Snopesism." He positions *The Mansion* as a Cold War novel that "engages at every level with the defining geopolitical condition of its era." Faulkner, he argues, must have keenly recognized the larger economic and geopolitical connections between the Cold War and Western imperialism, particularly as those were articulated in the U.S. rhetoric of freedom versus the Soviet rhetoric of social justice. This conflict of ideologies between liberal democracy and communism embodied in the struggle between the two superpowers is reflected in *The Mansion*, a novel that expresses Faulkner's longings for "a more authentic freedom, in which liberty and justice need not conflict, where the discrepancy between the idle rich and the imprisoned worker need not end in murderous confrontation." Leigh Anne Duck takes up this concern with global (post)modernity to show that Faulkner was intensely aware of the power and mobility of global capital. Like Matthews, Duck uses a Cold War novel, *Requiem for a Nun* (1951), to examine how Faulkner approaches globalization from a regional perspective and Southern regionalism from a global perspective. Duck reads *Absalom, Absalom!* (1936) back through *Requiem for a Nun* in order to suggest that

"Faulkner's concerns about global capital—so fully bodied forth in the later work—may have shaped his understanding in ways he was not previously ready to name." She takes her reading strategy from Faulkner's own technique of accrescence, a process of layering and sedimenting narratives that allows her to read the contemporary moment in *Absalom, Absalom!*—the 1930s and the U.S. occupation of Haiti—from the vantage point of the 1950s and against the novel's historical past centered on the 1804 Haitian Revolution. In her essay, these moments are shuffled together to "reveal something by way of indirection" about the author's insights into the psychological and economic effects of the global South's plantation culture. Faulkner's view of global South economics is also the topic of Melanie Benson's essay. Benson argues that "in the postplantation South" of *Go Down, Moses* (1942) the ledgers in "The Bear" are no longer "operative mechanisms of a fiscal order, but residues of what their obsolescence signifies: the certainty of hierarchy under slavery, the moral satisfaction of balance, and the allure of profit by engineering surplus value." The ledger entries have a double function: they point to a specifically Southern legacy of slavery, *and* they are associated with Northern industrial interests and modern commercial practice. This double function offers "the chilling recognition that the plantation's priorities carry over into the New South's global economic exchanges including the principles of exclusion, privilege, and contrivance." Together the essays by Matthews, Duck, and Benson examine Faulkner's understanding of the global South's economy and its implication in American imperialism and the history of New World colonialism.

To study the global dimensions of Faulkner's fiction involves a careful rereading of his texts. The global Faulkner, George Handley suggests, calls for a new kind of reader who abandons the regional and national models of literature and instead probes Faulkner's relevance to New World cultures. This kind of reading, he argues, "makes the boundaries of one's community tenuous since the reader is brought out of bounds, beyond the confines of accepted knowledge and into the uncertain terrain of calls and echoes between and among communities, near and far." Handley's essay brings two communities of readers into contact with each other. The translation of the parchments in Gabriel García Márquez's *One Hundred Years of Solitude* functions similarly to Ike's "translation" of the ledgers in "The Bear": these documents are "repositories of the communities' fragmented histories, transgressions, and genealogies—each containing the secret of incest and the implication of the reader in a history of transgressions." For Handley, reading the ledgers or the parchments is neither purely an act of decoding a text nor an act of the imagination, but recognition that all knowledge is produced *between* author and reader, between "revelation" and "translation." The idea of cultural translation and revelation also plays a key role in Keith Cartwright's comparative study of Faulkner and Wole Soyinka. By drawing global South connections between Mississippi and Nigeria, Cartwright maps Yoknapatawpha's local racialized violence in stories like "Red Leaves," "That Evening Sun," and "Delta Autumn" onto a larger transnational grid of ethnic economies shared by Soyinka's Africa. Cartwright analyzes the "carriers" of ritual cleansings (often African American or Native American characters in Faulkner) and the "medicinal models" of healing in the fiction of Faulkner and Soyinka, who move their readers to "cathartic responsibility" by triggering a startling recognition of the reader's own participation in repeating the violence. The cross-cultural comparison of Cartwright's essay testifies to Faulkner's dense and evocative African intertextuality.

Comparative approaches and methodologies to Faulkner model particularly well the idea of reading as transcultural "translation," and they highlight the global polyphony of his fiction. Questions of intertextuality and influence remain central for a study of the global Faulkner, prompting us to ask, how does this Southern writer appear in a global network of texts? And in this global network, what is the status of the "original" versus the "translation"? The question of Faulkner's global reception, so important twenty-five years ago, has shifted to address not only how each culture reads and translates his works, but more so how we can reread Faulkner for the relationship between cultures. Three contributors—Manuel Broncano from Spain, Takako Tanaka from Japan, and Mario Materassi from Italy—present a comparative international approach to reveal "the world's Faulkner." Broncano argues that the kinship between Faulkner and Cervantes is not primarily a question of European "influence" but of dense cultural intertextuality and translatability. He suggests that Spanish readers of Faulkner's time found in his fictional treatment of the American Civil War (1860–64) a way of dealing with their own civil war (1936–39). In that sense, Faulkner was crucial to the readers and writers of Spain. But Spain, too, provided inspiration for Faulkner. Many of Faulkner's works, from *Pylon* (1935) to *The Mansion* (1959), were inspired by *Don Quixote*, a novel he admired and reread on a regular basis. Broncano's essay takes us on a tour of the many surprising connections between Renaissance Spain and the post–Civil War South to show that the characters of La Mancha share a number of social concerns with those of Yoknapatawpha. Like Boncano, Takako Tanaka also begins by mapping "situational similarities" between two cultures. In the context of Tanaka's transpacific comparison, Japan and the U.S. South are two cultures that share the trauma of mod-

ernization and the burden of patriarchy. Tanaka writes that at roughly the
same time as the Southern plantation system collapsed and the South lay
in shambles after the Civil War, the Tokugawa Shogunate, a feudal system
that had governed Japan for more than 250 years, collapsed in 1868. Both
places experienced the trauma of losing their traditional cultures under
the pressures of Western imperial and Northern industrial powers. Like
the South, Japan experienced problems with the exploitation of minority
groups in the name of modern development and with the long lasting effects of patriarchal power. Tanaka reads the stories in *These Thirteen* and
traces Faulkner's influence on contemporary Japanese writers, especially
Kenji Nakagami. Mario Materassi shares Tanaka's interest in Faulkner's
early fiction in an essay that spans a wide arc, both geographically and
chronologically, as he discusses the place of creativity and the artist figure
in *Mosquitoes* (1926). Like Broncano, Materassi foregrounds the European context for a global Faulkner and the long history of transatlantic influences and shared cultural paradigms, including the Pygmalion myth.
Materassi probes Faulkner's use of the myth that presents women as the
objects and creations of men's fantasies.

Globalization is not a homogenous phenomenon in the way it impacts
gender, race, and ethnicity as well as patterns of relating across differences
more generally. Elizabeth Steeby, Jeff Karem, and Tierno Monémembo
move the discussion of the global Faulkner into the context of the Black
Atlantic to explore some of these differences. Steeby, who shares an emphasis on gender with Materassi, reads Charles Bon as a character who expresses not only Faulkner's interest in sexuality but in a specifically queer
imperial desire. Steeby recontextualizes Bon's "ambiguous identity," which
"works toward the dissolution of the very building blocks of empire itself."
She argues that the international political practices that have governed the
U.S. attitude towards Haiti also govern, on a local level, the Supten dynasty's relationship to Bon. In both contexts, the sexually "deviant" expression is displaced onto a racial difference that is then policed by the rule
of whiteness. For Jeff Karem, too, *Absalom, Absalom!* plays a central role
for understanding Faulkner's vision of the Caribbean and Africa. Karem
argues that this vision evades "specific historical knowledge, in favor of
a mythic projection of guilt that is symbolically rich but historically impoverished." By comparing the archival texts of *Absalom, Absalom!* and
the screenplay *The Last Slaver*, published in the same year, Karem traces
Faulkner's depiction of African slavery in the Caribbean in a movement
that "both recalls and obscures" Black Atlantic history. The revision history of Faulkner's Caribbean and African passages in both texts reveals the
author's desire for mythmaking. Faulkner, Karem concludes, "succeeds

in exposing deep legacies of guilt in each text, but he is less successful in recalling anything deeply historical" (13). The volume concludes with a personal essay by Tierno Monémembo, who writes about Faulkner's impact on French West Africa. What was the encounter with Faulkner's fiction like for the writer from the Ivory Coast? Monémembo remembers this encounter in the recently postcolonial Africa of the 1970s. In his essay, he recirculates and rereads Faulkner back though the Caribbean via Édouard Glissant and through France via Maurice Coindreau. He believes that West African writers can identify with the concerns in Faulkner's fiction because "he tackles two primordial questions of the literature of young nations: language and the relationship with history." Monémembo's provocative suggestion that Faulkner's "verbal alchemy" resembles the dilemmas of Africa's postcolonial languages opens new questions for further discussion as it brings to a close this volume on the Global Faulkner.

Annette Trefzer
The University of Mississippi
Oxford, Mississippi

NOTES

1. Doreen Fowler and Ann J. Abadie, eds., *Faulkner: International Perspectives* (Jackson: University Press of Mississippi, 1982), xii.
2. Édouard Glissant, *Poetics of Relation* (Ann Arbor: University of Michigan Press, 2006), 31.
3. James L. Peacock, "The South and Grounded Globalism," in *The American South in a Global World*, ed. Peacock, Harry Watson, and Carrie Matthews (Chapel Hill: University of North Carolina Press, 2005), 269.

Note on the Conference

The Thirty-third Annual Faulkner and Yoknapatawpha Conference sponsored by the University of Mississippi in Oxford took place July 23–27, 2006, with more than two hundred of the author's admirers from around the world in attendance. Eleven presentations at the conference are collected as essays in this volume. Brief mention is made here of other conference activities.

The conference began on Sunday with a reception at the University Museum and two lectures, followed by a buffet supper at the home of Dr. M. B. Howorth Jr. That evening, after a welcome by Andrew K. Howorth, Circuit Judge, Mississippi Third Judicial District, Donald M. Kartiganer, director of the conference, announced winners of the William Faulkner Society Award for conference fellows and introduced Campbell McCool, who presented the Frances Bell McCool Faulkner Dissertation Fellowship to Stephen Monroe. Charles Reagan Wilson, director of the Center for the Study of Southern Culture, presented the twentieth annual Eudora Welty Awards in Creative Writing. Roxann Jackson, of St. Andrew's Episcopal School in Jackson, won first prize, $500, for her poem "The Man in the Moon." Jackson's teacher is Bill Albright. Christi Positan, a student at Clinton High School in Clinton, won second prize, $250, for her short story "What Wondrous Love Is This." The late Frances Patterson of Tupelo, a longtime member of the Center Advisory Committee, established and endowed the awards, which are selected through a competition held in high schools throughout Mississippi. The rarely seen film *Impressions of Japan*, based on Faulkner's 1955 visit and scripted by the author, was shown, after which local actors presented *Voices from Yoknapatawpha*, readings from Faulkner's fiction selected and arranged by actor George Kehoe.

George Handley, John T. Matthews, and Mario Materassi presented lectures on Monday. The day's program also included sessions during which Seth Berner, a book dealer from Portland, Maine, talked about "Collecting Faulkner"; James B. Carothers, Charles A. Peek, Terrell L. Tebbetts, and Theresa M. Towner discussed "Teaching Faulkner"; and Elizabeth Steeby, Jeffrey Stayton, and Bart H. Welling made presentations for the first of three panels featuring short papers selected through an annual call for papers. Registration for panelists was funded in part through an anonymous gift made in honor of Faulkner biographer Joseph Blotner. The day's activities ended with Colby Kullman moderating the sixth Faulkner Fringe Festival, an open-mike evening at Southside Gallery on the Oxford Square.

Guided tours of North Mississippi, the Delta, and Memphis took place on Tuesday, as did an afternoon party at Tyler Place, hosted by Charles Noyes, Sarah and Allie Smith, and Colby Kullman. The day ended with Manuel Broncano's lecture. On Wednesday, after lectures by Takako Tanaka and Leigh Anne Duck and a panel with presentations by Mariko Hiwatashi, Ugo Rubeo, and Jo K. Galle, Elizabeth Nichols Shiver brought together current or former Oxford residents Harter Williams Crutcher, Carl S. Downing, Byron Gathright, and Mildred Murray Douglass Hopkins to reminisce about Faulkner. Attendees then gathered for the annual picnic at Faulkner's home, Rowan Oak. Program events on Thursday were "Teaching Faulkner" panels, Melanie R. Benson's lecture, and presentations by Jeff Karem, Katie Woolsey, and Laura Martin. The conference ended with a party at Off Square Books.

Three exhibitions were available throughout the conference. The Department of Archives and Special Collections at the University's John Davis Williams Library sponsored *Mississippi Matinée: An Exhibition of the State and the Silver Screen*, with cases related to film adaptations from Faulkner, Tennessee Williams, Larry Brown, Willie Morris, and others, as well as films made in or related to Mississippi. Also on display were annotated manuscripts of screenplays and documentaries of bluesmen and women. The University Museum sponsored *Journey of the Spirit*, a fiber quilt exhibition by Gwendolyn Magee of Jackson, Mississippi. *Southern Towns, Southern Cities*, a collection of twenty-three black-and-white photographs by photographer David Wharton, assistant professor of Southern Studies and director of documentary projects at the University of Mississippi, were on exhibit at Barnard Observatory's Gammill Gallery. The University Press of Mississippi exhibited Faulkner books published by university presses throughout the United States.

The conference planners are grateful to all the individuals and organizations that support the Faulkner and Yoknapatawpha Conference annually. In addition to those mentioned above, we wish to thank Square Books, St. Peter's Episcopal Church, Mr. and Mrs. William Lewis and the Downtown Grill, the City of Oxford, and the Oxford Tourism Council. Also, we thank the *Memphis Commercial Appeal* for use of the December 6, 1950, photograph of Faulkner to illustrate this year's conference materials.

Global Faulkner

FAULKNER AND YOKNAPATAWPHA
2006

Many Mansions:
Faulkner's Cold War Conflicts

John T. Matthews

In my Father's house are many mansions: if it were not so, I would have told you. I go to prepare a place for you.
—John 14:2 (King James Version)

In my father's house are many mansions
If it were not true he would have told me so
He has gone away to live in that bright city
He's preparing me a mansion there I know.
—(Arranged and adapted by Elvis Presley)

Had Faulkner completed the Snopes saga as he first imagined it in the mid-1920s, Flem's story might have remained simply a satire about the rise of a redneck—a bemused caricature of the implausible rural success stories made possible by novelties of modernity like speculative capitalism and a culture of consumption.[1] *The Great Gatsby* chez Frenchman's Bend. But *The Hamlet*, appearing at the end of the decade of the Great Depression, also takes note of the corresponding plight of the dispossessed, even if it still laughs at the grotesques serving Mammon. *The Hamlet* sounds proletarian overtones: the rage of the landless debtor classes who have been reduced to wage labor and nomadism, the resentment at changes in social relations caused by rampant commodification and an emergent culture of consumption, the hypocrisies of a smug bourgeoisie. In 1940 *The Hamlet* counterpoints the despair of an underclass, the indifference of the prosperous, and the equivocations of the professional observer.[2]

The Hamlet's sympathies suggest that it belongs to the moment of late proletarian fiction. Faulkner's open-ended diagnosis of class conflict measures the unresolved contradictions of American capitalism laid open by the Depression. In the 1939 short story "Barn Burning," Faulkner elaborates on the tenant Ab Snopes's confrontation with his new employer, Major de Spain, an episode referred to in *The Hamlet* but left unnarrated. "Barn Burning" gives voice to Ab's resentment at the mastery of money, at the planter's alchemy of the laborer's sweat into French décor. But at the

3

end of the story, Ab's son Sarty betrays his father's plot of crude revenge, and disappears, lost amid contrary senses of justice—the rights of the disadvantaged versus the rule of law—and contrary senses of freedom—the opportunity to succeed versus the license to exploit.[3]

The Hamlet reflects a time of both national and global indetermination on the eve of World War II. The working-class Mink is left incarcerated while the managerial Flem is destined for dominance; the metropolis beckons while the provinces languish; the ambitious adopt national models of success—"Wallstreet," "Montgomery Ward"—while local patterns fade. The novel's lurch toward modernity corresponds with world developments as well: working-class retreat before corporate advance; the rise of state nationalisms; and the stirrings of anticolonialism, antiracism, and women's equality that contended uncertainly during the war years. But then in the decade and a half between *The Hamlet* in 1940 and *The Town* in 1957, however, many of these conflicts within modernity came to be subsumed under Cold War priorities. As Odd Arne Westad puts it in his recent study of the period, the global Cold War emerged after World War II as perhaps the central discourse of the later century's international history.[4]

Under Cold War pressure in the 1950s, Faulkner globalizes Snopesism. The later trilogy places the regional story of Flem's rise and Mink's resentment into the context of the conflict between the two principal narratives of Western progress: the spread of freedom and the advance of equality. As the Cold War hardened ideological differentiation, freedom became the watchword for U.S. capitalist democracy, while an egalitarian vision inspired Soviet-style communism. Faulkner himself understood the "battleground" between the era's "two mighty forces" in these terms. In a pamphlet addressed to Japanese students in 1955, he emphasizes that the only hope for humankind rests in the ideal of "freedom," though, he hastens to add, such liberty "must be complete freedom for all."[5] Elsewhere, speaking against U.S. racism, he insists that the defense of freedom cannot be separated from a commitment to equality: "we cannot choose freedom established on a hierarchy of degrees of freedom"; "belief in individual liberty and equality and freedom . . . is the one idea powerful enough to stalemate the idea of communism."[6]

Published in 1959, two years after *The Town*, *The Mansion* engages at every level with the defining geopolitical condition of its era, the global Cold War.[7] Faulkner expressed his alarm about the superpowers' antagonism in the age of the atomic bomb most memorably in his Nobel speech, in which he broods over the catastrophe of human destruction on a planetary scale. As well, Faulkner's overwrought Cold War allegory, *A Fable* (1954), issued from deep anxiety over the inexorable growth of military industrial capitalism.[8] The travel-averse Faulkner must have regarded the threat of atomic annihilation very seriously to have agreed to trips sponsored by the U.S. State Department, which he undertook as contributions to international good will and cross-cultural understanding. But as we might expect from someone whose pronouncements on political questions make John Kerry sound downright committal, Faulkner refused to side uncritically with USAism during the '50s standoff of superpowers. As the Cold War became a national preoccupation, Faulkner put difficult questions to capitalist democracy's certitudes.

Since Southerners of Faulkner's background had been both perpetrators and perceived victims of colonization, creating an internal colony of slaveholding, and then later suffering subjection to federal military reconstruction and northern capitalization, Faulkner could look at national history from both more global and more regional perspectives than many could.[9] The U.S. South reached the twentieth century as the First World's Third World. At the least this produced a kind of schizophrenic insight. Better than many, certain modern Southerners could see through delusions of ideological purity, colonial self-sufficiency, and regional denigration. We have recently come to appreciate how fully Faulkner confronted the legacy of New World plantation society in the U.S. South.[10] In his fiction through *Absalom, Absalom!*, Faulkner comes to see the South's implication in global European imperialism. In the Southern plantation's participation in transatlantic slave economies, in its indispensability to northern U.S. and European industrial capitalism, in its dependence on the colonial invention of race, Faulkner admits his South's place in the history of New World colonialism. Once Faulkner recognizes the South as a historical phenomenon of global imperialism, what does that recognition mean for his sense of the contemporary nation? What connects the Civil War to the Cold War?

My argument here will be that Faulkner surmised, on the basis of his reckoning with the Southern past, a truth about the superpowers' behavior in the 1950s: that the Cold War was the direct descendant of Western imperialisms, and that the U.S. and Soviet Union were pursuing conflicting projects of postcolonial modernity through neo-imperial presumptions. According to Westad, we may think of the Cold War as a continuation of European colonialism. As Western expansionism reinvented itself at the end of the nineteenth century to promote what it understood to be a mission of social progress and the advance of civilization, so its post–World War I hegemonic heirs, the U.S. and Russia, envisioned competing roads to utopian modernity. For Westad, the U.S. may be captioned as an "empire of liberty," Soviet Russia as an "empire of justice." The practical differences pitted the United States' commitment to urban-based growth, consumption, high technology, and an integrated global market, against Russia's confidence in state-fostered economic development, collectivized production, heavy industry, and independence of international markets (92). The operative distinction, as we shall see, involved what was meant by *freedom* and *justice*. But for the moment I want to highlight the other term in Westad's formulation, *empire*, since it was what the superpowers shared.

According to this view, both the United States and the Soviet Union approached their Cold War confrontation decisively conditioned by their imperialist histories. In the case of the U.S., the republic's founding on the principle of liberty cannot be separated from its insistence on the rights to private property and freedom of commerce. Over the course of the nation's early history, defense of the free market became the cornerstone of its foreign policy. To the extent that the purpose of U.S. foreign policy was to make the world safe for capitalism, as Westad puts it, then expansionism, interventionism, and colonization were key instruments of American success from the outset. As each superpower sought to "lift" the rest of the world toward its own image of modern prosperity, the U.S. understood its global mission as an Americanization of the world. Treating Third World countries as latter-day instances of its own native Americans and African slaves, to whom it believed it had offered the advantages of civilization, the U.S. carried the historical conceits of capitalist imperialism into the Cold War conflict.

The Soviet Union, likewise, stood on the shoulders of an expansionist empire. Westad observes that nineteenth-century Russian imperialism conceived its mission as the civilizing of Asia to the east and south, and that like the U.S. it resorted to genocide, particularly against Muslim minorities, and inner colonization, in the treatment of serfs. Over the course of the first half of the twentieth century, the Soviet Union fashioned a project of global socialist revolution. This involved constructing the Third World as instrumental to the advance of socialist modernity and directing worldwide leftist movements from Moscow, as the seat of working-class revolution. Although the Soviet Union explicitly attacked the remnants of European imperialism and fostered anticolonialist independence movements, it nonetheless functioned as an *"empire* for justice." A determination of such an empire was to neutralize U.S. interventionism and make the world safe for revolution.[11]

Seen this way, the Cold War was a phenomenon of postcolonialism, reorganizing classical imperialism as hegemonic neo-imperialism. Both superpowers managed relations to the Third World as functions of their own strategic interests. Their manipulation of Third World affairs replicated features of colonial administration: the "foreignness" of the state, the use of force, the preferment accorded cooperative elites, the illegitimacy of nonelective government (75).[12] The very term "third world" was coined by postcolonial nations to express their determination to protect their nonalignment, to mark out a third way between the monoliths of U.S. capitalism and Soviet communism, between global marketry and state collectivism.

Writing for the first time in his career as a world figure, and in years during which global geopolitics were creating an era of apocalypse, Faulkner in the 1950s responds to Cold War preoccupations. *The Mansion* addresses numerous contemporary issues: U.S. Communist Party activities, red-baiting, Greenwich Village bohemianism, artistic avant-gardism, European fascism. The result is the most topical of all Faulkner's novels. In the reading of *The Mansion* that follows, however, I want to suggest that Faulkner does more than offer reflections on contemporary world events; he undertakes a systematic exploration of conflicting Cold War principles. He shows how Cold War ideals on both sides represent legitimate aspirations for progressive change, yet how vestigial mentalities protect vested interests. Extending his earlier encounter with the history of colonialism, Faulkner now detects that history's horrific afterlife in the specter of planetary annihilation. Expanding the provincial story of Flem's rags-to-riches success, *The Mansion* may be taken as Faulkner's Cold War fable. In the later Snopes trilogy Faulkner criticizes the pieties of U.S. free worldism for disregarding the casualties of injustice strewing the path to ever more stately mansions.

Faulkner organizes his last Snopes novel as a standoff between two powerful motives: the demand for revenge and the desire for freedom. Mink Snopes, the protagonist of the novel, waits thirty-eight years before finally gaining his release from Parchman Penitentiary, whereupon he makes his way to Flem's parlor to even a very old score indeed. Faulkner tightens the bow of this narrative over the course of the entire trilogy; *The Hamlet* ends with Mink beginning his prison sentence, having been betrayed by Flem, stunned that his kinsman deems respectability thicker than blood. Mink neither forgives nor forgets. Flem knows what's coming when Mink gets out of jail, so he tricks Mink into attempting a premature prison break and gains a second term of protection for himself.

Unlike the earlier volumes of the trilogy, *The Mansion* actually tries to understand a Snopes. In *The Hamlet*, Faulkner shows pity for damaged Snopeses like Ike and Ab, as he ridicules soulless ones like Flem and I. O. But there's no getting inside those wolverine brains. In *The Mansion*, however, Faulkner devotes the first long chapter of the novel to Mink, using free indirect discourse to render his point of view and expressive habits. We begin to grasp the world as Mink does, and learn that his singular preoccupation is the question of fairness. He pays his court-imposed fine to Houston painstakingly, for example, all the while trying to convince himself that eventually he'll get a fair shake.

> He meant, simply, that *them—they—it*, whichever and whatever you wanted to call it, who represented a simple fundamental justice and equity in human affairs, or else a man might just as well quit; the *they, them, it*, call them what you like, which simply would not, could not harass and harry a man forever without some day, at some moment, letting him get his own just and equal licks back in return.[13]

Mink remains partial to homicide as the equalizer of choice, and his demands for "fundamental justice" never surpass his uncle Ab's bitter vengefulness. Mink serves as Faulkner's study of Southern farm laborers' underdeveloped capacity to reorganize agricultural capitalism through class pressure, whether as disadvantaged participants or as would-be revolutionaries. He gets into trouble initially because he has the audacity to launch a plot of his own, however misbegotten. Mink sets his scrawny cow free one fall, letting his prosperous neighbor Houston winter it, before claiming it again in the spring as a newly found "stray." To cover the implausibility of his ruse, Mink invents a story about selling the cow to a distant farmer, whom Mink claims to have reimbursed when he discovers the cow has wandered back. But Mink's scheme is motivated more by pure resentment than any bid to better his financial condition. He is goaded into action only because he cannot stand the sight of Houston's prosperity and, worse, the superior airs of Houston's black overseer. Mink hardly cares about the chance to turn a profit; he cannot get over the eight dollars he knows he will have to pay Houston to get his cow back, even though he knows he's far ahead on the wintering costs (and will be farther ahead if his cow is returned pregnant, as is likely). He rages at what might be called the temporality of capitalism, frustrated that he cannot gain "simple justice and inalienable rights" "at one stroke," but "must depend on the slow incrementation of feed converted to weight" (341). Mink's time is never more than mere waiting, without issue—"prolongation" it is called (341). The individual tenant cannot hope to turn a worthwhile profit; farming like this, as Flem puts it at the outset of his mercantile career, has no "benefit." Flem, on the other hand, understands that speculative time is fungible, figuring out, for example, how to collect nickels and dimes in perpetual receipt of interest from the uncomprehending victims of his usury.

Mink's imprisonment in the prison farm at Parchman just makes literal his economic confinement. Working the state's cotton fields under armed guard hardly differs from being indentured to Varner. He has heard of the "commonist" cause (416), as he once puts it, but he never develops a political consciousness. He fumes at Houston for "being a rich man too and all you rich folks has got to stick together or else maybe some day the ones that aint rich might take a notion to raise up and take hit away from you" (366). But he adds that that's not the reason he's murdered his nemesis; the killing was the result of Houston's gratuitous assessment of an "extry" dollar pound fee. Just as he swears to get even with Flem not for duping him into trying to break prison but for the unnecessary insult of providing a woman's dress and sunbonnet to do it in, Mink repeatedly acts on trivial motives and gains nothing from them but self-ruination. Notice how Montgomery Ward, who, unlike Mink, follows in Flem's commercial footsteps, describes what it means to be a Snopes: "I realized that I had come from what you might call a family, a clan, a race, maybe even a species, of pure sons of bitches" (87). All doubtless apt, but of course what's missing from the list is "class." The businessman Montgomery Ward embraces the myth of individualism as it sanctions predatory capitalism, but the tenant farmer Mink will only be driven into the ground by standing alone.

Faulkner molds Mink's story around the ideal of working-class justice that inspires communism.[14] "Commonist" solutions to the excesses of property appealed to Faulkner; he imagines them most sympathetically in Uncle Ike's dream of a return to the "communal anonymity of brotherhood" under which Native Americans held the land, before any white man had arrived to say, "Get away! This is mine." Later in *The Mansion*, Mink receives help according to his need from a communitarian Protestant congregation. Faulkner sharpens the issue of class conflict in *The Mansion* by adjusting his depiction of Houston. In *The Hamlet* Houston is barely getting by himself, having mortgaged most of his land to Will Varner, while in *The Mansion*, perhaps to underscore the tenant's resentment, he appears as a lordly man of wealth. As for Mink, Faulkner suggests that the sort of economic system that has evolved in the modern South has put the landless laborer into a state of arrested development. Mink is repeatedly described as a "small frail creature not much larger than a fifteen-year-old boy" (376). The "commonist" fails to attain majority status.

Historically, of course, Southern workers did organize unions and other collective organizations to defend their rights. A number of the more radical managed to affiliate with the Communist Party, though farmers were less likely to join than urban industrial wage laborers.[15] Faulkner knows that efforts to forge common cause along class lines were often sabotaged by ideologies descending from American imperial capitalism. To begin

with, there was the impregnable fiction of individual success.[16] When
Faulkner has two comic communist Finns show up looking futilely for Jefferson's "proletariat" (522), they never do learn that there is no proletariat
in Jefferson. There's not even a middle class, the poor "being convinced instead that it was merely in a temporary interim state toward owning in its
turn Mr Snopes's bank or Wallstreet Snopes's wholesale grocery chain or
(who knows?) on the way to the Governor's mansion in Jackson or perhaps
the White House in Washington" (523). I suppose the Finns would have to
wait for Mega Millions or *American Idol* to get the point. A second condition stalling class solidarity in the South, of course, was racism, a remnant
of colonial ideology, invented to rationalize slavery, reanimated to promote postemancipation peonage. Faulkner suggests this obstacle in having
Mink misdirect his animosity toward Houston's black employee: "I don't
listen to niggers: I tell them" (344). Mink's brain is as much his prison as
Parchman. He embodies the stubborn entrenchment of ruling class fictions even in those for whom they do nothing. Mink's story validates the
ideal of justice while suggesting how it has been thwarted by those who
profit from injustice. Faulkner tells the story of failed working-class "com-
monism" from the historical perspective of the 1950s, when the shib-
boleths of capitalist individualism and racism take on fresh life in the Cold
War nation, as well as when the reflexes of proletarian resentment and
class conflict seem as anachronistic as the time-capsuled Mink.

Over the course of *The Mansion*, Faulkner enlarges the narrative of
justice to touch on numerous other struggles for social equality. The novel
takes seriously the determination of communists like Barton Kohl and
Linda Snopes to fight against oppression.[17] Faulkner treats the couple's
involvement in the Spanish Civil War respectfully, and we recall that he
cared about this cause himself, donating his manuscript of *Absalom, Absalom!* to a fundraising campaign on behalf of the Spanish Loyalists, and
even subscribing to the anti-Franco, antifascist statement that accompa-
nied it.[18] As well, the novel makes much of Linda Snopes Kohl's personal
feminism: her military heroism, her wartime factory work, her physical
strength, and her sexual freedom. It is Linda who grows impatient with Jim
Crow education in Jefferson, and a gradualist African American principal
quoting Booker T. Washington who wants her to stop interfering. Later,
though, a younger black man sharply defends to the skeptical Mink Linda's
work on behalf of racial improvement.

In these episodes it seems clear that Faulkner understands how Cold
War communism was rightly pressuring traditional forms of American inequality. As Joanne Meyerowitz and other recent scholars of Cold War culture have begun to demonstrate, the American 1950s were not exclusively

years of domestic containment, customarily held to be a function of global political containment. Although the Cold War did provide rationalizations for shooing women back toward household duties and strengthening the defense of American economic and sexual "norms," social practices that violated the ideal of liberty and justice for all became points of ideological vulnerability during the Cold War. Truman and later John F. Kennedy were particularly sensitive to Soviet propaganda in the Third World about the shortcomings of U.S. civil rights. For many Cold Warriors, Southern desegregation, for example, mattered as much to global politics as to domestic ones. Civil rights activists seized the moment, while, likewise, numerous women's organizations "joined together to use the Cold War as an opportunity for collective action on behalf of women."[19]

What I find astute about *The Mansion* is the way Faulkner uses the vulnerabilities of the South to criticize capitalist Cold War certitudes. He insists that the South, as the forgotten subtext of national failure, exploitation, and hypocrisy, contradicts American pride in itself as the land of freedom, equal opportunity, and justice. The prevailing contemporary view of the South as the nation's *problem* functions critically for Faulkner as the country's Achilles heel.[20] As one of its central concerns, then, *The Mansion* is determined to recognize the longings for justice that fail to be answered by American democratic capitalism. Faulkner's portrait of Mink Snopes represents a global South's agricultural proletariat, a Third World composite who awaits recognition and recompense.[21]

If Faulkner bravely defends the claims of justice associated with the left at the height of the Cold War, he likewise criticizes the so-called Free World's perversion of freedom. Faulkner begins *The Mansion* with an eye-popping fusillade directed at the commodification of everything. For page after page the novel initiates us into the subhuman mentality that reduces everything to monetary valuation. Beginning with Mink's desperate cry for help—"I'll pay you—Flem'll pay you!" (333)—through the torturously obsessive calculations of Mink's cow scheme, down to an obscene allegory of market intercourse that has country preachers providing sexual favors to frustrated farmwives in exchange for home-style cooking ("the job of filling his hole in payment for getting theirs plugged . . . the wives coming because here was the best market they knowed of to swap a mess of fried chicken or a sweet-potato pie; the husbands coming not to interrupt the trading" [335])—Faulkner imagines the endless grotesqueries of the lust for money.

Faulkner responds to Cold War preoccupations by broadening the significance of Flem's career in *The Mansion*. If Flem was little more than a Lee Russell redneck in *The Hamlet*, by the 1950s he bids to become an

American icon. The key to Flem's ultimate ascent to the presidency of the Merchants and Farmers' Bank of Jefferson involves his adoption of national models of managerial capitalism.[22] When Flem succeeds to office, he makes a point of trading in his cloth cap for "a black felt planter's hat suitable to his new position and avocation" (453). That hat points to the financial lineage of Jefferson's wealth, to the founders Major de Spain and Will Varner, who represent, respectively, the planter class and the commercial class of landholders. But it evokes an even more august forebear as well, the nation's Founding Planter, who inspires the banker to do an extreme makeover of his digs so that it resembles Mount Vernon. Snopes sits idly in this "monument" the rest of his days, occupying what Faulkner calls "a colonial monstrosity" (513), the "Snopes-colonial-mausoleum" (645). At one point, Flem has a piece of wood affixed to the mantel where he props his feet, to remind him, Ratliff speculates, of his origins, but practically to protect the finish from wear. It's as if Flem imagines his place in the pantheon of American capitalists, his house already "the solid ancestral symbol of Alexander Hamilton and Aaron Burr and Astor and Morgan and Harriman and Hill and ever other golden advocate of hard quick-thinking vested interest" (470). Flem wants to be careful; someday there might be tours.

The utter vacuity of Flem's life calls into question what the U.S. thinks it is doing in the Cold War. As Faulkner suspects, the empire of freedom looks mainly like an imperial free market, its only rule the "trompling" of the poor on the road to the palace of leisure. If Flem's mansion stands as the culmination of New World plantation colonialism, then Faulkner has indeed unearthed the bloodline of Cold War capitalism. One character summarizes U.S. foreign policy after World War II as all a matter of dollars: "If they had let us lick the Russians too, we might a been all right. But they just licked the Krauts and Japs and then decided to choke everybody else to death with money" (427–28). Or as Montgomery Ward Snopes puts it drily, having been framed by his cousin Flem, he welcomes Parchman because at least he'll be "safe from the free world, safe and secure for a little while yet from the free Snopes world" (406).

Patterns of colonial domination organize modern American consumption as well. Even an expanding market does not enfranchise equally.[23] Montgomery Ward's infamous Atelier Monty brilliantly symbolizes Faulkner's conviction that profiting from the wants of the needy amounts to a sort of pornography, that behind the traffic in consumer desire is "what you might call a dry whorehouse" (379). French erotic postcards may enflame male lust in Jefferson, but they function like all capitalist spectacle to represent the barrier to gratification as itself the source of pleasure.

Miss Reba, the mistress of a bordello in Memphis who has heard about Monty's enterprise, underscores the distance between classes of consumers: "just looking at pictures might do all right for a while down there in the country where there wasn't no other available handy outlet but . . . sooner or later somebody was going to run up enough temperature to where he would have to run to the nearest well for a bucket of real water" (402).[24] It is the poor and distant who are excluded from metropolitan pleasure—at least until they break out and make a run for the real thing. Once Montgomery Ward grasps Miss Reba's point about the relation of his business to hers, he realizes that his franchise is just the "desert-outpost branch" (402). Faulkner anticipates views of global modernization that emphasize the power of U.S. marketing to Third World consumers. Figured by Montgomery Ward's repackaging of French postcards, extended in Mink Snopes's orgasmic consumption of cold Coca-Colas the minute he's out of prison, it is U.S.-driven market domination, Faulkner suggests, that the ideology of the Free World means to defend during the Cold War.

In probing modern American capitalism and its sustaining culture of consumption, Faulkner grasps another feature of its pathology, its fundamental reliance on the abuse of women. As deeply as any book Faulkner wrote, *The Mansion* sees how masculine "self-making" involves the forcible command of female bodies and labor.[25] The novel includes a number of episodes in which men batter women into submission: Mink, for example, having to compensate for his lost hours of work, "with vicious and obscene cursing drove the three of them, his wife and the two girls, with the three hoes out to the patch to chop out his early cotton" (364). Mink knows this drill intimately, since he once recalls from "deep in memory" (426) a scene in which his stepmother has been beaten so badly by Mink's father that she cannot eat. Mink remembers her as "always either with a black eye or holding a dirty rag to her bleeding" (426).

Such brutal violence is the bedrock of the more genteel forms of financial exploitation practiced on women in the trilogy. Faulkner understands that misogyny is not incidental, but instrumental to an American-style capitalism based on the rights of private property (to wives, land, slaves), the legal power to coerce labor, the lawful entitlement of men to women's financial resources. Flem's scheme to have Linda make him the beneficiary of her will simply literalizes the association between dead women and living patrimonies. Even Chick can see that "the record of success and victory behind [Flem] already had two deaths in it," Eula's suicide, but also Linda's incurable alienation. Faulkner provides a nearly anthropological grasp of the foundational commodification of women, tracking Eula's fungibility for her father and husband through numerous permutations, to its last word as real estate: Eula Acres.

When Faulkner gets to the cultural symbolism of misogyny, then, he makes us see sexual depravity as more than just a convenient image for capitalist corruption. Miss Reba's remark that her patrons "come in here to do business" (400) conveys a literal truth, Faulkner's extensive thematics of prostitution and promiscuity throughout his fiction suggesting the conflation of sexual and financial commerce. Consider the subplot involving Virgil Snopes's "really exceptional talent" to "take care of two girls in succession to their satisfaction or at least until they hollered quit" (398). Clarence Snopes capitalizes on his nephew's prowess by marketing him, and dreaming of his big future, "if the supply of two-dollar whores just holds out" (398). The practices of sexuality are so laced with economic language, and the practices of economics with the language of sexuality, that Faulkner seems to be suggesting more than a figurative relation between them. It's not analogy, or even homology, that aligns capitalism and sexual exploitation, but their mutual history as social institutions.

Faulkner evokes perhaps the most iconic representation of these matters in the portrait of the young Linda Snopes, who stands in a long line in American literature of fetishized nymphets representing a national psychosis: the transgressive consumption of unspoiled goods. Besides Faulkner's own Eula Varner, Temple Drake, and Little Belle Mitchell, we might think of Fitzgerald's Nicole Devereux Diver and Rosemary Hoyt in *Tender Is the Night* or Nabokov's Dolores Haze in *Lolita*. Such figures share defining features: they combine excessive desirability with prohibition against it, often in the form of incest taboos; despite their innocence, they are made responsible for their own violation by their purported seductiveness; they function as emblems for broader dynamics of consumption; and they are frequently associated with the vulgarity of mass culture.

Lolita may offer the most provocative context for what Faulkner is doing with Linda Snopes. Published in 1955, two years before *The Town*, *Lolita* bespeaks the seductions of American pop consumer culture. Humbert Humbert cannot maintain his high-mindedness in the face of Lolita's bewitching appetite for all kinds of stuff: "four books of comics, a box of candy, . . . two cokes, a manicure set, a travel clock with a luminous dial, a ring with a real topaz, a tennis racket, roller skates with white high shoes, . . . a radio set, chewing gum, a transparent raincoat, sunglasses, some more garments—swooners, shorts, all kinds of summer frocks" (140–42).[26] Lolita's consuming and eminently consumable body, then, in its forbidden inviting freshness, feeds (on) the fever of consumption under capitalism. In fact, Nabokov perceives that it is consumption itself that Americans are driven to consume. Humbert ricochets around the nation's interstates, a man made mad by the lust for the goodies America dreams up. Here is Devereux Warren's piggish incest, Dick Diver's preference for Daddy's girls, Quentin Compson's longing for Little Sister, Horace Benbow's fantasies of Little Belles, Popeye's voyeurism, and Flem's paternal proprietorship rolled into one all-consuming maniac. But if it took a Russian émigré to invent the consummate duo of Cold War U.S. consumptionism, his Dixie counterpart responded by bolshevizing the nymphet and making her admirers an ascetic and a Russian.[27]

Gavin Stevens wonders if he can't emancipate his Lolita instead of devouring her. Rather than succumb to temptation, Gavin perfects habits of renunciation. With her mother's encouragement, Linda meets the lawyer who is twice her age at the drugstore a couple of times a week, where "she et a ice-cream sody or a banana split and the ice melted into the unteched Coca-Cola in front of him" (134). Stevens undertakes Linda's informal education during these sessions, tutoring her in the poets, telling her about northern colleges, and mostly urging her to get out of Jefferson and leave everything Snopes behind. Stevens directs her toward New York City, not as the classic destination for materializing the American dream, but as the place where she can discover oppositional culture. Linda's escape to Greenwich Village yields her a Jewish lover, a communist sculptor committed to radical politics and experimental aesthetics. Already signaled by Gavin's refusal to touch his Coca-Cola, Linda's liberation constitutes a different kind of freedom; it repudiates "the free Snopes world" of money-making and consumption. She bids to emancipate herself from false norms of behavior attached to national origin, region, class, family, race, gender, marital relation—norms fetishized by Cold War America, but discredited here as functioning primarily to rationalize powerholding.[28]

I have argued that Faulkner's political fable in *The Mansion* exposes the shortcomings of U.S. Cold War conflict thinking on several counts. Not only does America's preoccupation with the defense of personal liberty deafen it to the claims of justice, but the assumption that freedom is synonymous with free marketry ignores the numerous fatalities behind capitalism's success story. Beyond this diagnostic insight, moreover, Faulkner manages to suggest longings for more authentic freedom, in which liberty and justice need not conflict, where the discrepancy between the idle rich and the imprisoned worker need not end in murderous confrontation. How instructive it would be these days to have a reminder that the "winds of freedom" may be more than the flutter of corporate invoices, that the Constitution, at least so far, does not contain the word "Halliburton."

Faulkner hints at possibilities for a progressive modernity not ade-quately represented by the ideologies of either democratic capitalism or Stalinist communism. Its general principle has to do with a fairer distribu-tion of the goods capitalism creates. In his paper on *The Mansion* at this conference last year, Jon Smith suggested that the handmade designer ties Ratliff buys in New York City might represent this element of market uto-pianism.[29] The Allanovna designs do indeed appeal to Ratliff's apprecia-tion for sensuous pleasure, as does Barton Kohl's modernist sculpture.[30] Faulkner presents such experiences inarguably as elevations of imagina-tion, expansions of spirit. Something similar occasionally lifts Mink out of his subhuman battle for survival. Mink has a thing for trains, cars, and mov-ies. Whenever he can, he spends a night at the depot, savoring the spec-tacle of motion and speed, the display of means and mobility, the em-bodiment of freedom and distance. Mink wants to be caught up in these intersecting narratives of modernity: narratives of movement toward the metropolis, of technological transformation, of revolutions in representa-tion. If only he could afford them.

The trilogy concludes with Mink in the midst of a reverie about the end of his life. In it, he tries to reconcile the powerful thirst for freedom with the undeniable demand for justice. He's already killed Flem, and he ex-ults *"I'm free now"* (720). He imagines finally being able to insert himself into the narrative of Western progress: he could head west now "since that was the direction people always went" (720). At the same time, Mink rec-ognizes that he'll never really catch up, never really have a mansion of his own. Only the dead are free—"the justice and the injustice and the griefs, leaving the folks themselves easy now, all mixed and jumbled up comfort-able and easy so wouldn't nobody even know or even care who was which any more, himself among them, equal to any, good as any, brave as any, be-ing inextricable from, anonymous with all of them" (721).

The Cold War offered conflicting roads to future reward. Behind Faulk-ner's title of the last Snopes novel it is difficult not to hear two familiar gospel tunes, "In My Father's House Are Many Mansions" and "I Have a Mansion Just Over the Hilltop."[31] Both were recorded by a young Elvis Presley in 1960. The first song is a setting of verses from the Gospel of John, in which Jesus promises a mansion in His Father's House for each of his followers. In the King James Version, Jesus explains that he must re-turn to heaven to prepare their places. In the King Elvis version, a line has been added about heading to the bright city instead. The other song con-curs: "I'm but a pilgrim in search of the city / I want a mansion, a harp and a crown." The idea of the city introduces a bit of equivocation about whether the mansions must necessarily be other-worldly, or might instead be over a nearer hilltop. The Elvis of Memphis and Hollywood might have endorsed the more material project, and certainly both songs picture bliss as involving plenty of silver and gold. Perhaps there was no word in Aramaic for suede.

Jesus uses the phrase "my Father's House" only one other time in the gospels, when he's clearing the temple of the moneychangers.[32] Someone does show up to clear Father Abraham's house of its moneychanger. Enabled by Linda Kohl, who aims her blow at the whole male principle of lying patriarchy,[33] Mink trespasses on a mansion so that he can say, "Look at me." The scene echoes another, Charles Bon's infiltration of the Sutpen mansion to insist that the planter recognize Bon's mixed blood as his own. Faulkner's fiction repeatedly stages moments in which the visibly invisible demand acknowledgment. In perhaps the most unsettling of all such episodes, Faulkner concludes *The Town* with an anecdote in which Byron Snopes's mixed Mexican/"Apache" offspring are mailed home to Flem by the fugitive embezzler.[34] The four inscrutably dark, silent, violent children terrorize Jefferson. A kinsman, paid by Flem to house the unwanted immigrants, has his face slashed one night when he sneaks into the children's room to see if they are asleep.[35] He doesn't even realize he's been cut until he feels two "streaks of fire," the "two slashes running from each ear, jest missing his eye on one side, right down to the corners of his mouth like a great big grin that would bust scab and all if he ever let his face go" (322). Flem gives up and mails the children back to El Paso, care of Byron.

This episode comes at the very end of *The Town*. It ruptures the narrative like a shard of the political uncanny. The children embody to the point of caricature every trait associated with the stereotype of "greaser." The McCarran-Walter Act of 1952 had severely tightened immigration policies, imposing measures that reflected McCarthy-driven paranoia and racism.[36] In 1954, Congress authorized a program to round up and repatriate illegal Mexican workers and to tighten border patrol. The project was known as Operation Wetback. El Paso was a center for return. But what makes the four "Snopes Indians," as they are once called, especially threatening is that they're not workers at all. Besides being adept at self-defense, they sneak into the Coca-Cola plant and drink the syrup; they also kill and devour a $500 show dog owned by a Yankee paving contractor's wife—"a Pekinese with a gold name-plate on its collar that probably didn't even know it was a dog, that rode in the Cadillac and sneered through the window not just at other dogs but at people too" (318). The children become suspects in the dog's disappearance when one is noticed wearing the collar as a necklace. I'd say this is Third World consumption with a vengeance.

Faulkner's uncontained fantasy here suggests the connections between Cold War defense of the American way of life and the threats sure to materialize from continued imperialist exploitation and inequality. At the end of *The Town*, it is as if Faulkner fully realizes the global framework of Snopesism, one that will require a more systematic consideration of Cold War conflicts in its successor. The American host's slashed face symbolizes the awful fiction of national innocence, a dopey grin that will dissolve into the wound it really is if ever he lets his face discompose. You'd like to think the aliens are safely pacified, but you're really working in the dark.

In these most political of his novels, whose time may finally have come, Faulkner invites us to imagine a day when a stunted Third Worlder, long out-of-sight-out-of-mind, will cross a border to say, "Look at me." If we indulge the conceit of a contemporary sequel to the late trilogy, I suppose we'd have to call it *The McMansion*. Here's the ending: Like Flem we watch the stuff just accumulate around us. Our boots are up on the mantel. We're enjoying global plutocracy exactly as planned. At the moment we're doing nothing, apparently thinking nothing—the casualties of our prosperity disregarded. Elsewhere, the Minks await release; the hybrid *bracero*—to whom it turns out we're related!—wants in. Things seem to be getting a little hotter. We know better, of course, but we prefer self-serving denial; we've even found a genius of incomprehension to lead us. When Mink's grandson, Enron Snopes, shows up, he won't get back what he's owed either. But imagine if the rest of us get what we deserve.

NOTES

I wish to thank the following individuals for instructive comments on the version of this paper presented at the conference: James Carothers, George Handley, Anne Goodwyn Jones, Noel Polk, Nina Silber, Jon Smith, and Theresa Towner. I also gratefully acknowledge the help of Gillian Cohen and Christie Ko, undergraduate research assistants at Boston University.

1. The earliest surviving version of Faulkner's Snopes fiction is a manuscript dating from late 1926 or early 1927, according to James B. Meriwether, editor of the text eventually published posthumously as *Father Abraham* (New York: Random House, 1984). The fragment contains narrative segments later reworked for *The Hamlet* (1940), primarily accounts of Flem Snopes's early successes, Eula's allure, and the auction of the spotted horses.

2. See Charles Hannon on Ratliff and developments in professional ethnography as reflected in *The Hamlet: Faulkner and the Discourses of Culture* (Louisiana State University Press, 2005), 104–30.

3. Four years earlier, in its portrait of a shiftless Jones who finally revolts against class abuse, *Absalom, Absalom!* superimposed the rage of 1930s tenants upon the resentment of

1860s peons. See my "Faulkner and Proletarian Literature," in *Faulkner in Cultural Context: Faulkner and Yoknapatawpha, 1995*, ed. Donald M. Kartiganer and Ann J. Abadie (Jackson: University Press of Mississippi, 1997), 166–90; Richard Moreland on repetition versus revision in dynamics of class conflict in "Barn Burning," in *Faulkner and Modernism: Rereading and Rewriting* (University of Wisconsin Press 1990), 7–20, 130–39; and Richard Godden on the racialization of class in the story, in *Fictions of Labor: William Faulkner and the South's Long Revolution* (New York: Cambridge University Press, 1997), 123–29.

4. *The Global Cold War: Third World Interventions and the Making of Our Times* (New York: Cambridge University Press, 2005). Subsequent references are cited parenthetically in the text.

5. "To the Youth of Japan" (Tokyo, 1955 [pamphlet published by the U.S. Information Service]), reprinted in *Essays, Speeches, and Public Letters*, ed. James B. Meriwether (New York: Random House, 1965), 84.

6. "On Fear: Deep South in Labor: Mississippi" (*Harper's*, June 1956), reprinted in *Essays, Speeches, and Public Letters*, 106, 102.

7. Peter Filene argues, on the contrary, that Cold War concerns were predominantly a matter for elites and ignored by the populace at large ("'Cold War Culture' Doesn't Say It All," in *Rethinking Cold War Culture*, ed. Peter J. Kuznick and James Gilbert [Washington, D.C.: Smithsonian Institution Press, 2001], 156–74).

8. See Richard Godden, "*A Fable* . . . Whispering about the Wars," *Faulkner Journal* 17.2 (Spring 2002): 25–88, for an analysis of how the novel explores the emergence of a post–World War II military-industrial complex.

9. See Joseph A. Fry, *Dixie Looks Abroad: The South and U.S. Foreign Relations, 1789–1973* (Baton Rouge: Louisiana State University Press, 2002), for a study of how these contrary experiences of subjugation fashioned a variety of Southern stances toward U.S. imperialism.

10. Among the major studies that have advanced this front of Faulkner studies, see Barbara Ladd, *Nationalism and the Color Line in George W. Cable, Mark Twain, and William Faulkner* (Baton Rouge: Louisiana State University Press, 1996); Édouard Glissant, *Faulkner, Mississippi*, trans. Barbara Lewis and Thomas C. Spear (New York: Farrar, Straus and Giroux, 1999); Deborah Cohn, *History and Memory in the Two Souths: Recent Southern and Spanish American Fiction* (Nashville: Vanderbilt University Press, 1999); and George Handley, *Postslavery Literatures in the Americas: Family Portraits in Black and White* (Charlottesville: University Press of Virginia, 2000).

11. I don't mean to exaggerate the symmetry of the superpowers' imperial designs. To be sure, Marxist commitment to economic *justice* appealed more readily to many emerging Third World nations. The Soviet Union supported anticolonial independence movements and offered an apparently less exploitative path to modernity via state-centered planning based on egalitarian ideals (Westad 80, 93). Social justice seemed intrinsic to decolonization. In the celebrated Bandung Conference of Third World nations, which gathered in Indonesia in 1955, Sukarno pronounced that the pertinent global forms of oppression were not based on class, but on race and colonial exploitation. Ho Chi Minh attacked "the hydra of Western capitalism" (Westad 83), and, later, when announcing Vietnam's repudiation of French colonial rule, quoted the U.S. Declaration of Independence on the principle that all men are created equal.

U.S. hegemonic capitalism, meanwhile, dictated Cold War policies that undertook the global defense of an economic system. Since the empire of freedom was fundamentally an empire of free marketry, the U.S. acted primarily to ensure stability and order in the Third World. U.S. policies rested on the conviction that such countries were underdeveloped and could be emancipated into modernity under U.S. guidance. Profiting from its successes in two world wars, the U.S. maximized its hegemonic status. To the Third World the U.S. functioned as a global metropolis, the command center of capital, administration, and production. Westad concludes that by "the late 1940s, when the United States produced a full half of the world's manufactured goods, it makes good sense to speak of an American capitalist world system" (30).

12. Given the record of forcible interventions by the Cold War superpowers, I do not

think it is overstating the case to say that many Third World nations must have continued to feel as they had under outright colonialism: that they were living within a giant prison (Westad 75).

13. *William Faulkner: Novels 1957–1962*, ed. Joseph L. Blotner and Noel Polk (New York: Library of America, 1999), 335–36. All subsequent quotations from *The Town* and *The Mansion* are from this edition.

14. See Eileen Gregory, "The Temerity to Revolt: Mink Snopes and the Dispossessed in *The Mansion*," *Mississippi Quarterly* 29 (Summer 1976), for an argument that Faulkner positions Mink against three fundamental narratives of suffering and redress, one of which is Marxist class revolution. Joseph R. Urgo argues that Mink "communicates in his thoughts and in his deeds the consciousness of the dispossessed proletarian farmer" (*Faulkner's Apocrypha: "A Fable," Snopes, and the Spirit of Human Rebellion* [Jackson: University Press of Mississippi, 1989], 203). Urgo examines the limitations of Mink's "individualistic response to injustice" (205), as well as the lamentable consequences of Flem's version of the American ethos of individualist success. Urgo notes that "individualism" carried ideological value in U.S. Cold War opposition to communism (209). Lawrence H. Schwartz studies how Cold War motives led U.S. intellectuals and cultural institutions to promote Faulkner after World War II as a quintessentially *American* writer, whose fiction seemingly pointed to an ethics of individualistic freedom, and whose modernist aesthetics illustrated the liberty of the individual imagination under democracy (*Creating Faulkner's Reputation: The Politics of Modern Literary Criticism* [Knoxville: University of Tennessee Press, 1988]). Schwartz interprets the uses to which Faulkner's fiction was put during the Cold War, but he chooses explicitly not to analyze the fiction itself. Schwartz's study ends with the early 1950s; Faulkner may be responding to the excessive "USAization" of his earlier fiction in his more balanced, even sympathetic reflections on leftism in *The Town* and *The Mansion*.

15. See Robin D. G. Kelley's *Hammer and Hoe: Alabama Communists during the Great Depression* (Chapel Hill: University of North Carolina Press, 1990). Kelley documents numerous communist activities in Alabama during the interwar years, some in the countryside, with major ones in Birmingham. I have been unable to find a corresponding study of communist participation in Mississippi by white tenant farmers like Mink, though among Alabama farmers African Americans constituted the vast majority of participants in communist undertakings, poor whites only sporadically overcoming longstanding racism.

16. See Urgo on individualism as a Cold War–era ideology. Faulkner touted individualism as the nonideological alternative to communism, an ideal resting on society's ensuring equal opportunity for all, but requiring each individual make something of the responsibility of personal freedom.

17. James Watson includes Linda's communist activism as part of Faulkner's favorable depiction of her "transcendent humanistic love" (*The Snopes Dilemma: Faulkner's Trilogy* [University of Miami Press, 1968], 228).

18. Frederick Karl, *William Faulkner: American Writer* (New York: Weidenfeld and Nicolson, 1989), 630.

19. For an authoritative version of the "containment" theory of domestic Cold War culture, see Elaine Tyler May's *Homeward Bound: American Families in the Cold War Era* (New York: Basic Books, 1988; rev. ed. 1999). Jane Sherron De Hart affirms the suitability of the metaphor of containment, but goes on to suggest how opportunities for racial and gender progress materialized against the era's pressures to conform ("Containment at Home: Gender, Sexuality, and National Identity in Cold War America," in *Rethinking Cold War Culture*, 124–55). Joanne Meyerowitz goes farther in detailing the activities of women's groups, activists for the rights of homosexuals, and sexual libertarians to press for greater freedoms ("Sex, Gender, and the Cold War Language of Reform," in *Rethinking Cold War Culture*, 106–23; quotation, 111).

20. Leigh Anne Duck, *The Nation's Region: Southern Modernism, Segregation, and U.S. Nationalism* (Athens: University of Georgia Press, 2006), discusses the tradition of casting the South as the deficient Other in the conception of national identity. See also Charmaine Eddy,

"Labor, Economy, and Desire: Rethinking American Nationhood through Yoknapatawpha," *Mississippi Quarterly* 57 (Fall 2004): 569–91, on a national fantasy of homogeneity and self-sufficiency that requires the misrecognition of compromising reliance on coerced labor, oppression, displacement, inequity—all repressed via a Lacanian exercise of desire on behalf of "the national ego-ideal" (574). She argues that the Snopes trilogy exposes the South as a site where such misrecognition fails.

21. See Hosam Aboul-Ela's discussion of the Snopeses in terms of broad Third World class structure, in particular of Flem Snopes as a representative of a global *comprador* elite that cooperates with foreign Northern metropolitan "development" and administers the foreign exploitation of local labor and resources (*Other South: Globalization, Faulkner, and the Mariátegui Tradition* [University of Pittsburgh Press, 2007]). Faulkner may be inscribing Third World contexts in some details of plot. There's the fact of Manfred de Spain's scar, sustained in Cuba during the Spanish-American War, but signifying ambiguously as either the result of a battle wound or a gambling one: the difference perhaps suggests the ambiguity of American imperial projects—freedom fighting or opportunism.

22. See Eddy on the conflict between regional and national patterns of success in the novel. She contends that Flem represents a new attitude toward labor and profit that introduces the function of *management* to the region's economic ways. Eddy also sees Flem as a practitioner of colonial mimicry; she anticipates the direction of Aboul-Ela's analysis, though not his use of Latin American development theory.

23. Recent scholarship on the growing opportunities for consumption enjoyed by the poor and blacks in the South only qualifies relatively, of course, the staggering inequity of means, access, and effects of such consumer activities. See Grace Elizabeth Hale, *Making Whiteness: The Culture of Segregation in the South, 1890–1940* (New York: Vintage, 1999) for an account of African American practices of consumption and their relation to Jim Crow strictures. Ted Ownby charts Faulkner's ambivalence to the culture of consumption in "The Snopes Trilogy and the Emergence of Consumer Culture," in *Faulkner and Ideology: Faulkner and Yoknapatawpha, 1992*, ed. Donald M. Kartiganer and Ann J. Abadie (Jackson: University Press of Mississippi, 1995), 95–128.

24. Fredric Jameson proposes the pornographic dimensions of late capitalism in *Postmodernism, or, The Cultural Logic of Late Capitalism* (Durham: Duke University Press, 1991). The spotted horses episode of *The Hamlet*, also published separately as a short story, remains Faulkner's classic study of the phenomenon. For a reading of the episode from this standpoint, see John Lutz, "That Texas Disease: Commodity Fetishism and Psychic Deprivation in *The Hamlet*," *Literature Interpretation Theory* 13 (2002): 69–90.

25. Faulkner wrote to Saxe Commins as he worked on *The Town* that "I still think it is funny, and at the end very moving; two women characters I am proud of" (*Selected Letters* [New York: Random House, 1977], 400); to Jean Stein he confided, "Just finishing the book. It breaks my heart, I wrote one scene and almost cried. I thought it was just a funny book but I was wrong" (SL 402). Keith Louise Fulton shows how Faulkner dramatizes the damaging effects of patriarchal "hegemony" and how Linda may be understood as taking justice into her own hands when she countenances Mink's murder of Flem since the law favors male interests ("Linda Snopes Kohl: Faulkner's Radical Woman," *Modern Fiction Studies* 34 [Autumn, 1988]: 425–436). Dawn Trouard ("Eula's Plot: An Irigararian Reading of Faulkner's Snopes Trilogy," *Mississippi Quarterly* 42 [Summer 1989]: 281–97), examines the desperate efforts Eula makes to free herself from being "the primary metaphor of both misogyny and patriarchal economy in the trilogy" (283). Hee Kang analyzes Linda as seizing male prerogatives of speech and fashioning them to her own disruptive ends, in "A New Configuration of Faulkner's Feminine: Linda Snopes Kohl in *The Mansion*," *Faulkner Journal* (Fall 1992): 21–41. Holly Levitsky reads Eula's suicide as a distinctively female gesture dedicated to staging the tragedy of women's lives at the hands of men, in "Suicide and Sex: The Cost of Desire (Is Death)," *Southern Quarterly* 41 (Fall 2002): 29–38.

26. Vladimir Nabokov, *Lolita* (New York, 1997); originally published in 1955 in France (Olympia Press) and in 1958 in the U.S. (Random House). See Susan Mizruchi, "*Lolita* in

History," *American Literature* 75 (Summer 2003): 629–52, for an examination of a distinctively American feature of the novel: its mediation of the subtextual memory of the Holocaust by the rites of the U.S. culture of consumption. Mizruchi quotes the passage from *Lolita* I excerpt here (631).

27. Randy Boyagoda, "From Revolutionary through Cold War: The Russian Outlanders of Faulkner's South" (unpublished essay), considers the importance of Ratliff's Russian heritage as symbolizing an original U.S. hybridity in the later trilogy, where it is revealed for the first time.

28. A portion of *The Mansion* was published as the short story "By the People" in *Mademoiselle* (October 1955). It recounts the episode of Clarence Snopes's withdrawal from his congressional candidacy as a result of a prank Ratliff pulls, in which dog scent surreptitiously left on Clarence's trousers attracts a four-footed crowd during his announcement speech. Gillian Cohen reports that *Mademoiselle* in the mid-1950s contained numerous stories and advertisements reinforcing the image of suburban nuclear families run by housewives, but also increasingly grew interested in questions of college education for young women. In view of Faulkner's distaste for Joseph McCarthy, the story works as a satirical portrait of demagoguery, but it is also interestingly addressed to an audience of women who might have been particularly attuned to Eula's and Linda's situations in *The Mansion*.

29. "Faulkner, Metropolitan Fashion, and 'The South,'" in *Faulkner's Inheritance: Faulkner and Yoknapatawpha, 2005* (Jackson: University Press of Mississippi, 2007), 82–100.

30. In *Creating Faulkner's Reputation: The Politics of Modern Literary Criticism* (Knoxville: University of Tennessee Press, 1988), Lawrence Schwartz argues that during the Cold War prominent U.S. intellectuals abetted national interests by promoting modernist experimentalism as an expression of the freedom of individual imagination under U.S. democracy, as opposed to the regimentation required of social realist writers in the Soviet Union. Associating the communist Kohl with experimental nonrepresentational sculpture may be part of Faulkner's resistance to Cold War cooptation of modernist aesthetics. See also Serge Guilbaut, *How New York Stole the Idea of Modern Art: Abstract Expressionism, Freedom, and the Cold War*, trans. Arthur Goldhammer (Chicago: University of Chicago Press, 1983). Catherine Gunther Kodat interprets *A Fable* as Faulkner's attempt to bridge the gap between modernist and mass cultural modes via an intermediate "sentimental modernism": "Writing *A Fable* for America," in *Faulkner in America: Faulkner and Yoknapatawpha, 1998*, ed. Joseph R. Urgo and Ann J. Abadie (Jackson: University Press of Mississippi, 2001), 82–97.

31.
I've got a mansion just over the hilltop
In that bright land where we'll never grow old
And some day yonder we will never more wander
But walk on streets that are purest gold.

Don't think me poor or deserted or lonely
I'm not discouraged I'm heaven bound
I'm but a pilgrim in search of the city
I want a mansion, a harp and a crown.

I've got a mansion just over the hilltop
In that bright land where we'll never grow old
And some day yonder we will never more wander
But walk on streets that are purest gold.
    (Words and music by Ira Stamphill, as sung by Elvis Presley)

32.
And the Jews' passover was at hand, and Jesus went up to Jerusalem.

And found in the temple those that sold oxen and sheep and doves, and the changers of money sitting:

And when he had made a scourge of small cords, he drove them all out of the temple, and the sheep, and the oxen; and poured out the changers' money, and overthrew the tables;

And said unto them that sold doves, Take these things hence; make not my Father's house an house of merchandise.
    John 2:14–16 (KJV)

Forasmuch therefore as you trample on the poor, and take taxes from him of wheat: You have built houses of cut stone, but you will not dwell in them. You have planted pleasant vineyards, but you shall not drink their wine.

For I know how many your offenses, and how great are your sins—you who afflict the just, who take a bribe, and who turn aside the needy in the courts.
    Amos 5:11–12 (KJV)

33. Noel Polk argues that though Mink's sense of grievance may be rendered sympathetically by Faulkner, a murder is still a murder, and represents more the repugnant corruption of the ideal of honor and individualism than their admired fulfillment: "Idealism in *The Mansion*," in *Faulkner and Idealism: Perspectives from Paris*, ed. Michel Gresset and Patrick Samway, S.J. (University Press of Mississippi, 1983), 112–26. Theresa Towner wonders if Linda's complicity in Flem's murder and her surprising departure in a new Jaguar cast doubt on the purity of her motives in working on behalf of Jefferson's African Americans; perhaps, Towner proposes, Linda cares mainly about embarrassing "the whitely 'respectable' Flem'" by her activities (*Faulkner on the Color Line: The Later Novels* [Jackson: University Press of Mississippi, 2000], 116).

34. The Jicarilla were part of the Apache nation, indigenous to the southwest. U.S. Jicarilla were eventually confined to a reservation in New Mexico in 1897. Few would have been left in Old Mexico at the time Byron claims to have found his wife there, but border-crossing from Mexico escalated during World War I, and Faulkner's depiction of mixed race borderline relations is historically resonant. (See www.crystalinks.com/apache.html and www.jsri.msu.edu/museum/pubs/MexAmHist/chapter15.html. Information provided by Christie Ko.)

35. Polk suggested to me in conversation that the children's host, Dewitt Binford, may also have molestation on his mind when he sneaks into the room and "reached out easy and found the hem of that nightshirt with one hand" (*The Town* 322).

36. David M. Reimers, *Still the Golden Door: The Third World Comes to America*, 2nd ed. (New York: Columbia University Press, 1992). However, the McCarran-Walter Act was weakened, according to many contemporary observers, by executive and congressional exceptions to it that catered to southwestern growers' demand for cheap undocumented workers from Mexico.

From Colony to Empire:
Postmodern Faulkner

Leigh Anne Duck

Faulkner's work is renowned for its attention to the presence of a regional past, a theme unquestionably central to his fiction. No matter what period his narratives represent, his fictional worlds are saturated with the traces of past times, and he seems phenomenally attuned to accretion, the process by which the past—as a collection of conflicts and outcomes, choices and (more often) compulsive actions—produces the present. But the fame accorded this aspect of his work tends to obscure how these fictions record a past and present already sedimenting into a future. Many of Faulkner's texts explore early stages in phenomena considered endemic to our contemporary era, particularly the way in which the mobility of capital transforms local worlds. Throughout his oeuvre, he displays characters who confront a problem Achille Mbembe describes as typical of our own present: they find that "many arenas of everyday life have outrun the pedagogies in which [they] were trained," however informally.[1] As he stages their ensuing cognitive and psychological crises, Faulkner approaches globalization from a regional perspective, but his attention to global capital also informs his understanding of the South.

For this reason, his work seems to me an interesting study for the postmodern era (to be clear, I'm not trying to describe Faulkner as a postmod-ern*ist*), but given the claims of Faulkner's early critics, even my milder claim could seem absurd. How could this writer be expected to have insight into emergent cultural forms if, as Jean-Paul Sartre complained, Faulkner's vision encompassed no future?[2] For his initial reviewers—and for many since—Faulkner seemed to exemplify two traits distinctive to the modernist era, incommensurable with our own and also, paradoxically, with each other. On the one hand, reviewers read his novels as representations of a regional culture stuck in the past and thus distanced from modern time—a form of temporal isolation unthinkable in our famously globalizing world—and on the other, despite Faulkner's apparently provincial origins, liberal and leftist critics argued that his work typified the mood of despair, powerlessness, and futility characteristic of bourgeois metropolitan modernism.[3] Such tones have often been used to distinguish this earlier aesthetic mode from postmodernist work, which is supposedly characterized by playfulness and parody.

But debates over our current era teach us nothing so definitively as to be skeptical of boundaries, whether in space (between center and periphery) or in time (between modern and postmodern). In one such destabilizing irony, Fredric Jameson notes that, in relation to Anglo-American literature, at least, the term "modernism" was not coined in an industrial metropolis of England or the northeastern U.S., but emerged instead in the relatively undeveloped U.S. South among a group of self-styled "Fugitive" poets.[4] While Jameson uses this aesthetic history to trouble the border between metropole and hinterland, Martyn Bone shows how this same group of thinkers, in their subsequent incarnation as Southern Agrarians, disrupt efforts at periodization (as well as most understandings of the political spectrum) by promoting cultural values later shared by Marxist critics of postmodernity. Each group protests that finance capitalism alienates individuals from tangible objects and their use value; each also worries that boundary-effacing flows of culture, products, and people might produce crises in individuals' senses of place and identity.[5] Finally, though postmodern writing—both literary and theoretical—was once considered relatively buoyant in comparison with that of the modernist era, that energy seems to be dissipating, as many current thinkers—particularly leftists—testify to pervasive melancholia, attributed to a loss of faith in the idea of social and political progress and a difficulty imagining what might replace such hopes and expectations.[6] In other words, present-day leftists, like high modernists before them, find it difficult to imagine "potentiality"—Georg Lukács's word for a future shaped, at least in part, by human agency.[7]

Though scholars disagree, then, about what to call or how to describe the contemporary era, one of its primary lessons is that we must reexamine our narratives of modernity and its discrete locales in order to produce a "global and relational" understanding of both past and present.[8] Studies of Faulkner and of the U.S. South have been vigorous and vital in these efforts, largely because the latter is, as Jon Smith has argued, "simultaneously center and margin, colonizer and colonized, global north and global south."[9] These structural dualities have been productively probed by scholars and writers including Deborah Cohn, Barbara Ladd, George Handley, Keith Cartwright, and Édouard Glissant, in work that has created new cultural and historical maps for contextualizing Faulkner's fiction.[10] Meanwhile, other critics have used his novels to debunk the idea that modernism and postmodernism could be rigidly demarcated. Brian McHale, for example, describes *Absalom, Absalom!* as "an ambiguously modernist-postmodernist text" and Richard Moreland notes the postmodern sensibility often evident in *Requiem for a Nun*.[11]

But while we have reconfigured Faulknerian space and acknowledged the degree to which the author's styles and philosophical concerns align with those of the present, we have been slower to recognize the degree to which *his* sense of space—both local and global—may have been shaped by an awareness of transnational dynamics, the likes of which have intensified in our own age. This hesitation is nowhere as evident as in readings of *Absalom, Absalom!*'s sojourn into nineteenth-century Haiti, where the fictional Thomas Sutpen claims to have "subdued" an uprising of plantation laborers in the 1820s. Interpreting this revolt as a slave rebellion, critics long ignored the concomitant anachronism—as slavery was abolished with Haitian independence in 1803—or treated the novel's chronology as a simple mistake.[12] Intervening in this general disregard for Haitian history, Richard Godden argued in 1994 that Faulkner erred intentionally, distorting the past in order to clarify its dynamics. In this argument, the mere mention of "Haiti, the only successful black revolution" enabled Faulkner to reference the "continuous potential for revolution within the institution of slavery" while insisting that the most essential characteristic of the "plantocracy" is its work to "suppress revolution"—the latter by having his "ur-planter," Sutpen, consistently defeat Haitians who, chronologically, should already be free.[13] Arguing against the idea that Faulkner's novel is "counter-revolutionary," Godden refrains from considering that such willful misrepresentation of Haiti's struggle for independence might be considered imperialistic no matter what the novelist's aims, and subsequent scholarship on this question has struggled to determine whether colonialism is strictly critiqued by or also enacted within the narrative.[14] It was not until 2004 that John T. Matthews argued that Faulkner may not have erred at all; he notes that the rebelling laborers are never definitively described as slaves, and suggests that "Sutpen and his narrators ignore historical truths that they are in a position to admit plainly."[15]

I want to consider this textual silence in relation to Faulkner's exploration of globalization, which—in his work as in our present—emerges as a centuries-long and continuing process, perpetually forcing its inhabitants to reinterpret the circumstances of their lives. The facts that Sutpen and those who observe him refuse to name shape not only Sutpen's era—which is to say, Quentin and Shreve's past, as well as Faulkner's—but also, and perhaps even more profoundly, Faulkner's present, which included the Great Depression and the end of the U.S. occupation of Haiti. In other words, the disavowal that takes place in *Absalom, Absalom!* may concern not only history and a sense of colonial complicity—as insightfully analyzed by Matthews—but also the perception of new social forms, engendered but not contained by past structures of injustice. I confess that my reading is informed in part by *Requiem for a Nun*, which situates an episode from *Absalom, Absalom!* in relation to forces that shape not only Faulkner's later present—now the Cold War—but also our own. Thus I read *Absalom, Absalom!*, published in 1936, through a novel published in 1951, in order to suggest that Faulkner's concerns about global capital—so fully bodied forth in the later work—may have shaped his understanding in ways he was not previously ready to name. And if all of this seems recklessly antihistoricist, I counter with the proposition that these novels urge us to think differently about history, which becomes in Faulkner's work not a linear progression so much as a shifting set of vortices, forces, and incidents which reach across periods to transform consciousness and society. Unseating his work from linear time, then—if ever so gently and provisionally—enables us to recognize him not only as a regional writer describing lost locales, but also as a regional writer describing incipient global transformations. Looking backward, one sees his work stage the progression from colonies, which were cleaved by enslaved African Americans from Native American lands without regard for the environmental or human toll, to a less clearly differentiated and potentially unlimited empire, which institutionalizes a similar disregard for the planet and its people while forging ever more intangible and implacable networks for extracting wealth. Such a project helps to underscore the contemporary relevance of Faulkner's vision, but it seeks more urgently to denaturalize his fiction's apocalyptic tones—a project that, in our current circumstances, may be somewhat more difficult.

One would expect Faulkner to be attuned to uneven economic development, given that he was surrounded for most of his life by discussions concerning the relationship between the vigorously industrializing U.S. North and the relatively agricultural U.S. South. This difference, in combination with the history of the South's defeat in the Civil War, often inflected discussions of Southern modernization with the language of conflict and loss. The Southern Agrarians, for example, were hardly the only figures in 1930 to express concern that industrialization and commercial culture might damage rural communities; such worries had long been central to U.S. discourse, and, in this period, much anxiety concerning the potential for cultural dissolution seemed to be directed toward the Midwest.[16] But a Midwestern regionalist could not so readily suggest—as the Agrarian John Crowe Ransom did—that concerned local citizens stimulate the "natives . . . to revive ancient and almost forgotten animosities," perhaps by "proclaiming to Southerners that the carpet-baggers are again in their midst."[17]

This belief that Southern poverty and suffering were caused directly and chiefly by Northern exploitation was not restricted to Agrarian partisans. Sherwood Anderson's 1935 travelogue *Puzzled America* suggests that some observers from outside the region felt guilty about its circumstances: as Anderson and a companion traveled "the back country of the deep South," for example, his friend "kept saying," " 'Look what we Northerners did to the South.' "[18] This view was granted federal and social scientific authority when Roosevelt's National Emergency Council, in its 1938 *Report on Economic Conditions of the South*, described the use of the region's natural resources and the development of its industry using the paradigm of intranational colonial exploitation.[19] As of 1929, Faulkner seems not to have embraced such perspectives whole-heartedly: when young Jason Compson complains, in *The Sound and the Fury*, that "fellows . . . sit up there in New York and trim the sucker gamblers"—manipulating farmers and others who lack "inside information"—readers nonetheless recognize that many of his problems are rooted much closer to home.[20] Nonetheless, this moment in the novel implies a world in which beliefs about internal U.S. colonialism shape many white Southerners' ideas about their local economy.

By 1951, Faulkner would expand this concept into a tendentious—if often parodic—history of the nation, presenting a Mississippi's eye view of U.S. progression from colony to empire. *Requiem for a Nun* encompasses regional history from the Ice Age to the present, situating Jefferson in relation to an ever-expanding United States "moving faster and faster," finally constituting "one nation: no longer anywhere, not even in Yoknapatawpha County, one last irreconcilable fastness of stronghold from which to enter the United States . . . one universe, one cosmos: contained in one America."[21] These descriptions—in which a single sentence, replicating the growth of U.S. influence, proceeds inexorably for pages—seem to outstrip other complaints from the period about the spread of mass culture or American expansionism. Faulkner's prose is, in contrast, replete with imagery associated with our contemporary era.

These portentous attributes include David Harvey's sense of "time-space compression," in which "the world suddenly feels much smaller, and the time-horizons over which we can think about social action become much shorter."[22] They also feature Michael Hardt and Antonio Negri's "smooth space," in which cultural and geopolitical boundaries are ineffectual from the perspective of capital, however meaningful they may be to those Faulkner sardonically deems "intractable and obsolescent."[23]

Faulkner further describes the cultural commodification that Michel-Rolph Trouillot considers a "tacit but pervasive" belief about contemporary globalization—the idea of "a shopping mall of cultures within which individuals and groups will be able to pick their preferred components and return home . . . to self-construct the culture(s) of their choice."[24] Accordingly, *Requiem* depicts "the old deathless Lost Cause" as a "social club or caste, or form of behavior when you remembered to observe it on the occasions when young men from Brooklyn, exchange students at Mississippi or Arkansas or Texas universities, vended tiny Confederate battle flags among the thronged Saturday afternoon ramps of football stadia" (212). Finally, Faulkner's argument that the development of the United States occurred through one "boundless immeasurable forenoon" in which "men's mouths were full of law and order, all men's mouths were round with the sound of money . . . profit plus regimen equals security" suggests the contemporary ascendance of neoliberal values, which involve, as Wendy Brown argues, not only "facilitating free trade, maximizing corporate profits, and challenging welfarism," but also, more radically, "extending and disseminating market values to all institutions and social action."[25]

To be clear, all of these changes are said to have taken place since approximately 1970, and I do not mean to elide the important and previously unpredictable economic, cultural, and geopolitical changes that have taken place between 1951 and the present. But Faulkner omits many economic and political realities of the mid-century United States: while Neil Smith argues that "postwar U.S. dominance was organized first and foremost through the world market," this moment in U.S. globalism was also shaped by the emerging Cold War—which foregrounded the need to align nation-states—and the continued influence of Keynesian economics and the New Deal.[26] Excluding these factors, Faulkner describes a global American empire that seems to have less in common with his own time than with today's neoliberal consensus, which is not strictly "American"—despite the centrality of U.S. economists and policies in this movement—but is rather shared among global corporations and nongovernmental organizations as well as diverse national governments pursuing this model for economic growth.[27] Like the Agrarians before him, then, Faulkner hardly distinguishes between America the nation-state and America the aggregate of corporations, industries, and communications networks, and he focuses his critique on the latter. Accordingly, even as the novel demonstrates how peoples are displaced and ways of living are destroyed by U.S. expansion, it associates these effects less with territorial changes—as it narrates the frontier era in a largely comic mode—than with economic development, which "dispossess[es]" not only the Chickasaw but also the "frontiersman" and, later, both white and black agricultural laborers (90, 210–1).

But while Faulkner's understanding of U.S. nationhood appears to have been shaped, to a significant extent, by resentment of how national capital had reshaped his region—both through wealth extraction in the late nineteenth and early twentieth centuries and substantial assimilation after World War II—that does not deprive it of insight. And his perspective on globalization appears also to have been informed by such factors as U.S. incursions into Caribbean nations—occupations that many theorists cite as precursors for contemporary military actions (so named to assert motives of assistance as opposed to aggression).[28] Unlike earlier European imperialists, the U.S. in the early twentieth century claimed the objective of preserving stability in occupied nations, but it sought more urgently to preserve its strategic interests in the hemisphere and to serve the needs of U.S. capital. This pattern was amply demonstrated by its 1915 occupation of Haiti, which elicited increasing protest in both countries over its nineteen-year duration.[29] Faulkner may have been attentive to this occupation long before he began work on *Absalom, Absalom!*, because early U.S. representations of the Haitian occupation echoed paternalist images of the pre–Civil War U.S. South; further, the brutality of the occupation was often attributed to the purportedly disproportionate number of Marines—solely white at this time—from the racially segregated U.S. South.[30] Continuing protests often noted that U.S. military and governing officials introduced into Haitian social clubs a "Jim Crow" style of racial segregation, enforcing a strictly dualistic understanding of racial identification that was both offensive and largely new to the Haitian public.[31]

Some recognition of such histories seems implicit in *Requiem for a Nun*, at any rate, because its global U.S. empire, while effacing geopolitical, economic, and cultural boundaries, institutionalizes racial ones. Faulkner interrupts his telescopic narration of the movement from "one nation" to "one world" in order to demonstrate new forms of racial division and exploitation, including a clause about the accomplishment of Japanese-American soldiers in World War II, "whose mothers and fathers at the time were in a California detention camp for enemy aliens" (212). He further notes how racial boundaries align with economic ones in this "new age" when he clarifies that technological change, in the form of air conditioning, has improved the lives of "people (white people)" (212, 207). (Incidentally, returning to *Absalom, Absalom!*'s theme of exploiting Caribbean laborers, *Requiem* reveals that the Jefferson courthouse was designed by the architect from Martinique, whom Sutpen brought to Mississippi, tied to slaves at night, and hunted with dogs when he escaped.[32])

I point to these moments because they suggest a significant difference between the perspective Faulkner derived from the relationship between the U.S. South and the larger nation, on the one hand, and that promulgated by the Agrarians, on the other. The latter vigorously insisted on their status as an internal colony of the United States: eschewing the possibility of "an independent political destiny," they nonetheless complained, "How far shall the South surrender its moral, social, and economic autonomy to the victorious principle of Union?"[33] But for many of them, disfranchisement and exploitation of African Americans constituted a vital element of this "autonomy." Frank Owsley, for example, described efforts to desegregate Southern juries as federal attempts to dominate the South on behalf of capitalist "industrialism."[34] Such arguments criticized internal colonization conducted according to region while often celebrating internal colonization conducted according to race. Sharing some insight with the Agrarians, *Requiem for a Nun* is much more rigorous in its anticolonial critique: ambivalent in its representation of race, it is nonetheless astute in observing how racial policies restrict and contain populations—often laborers—even as capital achieves unprecedented ability to transcend and eradicate other borders.

A reader of Faulkner's early fiction might not have predicted such acuity. *Flags in the Dust*, Faulkner's first novel set in Yoknapatawpha (which he called, at the time, Yocona County), both stages and encodes white supremacy. With few exceptions, this novel, published in edited form in 1929 as *Sartoris*, naturalizes Southern racial segregation through tropes from the tradition of plantation romance; it represents an "organic society" in which all residents—aside from those who have been disoriented by their travels in World War I—are accustomed and attached to their social roles.[35] Faulkner's subsequent novels—particularly *The Sound and the Fury* (1929) and *Light in August* (1932)—powerfully and much more critically explore the psychological effects of racism among white and possibly mixed-race Southerners, as Joe Christmas's racial background remains forever indeterminate; in that process, Faulkner reveals race to be a social construction. But he does not devote extended attention to the economic and political effects of that construction—the ways in which, for example, it constrains or enables choices, and marginalizes or legitimizes viewpoints—until *Go Down, Moses* (1942) and later novels.

Absalom, Absalom!, situated between these two phases, is strangely muted on these questions: their import repeatedly rises to the surface of the narrative, and at these moments, meaning seems almost deliberately to be silenced or occluded, a pattern many critics attribute to the emergence of overwhelming historical knowledge.[36] Without denying these arguments, I want to argue that *Absalom, Absalom!*, rooted in a short story profoundly relevant to Depression-era debates about Southern labor, also contains—that is, includes and constricts—important and perhaps destabilizing observations about race in Faulkner's *contemporary* social structure. In this novel, Faulkner implicitly moves from seeing race as a social and subjective division deeply rooted in local cultures to seeing it, in addition, as a political and economic division that organizes and sustains capital and oppressive labor relations across national contexts. He makes this move by sending his poor white protagonist to Haiti.

As Richard Godden notes, one kernel of *Absalom, Absalom!* lies in the short story "Wash," published in 1934; here, a stereotypical "white trash" man—without property or work, and nothing to sustain him but his racial identification with a wealthy white man who allows him to live in a decayed shack on his plantation—finally realizes that the plantation owner is neither heroic nor his ally.[37] Having lost much of his family and land during the Civil War, the once wealthy Thomas Sutpen impregnates Wash Jones's granddaughter, Milly, and then refuses to marry her once she delivers a girl; having hoped for a boy who might replace his lost heir, he dismisses Milly with the comment, "Too bad you're not a mare. Then I could give you a decent stall in the stable" (535). Though deeply troubled that "Negroes, whom the Bible told him had been created and cursed by God to be brute and vassal to all men of white skin, were better found and housed and even clothed than he and is," and sensing "always about him mocking echoes of black laughter," Jones has in the past consoled himself by visualizing Sutpen as "his own lonely apotheosis" (538). When Sutpen abruptly denies the possibility of a transclass white racial alliance by viewing Milly as less worthy of housing than his livestock, Jones kills Sutpen and, later, Milly; he then burns his shack and great-grandaughter, rushing out to challenge—with Sutpen's scythe—the sheriff, the police, and their guns.

As Caroline Miles has argued, the class resentment enacted here suggests a "radical" commentary; in its exploration of race and psychology, this story also asks vital questions about Southern labor relations in the 1920s and 30s.[38] During this period, conservative and liberal analysts agreed that the rigid triangulation of race and class was crucial to the white supremacist status quo in the South: they differed only as to whether poor whites were congenitally convinced or manipulatively persuaded to forego the sorts of economic and political rebellion that would acknowledge their shared class interests with poor African Americans.[39] Though hardly new to this period, questions about how and why racial identification might preempt class identification emerged with new urgency amid economic depression and increasing national anxiety over Southern social structures. Accordingly, for example, both "Wash," published in 1934, and C. Vann Woodward's *Tom Watson, Agrarian Rebel*, published in 1938, consider a troubling contemporary dynamic by tracing or imagining its manifestations in the past. *Absalom, Absalom!* deepens this implicit critique by providing Thomas Sutpen a past in which he exploits both slaves and Milly Jones in the pursuit of class revenge—as Faulkner later argued, "for all the redneck people."[40] Rather than rebelling against an oppressive system, however, Sutpen seeks wealth that would rival the holdings of the most established Southern aristocrat.

For where Wash Jones only occasionally suspects that his status might be lower than that of slaves and, later, free African Americans, young Thomas Sutpen briefly loses all his illusions about social status. Growing up in a remarkably undifferentiated hill society, he subscribes, effectively, to the frontier myth that often underwrites celebratory accounts of capitalism and opportunity in the U.S.[41] Faulkner complicates this myth by noting that the relative homogeneity of Sutpen's Appalachia is achieved through the systematic murder of Indians, but that does not lessen its psychological impact on young Thomas, who "didn't even know there was a country all divided and fixed and neat with a people living on it all divided and fixed and neat because of what color their skins happened to be and what they happened to own" (179). As his family moves into a plantation region, however, he very quickly determines that race can be expressed as species difference, and refers to African Americans as "bull[s]" and "monkey[s]" (182, 186–90). Separating slaves from the racial classification shared by himself and the wealthy initially helps to defer his awareness of class difference among whites—the idea that "any man should take any such blind accident" as birth into a propertied family "as authority or warrant to look down at others" (180). But this strategy collapses when, seeking to relay a message to his father's boss, Sutpen is told by the slave/butler who answers the door that he must go to the back—presumably the door slaves would use, and certainly the door African Americans were required to use at white homes during Faulkner's lifetime.

As Hortense Spillers argues, this event utterly disrupts Sutpen's understanding of both self and society: as it happens he "seem[s] to kind of dissolve," and he concludes that he and his family also, from the plantation owner's perspective, occupy a distinct species category—"cattle, creatures heavy and without grace, brutely evacuated into a world without hope or purpose for them."[42] (To be clear, from the colonial era through Faulkner's period, Southern "poor whites" were often distinguished from other financially troubled white people by their supposed psychological and physical difference.[43]) Because Sutpen, in his racism, has already accepted and even embraced belief in such differences among humans, he finds this new understanding of his own status unbearable. Unlike his father, who beats the plantation owner's slaves when confronted with such frustration, Sutpen seeks to become a plantation owner, thereby changing categories. Nonetheless, because he believes that his white racial identification allows him the potential for economic mobility, Sutpen serves, at this point, as a near model for Depression-era critiques of how "poor whites" fail to understand their class interests.

Like so many protagonists of U.S. novels, Sutpen determines that, in order to escape a restrictive class or ethnic identity, he needs only to leave his restrictive locale; he sets out on what he imagines will be a sort of imperialist adventure to "a place called the West Indies to which poor men went in ships and became rich, it didn't matter how, so long as that man was clever and courageous."[44] (Here, the tone of abashed romanticism resonates with the novel's systematic critique of the plantation tradition, for the heroic imperialists of late nineteenth-century U.S. fiction were built, according to Amy Kaplan, from the tropes of Confederate mythology.[45]) But where Sutpen expects to find unlimited agency in this foreign venue, he ultimately discovers that the white class privilege to which he aspires is not global in reach. Though he believes that plantation owners must unquestionably be white, and that laborers must unquestionably be black slaves, both certainties are exploded in Haiti, where a successful revolution had ended slavery two decades before Sutpen's arrival and white landownership was constitutionally prohibited.

These differences are initially invisible to Sutpen, however, because closely aligned class and color divisions between *les mulatres et les negres* served to sustain a Haitian plantation labor system structurally quite similar to that existing in the colonial era. Certainly, as C. L. R. James demonstrates, postrevolutionary Haiti was shaped by liberatory hopes: the idea that racial unity could help to bind citizens of the new nation was suggested, for example, by Dessalines's constitutional declaration rendering all Haitians officially "black"—a strategic use of the term that, encompassing also those Europeans who had fought for Haitian independence, would nicely debunk Sutpen's understanding of race as species difference.[46] Nonetheless, as Matthews notes, postrevolutionary Haitian agriculture was, particularly during the 1820s—the period when Sutpen would have worked in Haiti, characterized by the establishment of mulatto-owned plantations and the systematic denial of rights to peasants.[47] President Jean-Pierre Boyer's Rural Code, enacted in 1826, not only restricted agricultural laborers from moving into cities and across regions but also stipulated arrest and forced labor for the unemployed.[48] In sum, Thomas Sutpen travels to a locale shaped by economic and legal structures that prefigured post–Civil War sharecropping in the U.S. South—the form of labor still experienced, in Faulkner's era, by up to 80 percent of farmworkers in some regions.[49] And Faulkner likely knew of this developmental similarity between post-revolutionary Haiti and the post–Civil War U.S. South, because occupation-era discourse concerning each area observed that, in the words of Jean Price-Mars, one of Haiti's foremost intellectuals, "legal slavery had given place to a hybrid form of serfdom."[50]

This convergence in economic history seems too thematically central to Faulkner's oeuvre to be a mere coincidence; a writer who so insistently probed the psychological relationships between wealthy and poor white Southerners could hardly fail to be interested in the class stratifications shaping a nation often called—among both admirers and detractors— "The Black Republic." Given the insistent concern with racial and class identifications staged in both *Absalom, Absalom!* and "Wash," Sutpen's trip to Haiti seems to open the door for a revelatory moment, as Faulkner brings his protagonist to a locale where his understanding of race no longer aligns him with those in power. But rather than revisiting his alliances and interests, Sutpen, as well as all who encounter his story, disavows the alignments that Faulkner's chronology has inexorably produced: in pondering Sutpen's story, no one in the novel ever acknowledges that the Haitian workers were—to some extent, at least—free, or that, in the dualistic Southern U.S. system of racial identification, the plantation owner for whom Sutpen works would be considered black. And yet there can be no question about this point: though Sutpen calls his employer "French" and questions the racial background of his "Spanish" wife, all French landowners were exiled or killed in the Haitian Revolution, a history rendered notorious in the white U.S. South and unquestionably familiar to Faulkner and, implicitly, *Absalom, Absalom!*'s elite white characters.[51] Still, none of them correct or even seem to understand the previously uninformed Sutpen when he complains, in cryptic astonishment, that his marriage to the Haitian plantation owner's daughter proved "not . . . adjunctive to the forwarding of [his] design"—which was, all along, the creation of a white U.S. Southern dynasty, which might allot him some control over the social categories that render some men impervious to scorn and others, in Sutpen's terms, "brutes" (211–12).

Thus *Absalom, Absalom!* goes much further, both spatially and thematically, than "Wash" in describing how racial identifications lead poor whites to make economic, political, and social decisions poorly suited to their own interests. It is not only the case that Thomas Sutpen's efforts to disavow his past alliances with Haitian elites lead to the demise of his design and his descendants, but also that, in turning to Haiti, Faulkner utterly disrupts the way racial categories were understood in the U.S. Finally, the novel implies that transnational alliances of capital and power *are* willing to transcend racial boundaries when such adjustments facilitate local control of laborers. For despite the country's history of racial conflict, the Haitian landowner is quite happy to accept Sutpen's services in suppressing a labor revolt, and Sutpen responds with oblivious zeal, leaving his rifle by the door of the barricaded house as he goes out to conquer, through sheer force of will, men whose socioeconomic position is identical to that from which he had just fled.

And his victory seems dependent on their recognition of his class betrayal, because the explanation offered by General Compson—Sutpen's "yelling louder . . . bearing more than they believed any bones and flesh could or should . . . containing an indomitable spirit which should have come from the same primary fire which theirs came from but which could not have"—is extravagantly absurd, yet another instance of his infinite disavowal concerning the long and violent Haitian Revolution (205). Indeed, it is difficult to understand what happens here: we know only that these workers revolt, appear to be winning, and then stop. In association with other themes in the novel, I can only understand this scene as suggesting some kind of revolutionary exhaustion on the part of the laborers, who would thus manifest, in a muted but absolute form, the belief that had previously traumatized Sutpen himself—the idea that *"there aint any good or harm either in the living world that"* laborers can execute upon the elite (192). Sutpen's ability to convey this message would emerge from his lack of identification with the parties in this struggle: Faulkner surely knew that the racism of white U.S. Southerners was notorious among twentieth-century Haitians, and that may have shaped his representation of these nineteenth-century laborers, who here observe an avowed white supremacist risking his life to protect a mulatto class opponent. Thus Sutpen demonstrates not the power of whiteness but that of the propertied class; especially relevant for Haitian laborers in the nineteenth and twentieth centuries, he exemplifies transnational networks protecting that power.

Here again, Faulkner may have turned to his contemporary era or to nineteenth-century history for inspiration. On the one hand, some Haitian elites initially lauded the U.S. occupation of 1915 because they were disturbed by the popularity of a local radical politician; though most would come to oppose the marines' presence and actions in Haiti before its end in 1935, a significant portion of Haiti's economy—in which most of the public lived in devastating poverty—was by that time closely tied with U.S. capital.[52] On the other hand, even though postrevolutionary Haiti became, as Joan Dayan argues, "the outcast of the international community, jeopardized by the racism and greed of the developing imperial powers," Boyer's Rural Code was translated and published in London for the interest of imperialists; enacted as it was shortly before the abolition of slavery in the British Empire in 1833, it provided one potential model for restricting and controlling "emancipated" laborers.[53] But it seems most likely that this moment in *Absalom, Absalom!* was influenced by a virulent and phenomenally popular representation of Haiti under the U.S. occupation—William Seabrook's *The Magic Island*, published in 1929—which devotes two chapters to the "Kiplingesque" tale of Faustin Wirkus, a Marine who had requested solitary posting on the island of La Gonave and had reportedly been crowned king.[54] Though I cannot say with certainty that Faulkner read this work, the parallels between Wirkus and Sutpen are striking: neither had any knowledge of the region before they arrived; both constitute exaggerated models of masculinity (Wirkus is said by his major to be able to "outcurse and outfight any tough baby I know in the whole service"); both are remarkably "self-contained" and eschew alcohol.[55] Whereas Seabrook's Wirkus achieves the "strangely potent dream" of "hold[ing] undisputed sway on some remote tropical island," Faulkner's Sutpen achieves only one small and almost inexplicable victory, after which his dreams are repeatedly disassembled; in each case, however, their "West Indies adventure" serves interests manifestly not their own.[56]

At least, the implicit and developing presence of global alliances of capital might help to explain one of this novel's most troubling characteristics, for *Absalom, Absalom!* seems repeatedly to introduce revolutionary energy only to dispel it: depicting how boundaries of class and race separate individuals from access to wealth or power, the novel cannot imagine any response to this knowledge that is not ultimately self-destructive or passive—from Charles Bon's apparent goading of his brother to kill him, to Henry Sutpen's acceptance of that charge, to the self-immolation of Wash Jones, to the repeated random fights of Charles Etienne de St. Valery Bon, to the inarticulate moans of Jim Bond, to the repeated denials of Quentin Compson. Critics have tended to attribute this pervasive sense of futility to the strict hierarchies of the U.S. South, and that is surely the main cause. But adding the silent surrender of Haitian laborers to this list suggests a contributing problem. In this novel where economic privilege is insistently tied to a sense of male psychological self-acceptance, that privilege is also shown, in multiple eras and national venues, to be nearly unassailable, despite not only the efforts of individuals such as Sutpen, but also such massive social changes as the end of slavery. While individual wealth and status can be gained or lost, any degree of redistribution or meaningful collective action seems unimaginable.

In taking a global, relational approach to plantation agriculture, *Absalom, Absalom!* suggests important insights about that economic form, but one must recognize the limitations of this novel's historical vision. For while Haitian laborers, like both black and white laborers in the U.S. South, did continue to be exploited, they also continued to revolt: Boyer's Code failed for precisely this reason, and later *caco* resistance to the Marine occupation received considerable attention in the U.S. press.[57] (Interestingly, from 1843 to 1848, peasants ironically seemed to acknowledge the potential for revolutionary exhaustion even as they defied it: an army of sharecroppers and rural dwellers calling themselves the "armée souffrante," or "Army of Sufferers," waged war while demanding broad economic and political reform.[58]) Similarly, the Depression-era South was characterized by renewed and biracial political activity among U.S. southern agricultural laborers.[59] Even *The Magic Island* can easily be read against the grain: though Seabrook's narrative mocks the Haitian "queen" of La Gonave and the "communistic" system of labor she leads, his conversations with Wirkus suggest that the latter supports this system of governance (185). Thus, though Seabrook describes Wirkus as "tyrannical" and reports that "these peasants looked up to him as a sort of God Almighty," his own account presents both as far more ambiguous.[60] Engaged in an imperialistic occupation backed by considerable military power, Wirkus is nonetheless open to negotiation; while he uses this process to introduce U.S. commodities into an established system (including, as Joan Dayan notes, the sort of pigs that cannot thrive in the Haitian setting), the peasants use his comparative respect for their social order to maintain some autonomy for their *coumbite*, a long-standing system of cooperative labor.[61] Faulkner's transnational analysis—enigmatic as it was—produced many of the benefits one might expect, particularly skepticism toward reflexive racial identification and an acute sense of how even agricultural capital organizes local space; furthermore, it may have facilitated Faulkner's more direct representation of southern labor and race relations in later novels. But it also yielded one problem that contemporary thinkers must still struggle to overcome—a totalizing view of inequity in which local struggles seem almost inevitably ineffectual.

NOTES

1. Achille Mbembe, "Theorizing the Present: Notes from South Africa," presented at AUETSA/SAACLALS/SAVAL Conference, "Forging the Local and the Global," Stellenbosch, South Africa, 10 July 2006.

2. Jean-Paul Sartre, "A Propos de *Le Bruit et la Fureur:* La Temporalité chez Faulkner" (1939), *Situations I* (Paris: Librairie Gallimard, 1947), 80.

3. Sartre, 77; Lionel Trilling, "Mr. Faulkner's World," *Nation* 133 (1931): 491–92; Henry Seidel Canby, "The Grain of Life," *Saturday Review of Literature* 9 (October 1932): 153; Granville Hicks, *The Great Tradition* (New York: Macmillan, 1935), 262–68; Malcolm Cowley, "Poe in Mississippi," *New Republic* (November 1936), rpt. in John Bassett, ed., *William Faulkner: The Critical Heritage* (London: Routledge & Kegan Paul, 1975), 206; Philip Rahv, review of *Absalom, Absalom!, New Masses* (1936): 20–21, rpt. in Bassett, 208–10; Louis Kronenberger, "Faulkner's Dismal Swamp," *Nation* 146 (1938): 212, 214; Alfred Kazin, "Faulkner: The Rhetoric and the Agony," *Virginia Quarterly Review* 18 (Summer 1942): 398–402.

4. Fredric Jameson, *A Singular Modernity: Essay on the Ontology of the Present* (London: Verso, 2002), 228–29 n. 4.

5. Martyn Bone, *The Postsouthern Sense of Place in Contemporary Fiction* (Baton Rouge: Louisiana State University Press, 2005), 13, 45–51.

6. Anne McClintock, "The Angel of Progress: Pitfalls of the Term 'Postcolonialism,'" *Social Text* 31/32 (1992): 85; Wendy Brown, *Politics Out of History* (Princeton: Princeton University Press, 2001), 1–17. For earlier accounts of postmodern "optimism," see Matei Calinescu, *Five Faces of Modernity: Modernism, Avant-Garde, Decadence, Kitsch, Postmodernism* (Durham: Duke University Press, 1987), 136–37.

7. Georg Lukács, "The Ideology of Modernism," in *The Meaning of Contemporary Realism*, trans. John and Necke Mander (London: Merlin Press Limited, 1962), 22.

8. Mary Louise Pratt, "Modernity and Periphery: Toward a Global and Relational Analysis," in *Beyond Dichotomies: Histories, Identities, Cultures and the Challenge of Globalization*, ed. Elisabeth Mudimbe-Boyi (Albany: State University of New York Press, 2002), 22.

9. Jon Smith, "Postcolonial, Black, and Nobody's Margin: The U.S. South and New World Studies," *American Literary History* 16.1 (2004): 144.

10. Deborah Cohn, *History and Memory in the Two Souths: Recent Southern and Spanish American Fiction* (Nashville: Vanderbilt University Press, 1999); Barbara Ladd, *Nationalism and the Color Line in George W. Cable, Mark Twain, and William Faulkner* (Baton Rouge: Louisiana State University Press, 1996); George Handley, *Postslavery Literatures in the Americas: Family Portraits in Black and White* (Charlottesville: University Press of Virginia, 2000); Keith Cartwright, *Reading Africa into American Literature: Epics, Fables, and Gothic Tales* (Lexington: University Press of Kentucky, 2004); Édouard Glissant, *Faulkner, Mississippi* (Paris: Éditions Stock, 1996). See also Jon Smith and Deborah Cohn, eds., *Look Away! Comparatist Approaches to U.S. Southern Cultures* (Durham: Duke University Press, 2004).

11. Brian McHale, *Constructing Postmodernism* (London: Routledge, 1992), 164; Richard Moreland, *Faulkner and Modernism: Rereading and Rewriting* (Madison: University of Wisconsin Press, 1990), 195–96, 228–33.

12. For readings that claim error, see Richard Godden, *Fictions of Labor: William Faulkner and the South's Long Revolution* (Cambridge: Cambridge University Press, 1997), 240 n. 3. For the general delay in discussion of this timeline, see John T. Matthews, "Recalling the West Indies: From Yoknapatawpha to Haiti and Back," *American Literary History* 16.2 (2004): 238–39.

13. Godden, 53. This essay was first published as "*Absalom, Absalom!*, Haiti, and Labor History: Reading Unreadable Revolutions," *ELH* 61.3 (Fall 1994): 685–720.

14. Maritza Stanchich, "The Hidden Caribbean 'Other' in William Faulkner's *Absalom, Absalom!*: An Ideological Ancestry of U.S. Imperialism," *Mississippi Quarterly* 49.3 (Summer

1996): 603–17; Handley, 137; Vera M. Kutzinski, "Borders and Bodies: The United States, America, and the Caribbean," *CR: The New Centennial Review* 1.2 (2001): 65–66.

15. Matthews, 250.

16. Susan Hegeman, *Patterns for America: Modernism and the Concept of Culture* (Princeton: Princeton University Press, 1999), 126–38.

17. John Crowe Ransom, "Reconstructed but Unregenerate," in Twelve Southerners, *I'll Take My Stand: The South and the Agrarian Tradition* (1930; Baton Rouge: Louisiana State University Press, 1977), 23.

18. Sherwood Anderson, *Puzzled America* (New York: Charles Scribner's Sons, 1935), 63.

19. National Emergency Council, *Report on the Economic Conditions of the South* (Washington: U.S. Government Publications Office, 1938), 54, 8. See also George Tindall, "The 'Colonial Economy' and the Growth Psychology: The South in the 1930's," *South Atlantic Quarterly* 64:4 (Autumn 1965): 465–77.

20. William Faulkner, *The Sound and the Fury* (1929; New York: Vintage International, 1990), 192.

21. William Faulkner, *Requiem for a Nun* (1951; New York: Vintage, 1975), 208, 212–13.

22. David Harvey, "Capitalism: The Factory of Fragmentation" (1992), in *Spaces of Capital: Towards a Critical Geography* (New York: Routledge, 2001), 123.

23. Michael Hardt and Antonio Negri, *Empire* (Cambridge: Harvard University Press, 2000), 190; Faulkner, *Requiem*, 216.

24. Michel-Rolph Trouillot, "The Perspective of the World: Globalization Then and Now," in *Beyond Dichotomies*, 4.

25. Faulkner, *Requiem*, 92; Wendy Brown, "Neo-Liberalism and the End of Liberal Democracy," *Theory and Event* 7.1 (2003), http://muse.jhu.edu/journals/theory_and_event/ (14 October 2005): par. 7. For the recent expansion of neoliberal influence, see David Harvey, *A Brief History of Neoliberalism* (Oxford: Oxford University Press, 2005), 2–3.

26. Neil Smith, *American Empire: Roosevelt's Geographer and the Prelude to Globalization* (Berkeley: University of California Press, 2003), 21.

27. Harvey, *A Brief History of Neoliberalism*, 8–9; Hardt and Negri, 31–32, 164–82.

28. Hardt and Negri, 175–79; Carole Boyce-Davies and Monica Jardine, "Imperial Geographies and Caribbean Nationalism: At the Border between 'A Dying Colonialism' and U.S. Hegemony," *CR: The New Centennial Review* 3.3 (2003): 151–55, 159–63; Neil Smith, *The Endgame of Globalization* (New York: Routledge, 2005), 50–79. See, for example, Woodrow Wilson's application of the Monroe Doctrine (as augmented by Theodore Roosevelt) in Mary A. Renda, *Taking Haiti: Military Occupation and the Culture of U. S. Imperialism, 1915–1940* (Chapel Hill: University of North Carolina Press, 2001), 91–100.

29. For a succinct description of motives for the occupation, see David Nicholls, *From Dessalines to Duvalier: Race, Colour, and National Independence in Haiti*, rev. ed. (New Brunswick: Rutgers University Press, 1996), 143–45. For a detailed history of discourse concerning Haiti and the occupation in U.S. culture, see Renda, 185–300.

30. J. Michael Dash, *Haiti and the United States: National Stereotypes and the Literary Imagination*, 2nd ed. (New York: St. Martin's Press, 1997), 27; Hans Schmidt, *The United States Occupation of Haiti, 1914–1934* (New Brunswick: Rutgers University Press, 1971), 143–45.

31. Schmidt, 136–40.

32. William Faulkner, *Requiem for a Nun*, 32–35; *Absalom, Absalom!* (1936; New York: Vintage International, 1990), 26, 178.

33. Twelve Southerners, "Introduction: A Statement of Principles," in *I'll Take My Stand*, xxxviii.

34. Frank L. Owlsley, "Scottsboro, the Third Crusade: The Sequel to Abolition and Reconstruction," *The American Review* 1.3 (June, 1933): 273.

35. For the prominence of such views among white Southerners in the 1920s and 1930s, see Joel Williamson, *The Crucible of Race: Black-White Relations in the American South since Emancipation* (New York: Oxford University Press, 1984), 478–82.

36. Hortense Spillers, "Who Cuts the Border? Some Readings on 'America,'" *Compara-*

tive American Identities: Race, Sex, and Nationality in the Modern Text, ed. Hortense Spillers (New York: Routledge, 1991), 9, 16; Matthews, 239; Godden, 49–79; Carolyn Porter, *Seeing and Being: The Plight of the Participant Observer in Emerson, James, Adams, and Faulkner* (Middletown, Conn.: Wesleyan University Press, 1981), 222.

37. Godden, 132; William Faulkner, "Wash" (1934), in *Collected Stories of William Faulkner* (1950; New York: Vintage, 1995), 535.

38. Caroline Miles, "Race, Anger, and Class Struggle in Faulkner's Short Story 'Wash,'" presented at the Society for the Study of Southern Literature 2006 Conference: "Labor, Literature, and the U.S. South," 31 March 2006.

39. W. E. B. Du Bois, *Darkwater: Voices from Within the Veil* (1920), *The Oxford W. E. B. Du Bois Reader*, ed. Eric J. Sundquist (New York: Oxford University Press, 1996), 530–32; William M. Brewer, "Poor Whites and Negroes in the South since the Civil War," *Journal of Negro History* 15:1 (1930): 26–37; Arna Bontemps, "Saturday Night: Portrait of a Small Southern Town, 1933," in *The Old South: "A Summer Tragedy" and Other Stories of the Thirties* (New York: Dodd, Mead and Co. 1973), 160; Robert Penn Warren, "The Briar Patch," in *I'll Take My Stand*, 260–61.

40. Frederick L. Gwynn and Joseph Blotner, eds., *Faulkner in the University: Class Conferences at the University of Virginia, 1957–1958* (New York: Vintage, 1959), 97.

41. On Faulkner's use and revision of Frederick Jackson Turner's "frontier thesis," see Robert W. Hamblin, "Beyond the Edge of the Map: Faulkner, Turner, and the Frontier Line," in *Faulkner and the Twenty-First Century: Faulkner and Yoknapatawpha, 2000*, ed. Robert W. Hamblin and Ann J. Abadie (Jackson: University Press of Mississippi, 2003), 154–71. For the role of this thesis in U.S. nationalist discourse, see Alan Trachtenberg, *The Incorporation of America: Culture and Society in the Gilded Age* (New York: Hill and Wang, 1982), 11–17.

42. Spillers, 11–14; Faulkner, *Absalom, Absalom!*, 190.

43. Leigh Anne Duck, *The Nation's Region: Southern Modernism, Segregation, and U.S. Nationalism* (Athens, Ga.: University of Georgia Press, 2006), 96–99.

44. Faulkner, *Absalom, Absalom!*, 199. See, in particular, Porter's comparison of Thomas Sutpen and Jay Gatsby (238–39).

45. Amy Kaplan, "Romancing the Empire: The Embodiment of American Masculinity in the Popular Historical Novel of the 1890s," in *Postcolonial Theory and the United States: Race, Ethnicity, and Literature*, ed. Amritjit Singh and Peter Schmidt (Jackson: University Press of Mississippi, 2000), 221, 238.

46. C. L. R. James, *The Black Jacobins: Toussaint L'Ouverture and the San Domingo Revolution*, 2nd ed. (New York: Vintage, 1989), 247–48, 261–62; Nicholls, 35–36.

47. Matthews, 252–53.

48. Joan Dayan, "A Few Stories about Haiti, or, Stigma Revisited," *Research in African Literatures* 35.2 (2004): 161–62.

49. Dayan, 162; Donald Grubbs, *Cry from the Cotton: The Southern Tenant Farmers' Union and the New Deal* (Chapel Hill: University of North Carolina Press, 1971), 8.

50. Jean Price-Mars, "La Vocation de l'Elite" (1919), quoted in Magdaline W. Shannon, *Jean Price-Mars, the Haitian Elite, and the American Occupation, 1915–1935* (New York: St. Martin's Press, 1996), 43.

51. Philippe R. Gerard, "Caribbean Genocide: Racial War in Haiti, 1802–4," *Patterns of Prejudice* 39.2 (2005): 138–61; Alfred Hunt, *Haiti's Influence on Antebellum America: Slumbering Volcano in the Caribbean* (Baton Rouge: Louisiana State University Press, 1988), 107–46; Matthews, 254.

52. Nicholls, 146.

53. Dayan, 158; Nicholls, 61.

54. William Seabrook, *The Magic Island* (New York: Harcourt, Brace, 1929), 178.

55. Seabrook, 174–76, 179; Faulkner, *Absalom, Absalom!*, 25.

56. Seabrook, 171.

57. Alex Dupuy, *Haiti in the World Economy: Class, Race, and Underdevelopment since 1700* (Boulder: Westview Press, 1989), 96.

58. Dupuy, 97; Mimi Sheller, *Democracy after Slavery: Black Publics and Peasant Radicalism in Haiti and Jamaica* (Gainesville: University Press of Florida, 2000), 128–40. They did not succeed on these terms: Faustin Soulouque, who emerged as Emperor following these battles, was relatively less oppressive to blacks than to mulattos, but his rule was autocratic.

59. See Grubbs; Caleb Southworth, "Aid to Sharecroppers: How Agrarian Class Structure and Tenant-Farmer Politics Influenced Federal Relief in the South, 1933–1935," *Social Science History* 26.1 (2002): 33–70.

60. Seabrook, 183, 186. For more on Wirkus's reflections concerning his term in Haiti, see Renda, 3–6, 84–88, 141–45, 155–58, 164–71.

61. Dayan, 171–72; Dupuy, 108.

The Fetish of Surplus Value;
or, What the Ledgers Say

MELANIE R. BENSON

*To such an end does bookkeeping lead. It is the numbering of a farm's
resources—its stacks of fodder, bushels of corn, bales of cotton, its stock
and implements, and the hundreds of things which make up its economy.
And as the only reason to number them is to turn them into cash . . . the
agrarian South is bound to go when the first page is turned and the first
mark crosses the ledger.*

—Andrew Nelson Lytle, "The Hind Tit"

Late in William Faulkner's *The Sound and the Fury* (1929), Jason Compson's boss accuses him of embezzling money from his own family: " '[A]
man never gets anywhere,' " Earl warns him, " 'if fact and his ledgers dont
square.' "[1] Jason's bitter defensiveness and sense of entitlement produce
a skewed sense of moral rectitude that allows him to condone his dishon-
est bookkeeping; but elsewhere in Faulkner's works, instances of fatally
botched accounts signify more encompassing crises of value in the scrupu-
lous New South. In the Summer 2002 issue of the *Mississippi Quarterly*,
Richard Godden and Noel Polk demonstrate brilliantly—by way of a fifty-
nine-page explication of the ledger entries in *Go Down, Moses*—that the
ledgers in Faulkner do, indeed, matter. The McCaslin family's "facts" become, under Godden and Polk's scrutiny, "cryptic" recordings filled with
"abbreviation and aporia," proffering meanings that are not absolute but
"necessarily provisional,"[2] and perhaps "uninterpretable."[3] But for Isaac
McCaslin as well as Jason, such hindrances do not preclude the desire for
definitive, self-enriching products—ones that might exalt Ike's sense of
personal honor as surely as they swell Jason's tightly guarded pockets. In
the *post*plantation South, the ledgers are no longer operative mechanisms
of a fiscal order, but residues of what their obsolescence signifies: the certainty of hierarchy under slavery, the moral satisfaction of balance, and the
allure of profit by engineering surplus value. At the same time, the ledgers
announce the succession of a mercantile order associated with Northern industrial interests and exclusions that incites Jason's representative sense of
divestment and distrust. Faulkner's Southerners respond to this historical

double bind in compromised attempts to balance the books: while Jason might doctor his ledgers to produce a compensatory excess, Ike overreads the account-book "facts" that will inflate his moral superiority.[4]

Between these familiar yet obverse objectives stands a single textual stratagem: the ledger. Rather than unearthing all of the suppressed histories and traumas that the ledgers themselves might ambivalently disclose, as Godden and Polk's reading encourages, it seems crucial instead to determine what the instrument of the ledger itself signifies in Faulkner's New South. That is, we should dwell not so much on what the ledgers say, but on what Faulkner's characters ask them to accomplish. In an age of expanding market relations and the advent of global economic exchange, the modern South famously retreated into its own sense of Agrarian nobility and exceptionalism. Yet the ledger, a relic dating from the earliest iterations of British and European mercantilism,[5] registers its relevance to both modern commercial practice and its anomalous perversions under chattel slavery. An encumbered symbol, it holds in purposeful collision the two social orders disgruntled new Southerners labored most to polarize.[6] Throughout Faulkner's novels, the ledger emerges irrepressibly to negotiate these antagonisms, disclosing its persistent entanglement with the twin objects of race and economics.[7] In what is by now a familiar trope of the neo-Agrarian South, déclassé aristocrats tended to disavow the intrusion of capital culture into their pastoral idylls; as a defensive, self-aggrandizing measure, they inflicted on low-class, "white trash" aspirants cultural demotion generally reserved for blacks. Often, the poor white "on the make" was equated with or below the black underclass.[8] But in the New South, as Myra Jehlen's influential argument reminds us, both neo-aristocrats and the striving poor "rightly viewed the other as a threat to its survival. . . . Faulkner was heir to both of these viewpoints and unable fully to approve either one."[9] In a more recent study, Kevin Railey locates Faulkner's compromise in a notion of "natural aristocracy" wherein individuals are judged by their ethical rather than material superiority, a quality conveniently innate to the social elite.[10] Railey's findings are compelling, but not quite complete; Faulkner's class loyalties are complicated by a growing awareness of America's persistently colonial culture. One of the most circulated clichés in Faulkner studies is his admission that "the past is never past," and his work tacitly unveils a South still very much shackled to an archipelago of occluded histories. In keeping with the transnational cues of both American and Southern studies, Faulkner's best critics—Jack Matthews, George Handley, Deborah Cohn, and others—are beginning to excavate Faulkner and the South's connection to other New World terrains and histories.[11] My work on the ledger suggests another conduit by which

Faulkner registers not only an awareness of a traumatic colonial legacy but also, because of the capital culture the ledger signifies, a chilling recognition that the plantation's priorities carry over into the New South's global economic exchanges, that the principles of exclusion, privilege, and contrivance encumber the national "free" market system as trenchantly as mercantilist savvy dominated the "humanist" order of chattel slavery. Burdened by a regional sense of expropriation and foreclosure,[12] Faulkner's novels witness again and again the doom of recognition that not only is the past never past, but the postcolonial is far from *post*colonial.[13] More than anachronism, more than encrypted historical "accounts," the revenants of the ledger in fact mark a neo-imperial order unable to dispense with the imperatives of a perverse, racially exploitative economic precedent. In their troubling returns, the ledgers constitute a fetish of compensation and restoration, an irrepressible enunciation of the return—*with interest*—of the indomitable master class.

To see this phenomenon fully, we need to recognize the porous peripheries from which the ledgers speak: beyond the actual commissary records that are the centerpiece of *Go Down, Moses* or the diurnal, double-columned fixations of Jason Compson, the ledgers become unmoored from their historical and textual origins to function like free radicals in the Southern body: the language of quantification infects the racially interpellated body of Joe Christmas, paralyzes the vulnerable ascendancy of Thomas Sutpen, and haunts the tormented, romantic Quentin. The instantiation of what I call a "calculating" discourse infiltrates not just Faulkner's writing but Southern discourse more generally,[14] as the recourse to precise numbers and figures in the wake of accounting signifies a way to validate not just social facts but gentlemanly honor and "credit."[15] When Jason's boss insists that a good man's "fact and his ledgers" must "square," he echoes a widespread conviction in genteel society that "moral rectitude . . . was signified by the balance and harmony so prominent in the double-entry ledger" and so cherished by God.[16] In a more literal and opprobrious migration, the ledgers also speak from the haunted soil of other New World terrains, testifying to the vestiges of colonial trauma in a continuous line from Haiti to Yoknapatawpha and back.[17] These are the moments, we shall see, when the calculations break down, when the evasions and exclusions of the ledger become clear, and when the despair of modernity's global, imperial entanglements fatally unsettles Faulkner's most ambitious characters.

Perhaps the most prominent of these strivers is Thomas Sutpen, known to many critics as the antebellum Flem Snopes:[18] a poor Appalachian white "on the make" certain to strike a hostile chord in Faulkner's divisive New

South.[19] As the young son of an indigent tenant farmer, Sutpen is inspired to ascend in a moment of racial sublimation at the front door of the wealthy white planter's house, where he is rebuffed by a Negro servant who orders him to the slave entrance around back.[20] Sutpen's shock of racial degradation forces him to confront his debased position within the South's social hierarchy as a white whose landless status renders him someone a slave might look down upon with impunity. He combats this debasement with an ambitious "design" to erect his own plantation and dynasty, and to elevate himself to mastery by careful economic and mathematical reckoning.[21] These calculations typify Sutpen's ledgerlike mentality: he manufactures a marriage, a house, children, and a social reputation out of carefully planned sums and equations. But the uninitiated Sutpen must first be schooled in what are to him, by birth, unnatural methods: his first arithmetic lessons are baffling, incompatible with his very nature. While he remembers that his "blood . . . forbade him to condescend to memorize dry sums," noticeably, his blood *does* "permit him to listen when the teacher read aloud [about the West Indies]" (195). As Jack Matthews has recently and persuasively argued, Haiti represents a periphery of colonial trauma that white Southerners avoid assimilating as an adjunct to the plantation South. Part of this process of fetishization, I would add, is Sutpen's eagerness to veil any interest in numbers—and, by extension, economic figures—with these more romantic, exotic narratives. He listens innocently but intently to his teacher's stories about the West Indies, not yet knowing that "I was equipping myself better for what I should later *design* to do than if I had learned all the addition and subtraction in the book" (195, emphasis added). While his desire to segregate these sites of imperial pedagogy signifies a commitment to protecting American exceptionalism and innocence, Sutpen soon learns that dry calculations are in fact the very language of these ominous Caribbean lessons. He adds to his design a wife, the daughter of a Haitian sugar planter, but learns too late of her occluded racial heritage; outraged, he registers her as a flaw in his accounts who must be subtracted: at first an "unknown quantity" (312), and then a dark "factor" not "adjunctive or incremental to the design" he has set out to accomplish (194).

Such a miscalculation will haunt, and in fact duplicate itself, over the remainder of Sutpen's attempts to replicate white mastery. As he admits uncannily from the start, it is his own morphologically tainted "blood" that prevents him from absorbing the arithmetic lessons in school, and presumably from accomplishing his presumptuous design—he very literally cannot master the ledger.[22] His first attempt a miserable failure, he returns from Haiti and sets to building his plantation anyway; accordingly, he converts his own body into a kind of ledger of exacting accounts: he spends thriftily and consumes food and drink frugally, "with a sort of sparing cal-culation as though keeping mentally . . . a sort of balance of spiritual sol-vency" (40). Yet such solvency connotes not just equilibrium but also a "dissolving" and "disintegrating" effect.[23] He clings to "his code of logic and morality, his formula and recipe of fact and deduction" but the "bal-anced sum and product declined, refused to swim or even float" (275). His wife is not, as he believes, a negation of his design as much as a reification of his own innate deficiency. That the mixed-blood Bon is the yield of this disastrous union only heightens the sense that his shortfall cannot be frac-tioned away but will go on reproducing itself. Bon is, quite literally, a prod-uct of Sutpen's botched books.

And yet, Bon is his father's son; in a stunning textual moment, he em-bodies the catastrophic delusion of compensatory bookkeeping. After tak-ing a proper white wife, Sutpen of course produces an unblemished son, Henry, to negate the error that was Bon; we know that this brotherly sum does not "swim or float" either, but rather engages in a murderous duel. Before the clash, however, and even prior to learning that Bon is his half-brother, Henry is enchanted by the mysterious Bon. Spellbound, he con-fesses, "You give me two and two and you tell me it makes five and it does make five" (94). Read in the context of Sutpen's ledgers, the calculation is telling: the miscegenated son inflates the product of a simple arithme-tic problem, effortlessly convincing his white rival that his math is indeed correct, that "five" might conceivably replace "four." By such rules, *sur-plus value* can be added to the simple product, a return with interest for what has been debited through racial or class accounting; he can make the product of two plus two something more than mandated, without having to "show the work"—a veritable aristocrat's dream.[24]

But is this Bon's math or Sutpen's? Is it the calculation of the decadent black son or that of the aspirant white master who controls the books and covets their increase? Either way, Faulkner drives home the point: such fabrications are as ineffectual from a black man's lips as a poor white im-postor's pen. The extravagant, dangerous Bon is the one who is eventually silenced in the text, not the innocently and temporarily duped Henry. The white heir, vessel and hope of Sutpen's continuing order, seems to wel-come the solution to Bon's innovative arithmetic; but by the end of the book, he lies wasted on a deathbed, replacing Bon's "five" with the same *"Four years"* (298) repeated over and over again like a mantra of futility. Henry expires knowing that "revenge could not compensate him" (274); neither can Sutpen's "payback"[25] for his original outrage at the planter's door balance out the minus-in-origin[26] that marks his birth. He is excluded from the ledger entirely, an expulsion mirrored by Sutpen's unexpected correlative, the ever-diminishing Rosa Coldfield who knows she will never be a wealthy planter's wife because she is not, by birth, a wealthy planter's daughter, a lament that fuels her own sentimental, poetic laments scribbled on "the *backsides* of the pages within an old account book" from her father's store (137, emphasis added). The substitution of a merchant's commissary book for a planter's ledger indicates powerfully that the South's new, commercial accounting belies the tenacity of the plantation code that belatedly excludes the likes of the Coldfields and the Sutpens.[27] The account book Rosa inscribes harbors these conflicted calculations, but Rosa rejects both the order that precludes her and the one that stymies her by recording her unspent desires only on the "backsides" of the ledger pages.

Back in Haiti, Sutpen crucially overlooked his opportunity to learn what Rosa seems to know. On the plantation that he oversees, he initially observes: "a soil manured with black blood from two hundred years of oppression and exploitation until it sprang with an incredible paradox of peaceful greenery and crimson flowers and sugar cane sapling . . . valuable pound for pound almost with silver ore, as if nature held a balance and kept a book and offered a recompense for the torn limbs and outraged hearts even if man did not. . . . And he overseeing it, riding peacefully about on his horse while he learned the language" (202). As Matthews has suggested, Sutpen oversees the workings of this New World plantation without precisely seeing it; but the text discloses in plain view the sobering recognitions that these peripheral scenes should arouse. Sutpen recognizes the black blood that "manures" the rich plantation crops, and sees the sugar cane burgeoning with the weight of its own value—nature's own reparations. Still, Sutpen knows that these gifts will be usurped by the white master who continues to appropriate and exploit them. His portentous response to this is simply to "oversee" it "peacefully" and "learn the language"—the calculating discourse of not just the overseer but the master himself. Yet he fails to see, as Matthews would suggest, that nature itself foretells his doom, fails to see the personal augury in this scene: those born to toil on the earth in colonial societies will not reap its rewards.

While Haiti's colonial lesson finds unsettling resonance in Sutpen's antebellum South, it also reflects the anachronistic anxieties of the New South's reluctant evolution. More deeply imbedded in the Haitian example is the imperial fiction that "nature" chooses its elite; in the new South, a sharpening commitment to the idea of "natural aristocracy" attempted to authenticate the exploitative rights of the master class. Neither Sutpen nor his sons can finally circumvent their social estrangement. His dream is brutally undone when Wash Jones, symbol of the white underclass Sutpen has fled, cuts down the ambitious impostor who pretends to master him: as Ramón Saldívar suggests, Sutpen "dies at the hands of a representative of the class he has forsaken."[28] Ultimately, the mobility made possible by American capital culture finds its fatal deadlock in the ledger's neo-imperial logic.

My reading of *Absalom, Absalom!* considers the ledger at least partially an anachronism, a narrative device to epitomize Faulkner's struggle to reconcile modern economic opportunism with the more occluded material order of plantation slavery. This crisis sharpens in *Go Down, Moses* (1942)[29] and Ike's updated quest to reject both the racial outrage and the fiscal boon that the faded, indomitable ledgers proffer. Ike's repudiation of his legacy comes with an ancillary profit: the notion that men do not need shamefully inflated dividends in order to be fantastically wealthy in gentle graces and honor. But Ike soon discovers that his birthright means not necessarily being able to separate currency from nobility.

Evocative of Sutpen's missed Caribbean lesson in colonial appropriation, Ike McCaslin has a more immediately cynical vision. Imagining a scene similar to the field of bloody outraged limbs Sutpen "oversees," Ike's more penetrating gaze surveys an analogous, ravaged Mississippi wilderness: "the tamed land which was to have been his heritage, the land which old Carothers McCaslin his grandfather had bought with white man's money from the wild men whose grandfathers without guns hunted it . . . and in their sweat scratched the surface of it to a depth of perhaps fourteen inches in order to grow something out of it which had not been there before and which could be translated back into the money he who believed he had bought it had had to pay to get it and hold it and a reasonable profit too."[30] Here, Haiti's blood-stained fields become a site of pure, American financial exchange, a transactional fiction to camouflage the brutal Amerindian genocide and removal that evacuated the Deep South's once-wild land for the agricultural baptism Ike describes. As he notes bitterly, the white man only "believed he had bought it" and now looks for a lucrative return on that investment. The transition from Sutpen's Caribbean parable to Ike's Mississippi iteration underscores the fetishized distance between these two global Souths: the blood of Haiti's vanquished is replaced by the noble "sweat" and toil of American settlers; the Indians simply evaporate with "white man's money" in hand and suffer no ostensible trauma. In America, neither the weak nor nature has a claim over the agency of the lusty pioneer poised to bleed the lands wrested from Indians and tilled by Africans. The two scenes present a purposeful intertextual slippage that has the effect of distancing New World colonialism from Southern Agrarian enterprise, but both Ike and Faulkner seem aware that the South's brutal origins are only thinly concealed by these sanitized fiscal transactions and the artifice of birthrights. The connections and substitutions Sutpen fails to make in the West Indies are implicitly supplied in this passage. Ike in fact mentions Sutpen in an immediately subsequent moment: "knowing better," he recalls, "old Thomas Sutpen" nonetheless indulges in this immoral colonial practice. Ike is right: Sutpen knows better, or at least he should know better, but his desperation compels him to spurn the evidence he refuses to assimilate.

Presumably, Ike believes he knows better too. In order to set the books right, he endeavors to reverse the usurious practice of agricultural profit extraction. He scours the family accounts for evidence of sexual and racial transgressions, decoding feverishly the books' irregular combinations of economic figures and journalistic jottings, which often evolve into cryptic, shorthand conversations between different bookkeepers.[31] He has read these ledgers before and knows already, either by force of memory or will, just what chronicles of perversion they harbor. Richard H. King echoes many of Faulkner's critics in suggesting that Ike's moral outrage over these offenses compels him to "transcend" his genealogical burden entirely, renouncing the land and property that is his birthright.[32] What Sutpen works so scrupulously to attain Ike casts off in a quest for ethical rather than monetary deliverance; but Ike is as duped as Sutpen in his subscription to a "characteristically American" belief that he might escape his heritage,[33] a desire that cannot ultimately combat the ledgers' fatal insistence on genealogical priority.[34]

One of Ike's signal mistakes comes in his assumption that "what the old books contained would be after all these years fixed immutably, finished, unalterable, harmless" (256). What, then, of the wreckage of postplantation disorder surrounding Ike, the disastrous living legacies of that incest and miscegenation and exploitation, and the novel's repeated instances of suicidal withdrawals from modern commerce and human relations? What the ledgers disclose are neither "harmless" nor "fixed" and "finished" chronicles at all; indeed, Faulkner tells us that Ike "would never need to look at the ledgers again nor did he; the yellowed pages in their fading implacable succession were as much a part of his consciousness and would remain so forever, as the fact of his own nativity" (259). Despite his "never" looking again, the next passage immediately features another ledger excerpt that Ike presumably mimeographs autonomically, the account of his family's sins already transcribed in his "consciousness." Or perhaps he is still reading, but is engaged in the act of "not seeing," in fact repressing what he already knows. This behavior is in keeping with what Matthews characterizes as an act of fetishized knowledge.[35] Such disci-

plined evasion would correspond exactly with Sutpen's own failure to reconcile the traces of global colonial trauma in Haiti, and indeed, the McCaslin ledgers burst geographic bounds as well, comprising the master register
of the entire South—"that record . . . that chronicle which was a whole land
in miniature, which multiplied and compounded was the entire South"
(280). In not just Ike's consciousness but in a collective New World landscape of sweating planters and violations of blood, the ledger testifies and
persists. In the corners of *Go Down, Moses*, it lingers to haunt Ike of his
empty, self-beguiling sacrifice. The discursive logic of the ledger is the sinister "birthright" that, despite its harrowing disclosures, neither Ike nor his
peers can repudiate as long as they live.

Tellingly, Ike is possessed by the language of plantation math even as a
boy: he refers to his age in "ciphers," a term originally designated to signify "zero" and only in modern usage applied to all numbers or figures;[36] as
a neutral term of reckoning, it applies the bookkeeper's computational activity to Ike's very person, while its association with a null set foreshadows
both his errant desire to nullify his birthright and the suicidal mechanisms
that are the only plausible means to accomplish it.[37] Ike's crisis is incited
early as he registers an incomplete shift from the notion of native entitlement to ascendance through work: in "The Bear," he interprets the role of
hunter as something to "earn," even though he believes he has "inherited"
the allegorical and elusive bear (184–85). If the Bear in its most prosaic interpretation represents nature, this tells us volumes about the birthright
Isaac believes has been given him, supported and mentored by the mystical black Indian Sam Fathers. Ike means for his desire to appear exculpa-
tory: with a convenient Indian ally resurrected from the obsolescence of
his earlier vision, he seeks to emancipate nature from man's proprietary
claims; but the endeavor is deeply compromised by his tacit assumption
that he has "inherited" the moral graces and the prey necessary to carry out
the noble task. A more mature Ike is known by the next generation of hunters for his self-promoting quip: "man is a little better than the net result
of his and his neighbor's doings" (330). He posits value not in bank state-
ments but in evidence of neighborly and communal goodwill—respectable
Southern traits by the most standard definitions. Yet his version of neighborly benevolence and moral decency does not extend to the light-skinned
black female who lives near the hunting camp and has a sexual tryst with
her own white cousin, Carothers Edmonds, producing yet another mixed-
race heir. Ike berates and dismisses her with a parcel of money, bemoaning
inwardly, *Maybe in a thousand or two thousand years in America. . . . But
not now! Not now!"* (361). For all his attempts to bury the past, Ike refuses
to move forward. It is not the bereft, lovelorn young woman he pities, and

his lament is not for the revivified dishonor and usury in the family line; rather, he evinces an almost classically supremacist disgust over the pervasive intercultural "breeding and spawning" the affair typifies (364).[38] The collision of races—*not* the system that drove them bitterly apart to begin with—is what Isaac McCaslin ultimately scorns. Indeed, Ike's next generation of entries in the commissary accounts actually serves to codify another line of modern slaves in the form of emancipated sharecroppers: in his merchant's log, he "ration[s] the tenants and the wage-hands for the coming week" (241). While he is distributing commissary goods on credit, the grammar here makes the tenants and wage-hands *themselves* the rations, converted into figures and entered into the columns that permanently subdivide the South's social classes, communities, and souls.

In the end, the novel's mixed-race offspring suffer most for their detention within the governing priorities of the ledger. Carothers's black mistress tries to spurn the money Ike hands her, wanting only an uncompromised love Ike promises her she will never receive. Lucas Beauchamp, part-black heir in the Edmonds line of the family, is more preoccupied with his own accounts, perhaps because he knows he is still not their primary custodian. After searching for a buried treasure night after sleepless night, Lucas finally capitulates. His surrender completes what seems to be a perverse trilogy: a third version of the Haiti-Mississippi plantation parables. He reflects: "a heap of what [man] can want is due to come to him, if he just starts in soon enough. I done waited too late to start. That money's there. Them two white men that slipped in here that night three years ago and dug up twenty-two thousand dollars and got clean away with it before anybody saw them. I know. I saw the hole where they filled it up again, and the churn it was buried in. But . . . I reckon that money aint for me" (126–27). The hardy sweat, toil, and ruthless profiteering Ike envisions become pure subterfuge in Lucas's estimation: instead of digging and raising crops, as both Sutpen and Ike variously witness, these white men simply steal a massive amount of money from the earth and then attempt literally to cover their tracks. And as in Sutpen's and Ike's chronicles, no one sees it happen. In a distinctly postplantation perversion of gathering coins rather than crops, ex-slaves and disenfranchised whites continue to fixate on what is "due to come" to them at last, until they are forced to admit defeat by white artifice, relinquishing their just rewards as money that "aint for" them.

But Faulkner's apparent sympathies for defeated men like Lucas are undercut by his more pronounced investment in the futility of Ike's noble sacrifice. What he and other Southern writers seem ultimately to register throughout their works is an ambivalent desire to both recuperate and renounce the contaminated social codes of plantation slavery, while bitterly critiquing the advent of a capitalist order that offers little better or different. What these unsettling, global purviews announce is the degree to which moral choice itself has been hijacked by a colonial nightmare that simply will not end but rather expands and replicates of its own accord. Whether any are willing to take responsibility for it is another, more troubling matter. For now, I'll end with a turn to Quentin, the archetypal proxy for Faulkner's own voice, and perhaps the most reliable vessel to conclude the colonial narrative Faulkner repeatedly unearths. In *The Sound and the Fury* (1929), Quentin is at Harvard but thinking

> of home, of . . . the niggers and country folks . . . and my insides would move like they used to do in school when the bell rang.
>   I wouldn't begin counting until the clock struck three. Then I would begin, counting to sixty and folding down one finger and thinking of the other fourteen fingers waiting to be folded down, or thirteen or twelve or eight or seven, until all of a sudden I'd realise silence and the unwinking minds, and I'd say "Ma'am?" "Your name is Quentin, isn't it?" Miss Laura would say . . . "Tell Quentin who discovered the Mississippi River, Henry." "DeSoto." Then . . . I'd be afraid I had gotten behind and I'd count fast and fold down another finger, then I'd be afraid I was going too fast and I'd slow up, then I'd get afraid and count fast again. So I could never come out even with the bell. (88)

Quentin evades the Southern schoolboy's imperial lessons; while he botches a simple internal counting exercise, another student effortlessly places the Spanish conquistador De Soto at the "discovery" of the Mississippi River, taking Ike's vision of Indian eviction one step further by implying that the Natives were never there at all. Significantly, it is a memory of "niggers and country folk" that prompts Quentin's classroom memory, continuing the comparative sweep with which Faulkner brings together the poor white, the ex-slave, and the Indian similarly divested by white imperialism. But Quentin resists this knowledge: he miscalculates his own digits absurdly ("fourteen" fingers?), literal somatic facts subsumed by the priorities of an imposed order he cannot master; but the ticking clock and tolling bell signify that he must move forward and learn how to keep up. His compulsion is to come out as "even" with the bell as his older brother Jason believes he might square with his own ledgers.

But Quentin is apparently not as good as Jason at faking it. I suggested earlier that Ike has no living hope of disqualifying himself from his birthright; and we know that Sutpen never survives to see his own ledger generate a surplus value. Alive, though, neither man seems able—or willing—to move forward. Perhaps Faulkner answers this plight with Quentin, creative reteller of Sutpen's tale and witness to its coda—Henry's dying body, the haunted house in flames—and now unable to move forward or backward or even to count himself accurately into the present. Significantly, the only math Quentin gets right is the calculation of how much weight it will take to sink his body to the bottom of the Charles River: "The displacement of water is equal to the something of something. Reducto absurdum of all human experience, and two six-pound flat-irons weigh more than one tailor's goose. What a sinful waste Dilsey would say" (90).[39] His equations are pointedly imprecise, exemplifying the unliveable, "reducto absurdum" of American experience, but ultimately his only escape from their ruthless dictates is suicide. Quentin's self-immolating calculations are disastrously revealing: not of honor or recompense or restoration, not of anything that the ledgers might utter, but rather of what Dilsey would say: "what a sinful waste."

NOTES

1. William Faulkner, *The Sound and the Fury* (1929; New York: Vintage, 1990), 229. Subsequent references will be cited in the text.

2. Richard Godden and Noel Polk, "Reading the Ledgers," *Mississippi Quarterly* 55:3 (Summer 2002): 301–59; 339.

3. Ibid., 359.

4. Godden and Polk suggest that Ike in fact manufactures the evidence he is invested in locating and disavowing in order to justify a rejection of a birthright he judges to be corrupt. Their reading attempts to evaluate the ledgers (and by extension, the novel) "on their own terms, rather than on Isaac's" (359).

5. For a thorough examination of the history of double-entry accounting and its profound influence on modern forms of knowledge, see Mary Poovey, *A History of the Modern Fact: Problems of Knowledge in the Sciences of Wealth and Society* (Chicago: University of Chicago Press, 1998).

6. Most notorious for circulating this position were the Nashville Agrarians (writing as "Twelve Southerners") who collaborated in 1930 on *I'll Take My Stand: The South and the Agrarian Tradition* (1930; Baton Rouge: Louisiana State University Press, 1977) in defense of "a Southern way of life against what may be called the American or prevailing way; and all as much as agree that the best terms in which to represent the distinction are contained in the phrase, Agrarian *versus* Industrial" (xxxvii).

7. John T. Matthews makes a similar point in "Touching Race in *Go Down, Moses*," in *New Essays on "Go Down, Moses*," ed. Linda Wagner-Martin (New York: Cambridge University Press, 1996), 21–47. Asserting Faulkner's "studied conviction that economic exploitation and racial oppression composed a double coil around the modern South," Matthews proposes the need for "a kind of double reading that demonstrates their mutual constitution" (25).

8. According to the *Oxford English Dictionary* (Online, Second Edition, 1989), the term "white trash" was first used in America in the antebellum South and to refer exclusively to "the poor white population in the Southern States of America." Early usages show, and a plethora of Southern literature corroborates, that the white trash Southern was often grouped with the region's blacks. In some instances, as Fanny Kemble notes in her 1835 journal, "The slaves themselves entertain the very highest contempt for white servants, whom they desig-

nate as 'poor white trash'" (*OED Online*). Antagonism between these two groups seems due to a heightened sense of competition in the free labor market that replaced slavery. In "The Briar Patch," his contribution to *I'll Take My Stand*, Robert Penn Warren confirms the commonly held belief in 1930 that "the fates of the 'poor white' and the negro are linked in a single tether. The well-being and adjustment of one depends on that of the other" (259).

9. Myra Jehlen, *Class and Character in Faulkner's South* (1976; Secaucus: Citadel Press, 1978), 21. Jehlen's seminal monograph continues to be influential in turning Faulkner criticism toward issues of class as "the underlying organizing principle in [Yoknapatawpha's] social structure . . . more precisely the division between two classes of white society, the planters and the 'rednecks'" (9). As Joel Williamson contextualizes in *William Faulkner and Southern History* (New York: Oxford University Press, 1993), "Faulkner was reared among an imperialized people, a people much reduced in power from what had been the case within living memory. In writing about their plight, he met the plight of the imperialized people of the world, the people whose land had been raped and labor taken to supply raw materials from the factories of the industrial powers" (363). This deep sympathy, I argue, also gives way to defensive competitiveness. A more recent book by Ted Atkinson situates Faulkner within the context of the Great Depression and interrogates more precisely his ambivalent perch between agrarian planter and landless poor. See Ted Atkinson, *Faulkner and the Great Depression: Aesthetics, Ideology, and Cultural Politics* (Athens: University of Georgia Press, 2005).

10. See Kevin Railey, *Natural Aristocracy: History, Ideology, and the Production of William Faulkner* (Tuscaloosa: University of Alabama Press, 1999).

11. See John T. Matthews, "Recalling the West Indies: From Yoknapatawpha to Haiti and Back," *American Literary History* 16:2 (2004): 238–62; George Handley, *Postslavery Literatures in the Americas: Family Portraits in Black and White* (Charlottesville: University Press of Virginia, 2000); Deborah Cohn, *History and Memory in the New South: Recent Southern and Spanish American Fiction* (Nashville: Vanderbilt University Press, 1999). Also, a recent collection edited by Deborah Cohn and Jon Smith provides a broader look at the U.S. South and New World Studies and includes essays on Faulkner by Matthews, Wendy B. Faris, Philip Weinstein, Dane Johnson, Helen Oakley, and Earl Fitz; see Smith and Cohn, eds., *Look Away! The U.S. South in New World Studies* (Durham: Duke University Press, 2004), 311–450.

12. There is ample support for the idea that the South functioned as a colony subjugated by Northern industrial, political, and cultural forces. See Gavin Wright, *Old South, New South: Revolutions in the Southern Economy since the Civil War* (New York: Basic Books, 1986); C. Vann Woodward, "The Colonial Economy," in *Origins of the New South, 1877–1913* (Baton Rouge: Louisiana State University Press, 1971); Morton Rothstein, "The New South and the International Economy," *Agricultural History* 57 (October 1983): 385–402; Joseph J. Persky, *The Burden of Dependency: Colonial Themes in Southern Economic Thought* (Baltimore: Johns Hopkins University Press, 1992). As Woodward reports, citing Henry Grady, "at least half the planters after 1870 were either Northern men or were supported by Northern money" (179); later, he concludes more dramatically that "The control exercised by the British merchant over the [Southern] tobacco colonies was extensive, but it never equaled that of the Northeastern banker" (318). By 1889, a sense that the South's resources and labor were being wholly exploited had become pervasive; Henry Grady, after attending the funeral of a Georgia man, remarked bitterly that "The South didn't furnish a thing on earth for that funeral but the corpse and the hole in the ground": the coffin, gravestone, and burial attire were all purchased ready-made from Northern manufacturers, even though their original materials may well have been extracted from Southern soil and factories [quoted in Glenn E. McLaughlin and Stefan Robock, *Why Industry Moves South: A Study of the Factors Influencing the Recent Location of Manufacturing Plants in the South* (Washington: Committee of the South, National Planning Association, 1949), 3].

13. According to the *Oxford English Dictionary* (Online, Second Edition, 1989), the term "postcolonial" began circulating in 1936, which coincides with the date of *Absalom, Absalom!*'s publication.

14. Indeed, while my focus here is on Faulkner's works, my investigation into the ledger's

discursive manifestations extends across the Southern canon; the larger project from which this talk is taken features readings of writers as diverse as Thomas Wolfe, Richard Wright, Frances Newman, James Weldon Johnson, Walker Percy, Dorothy Allison, Alice Walker, Louis Owens, and Toni Cade Bambara.

15. As Arjun Appadurai and others have argued, such practices are indicative of imperial societies, which resort to these and other mechanisms of "reason" not just to regulate but to justify and normalize their social hierarchies. For more on number as a technology of imperial control, see Arjun Appadurai, *Modernity at Large: Cultural Dimensions of Globalization* (Minneapolis: University of Minnesota Press, 1996). I would argue that examples of this calculating discourse are abundant throughout Southern history: under slavery, economics provided the motive, means, and the vocabulary for diminishing the wills and worth of human property at the expense of the master's literal and psychological profit margin. The technologies of oppression include the ledgers themselves, along with bills of advertisement and sale and census documents. These discourses gave way to other numerical iterations, such as the constitutional language of the "Three Fifths Compromise" declaring that African Americans might be "counted" most profitably as fractions. After emancipation, these mathematical modes proliferated, whether through racial-classification schemes like the "one-drop rule," often determined by elaborate mathematical equations and scientific proofs appearing in nineteenth-century pamphlets and periodicals [see, for example, Werner Sollors's excellent *Neither White Nor Black Yet Both: Thematic Explorations of Interracial Literature* (New York: Oxford University Press, 1997)], or in the (significantly contrary) massive blood quotients required to "verify" American Indian heritage. Data of social classification and control is calculated "scientifically," recorded in census rolls, government legislation, and official documents, and is used to police behavior, determine benefits, and in short, to regulate constructions of personal identity and worth.

16. Poovey, 11.

17. This phrase is a play on the title of John T. Matthews's recent article (n. 11), where he suggests that these global connections constitute the South's "fetishized knowledge" of its implication in a vast colonial order that white Southerners hold in plain view but overlook in failures of recognition that signify something more than repression (239).

18. Don H. Doyle, *The Historical Roots of Yoknapatawpha* (Chapel Hill: University of North Carolina Press, 2001), 294. For a useful comparison of the Snopes and Sutpen families, see Corinne Dale, "*Absalom, Absalom!* and the Snopes Trilogy: Southern Patriarchy in Revision," *Mississippi Quarterly* 45 (1992): 321–37.

19. Common folk trying to work their way up are a type Faulkner represents most fully and satirically by the upwardly mobile Snopes clan who ascend from shack to mansion in the course of three novels and countless unscrupulous exploits. A character like Flem Snopes constitutes for Faulkner an object of both fascination and derision, high satire and brutal wit; *Absalom, Absalom!* gives us the same social trajectory cast in radically different terms, akin to a Shakespearean tragedy. Such rises were not uncommon in Tidewater Virginia where Sutpen is born; in the 1830s, George Handley (n. 11) notes, this was "a region of considerable economic opportunity, where many poor white farmers were able to move slowly up the class ladder" (133).

20. William Faulkner, *Absalom, Absalom!* (1936; New York: Vintage, 1990), 184–88. Subsequent references will be cited in the text.

21. As Eric Dussere indicates, Sutpen "goes about making himself a gentleman planter according to his strictly quantitative system"—much like a ledger. See Dussere's *Balancing the Books: Faulkner, Morrison, and the Economies of Slavery* (New York: Routledge, 2003), 50.

22. Indeed, Sutpen finds his Haitian wife not "adjunctive or incremental" *to* his design because she fails to compensate for what Sutpen himself lacks in natural aristocracy. Sutpen embodies the "minus in the origin" that Homi Bhabha assigns to the subjugated; the subtraction factor in his imaginative books drives him compulsively to overcompensate, to find adjuncts and increments that will render him solvent.

23. While the state of being "solvent" means the ability to pay one's debts, it also connotes

"dissolving" or "laxative" properties, promoting the expulsion of undesirable elements or influences (*Oxford English Dictionary* Online, Second Edition, 1989). The fact that this process takes place within Sutpen's body is significant, as it indicates his attempts at forging balance nonetheless exacerbate his depletion as well.

24. This idea echoes a moment in William Alexander Percy's autobiography of unsettled aristocracy, *Lanterns on the Levee: Recollections of a Planter's Son* (1941; New York: Knopf, 1994): "maybe in time someone will pay us more for our cotton than we spend making it," he fantasizes (24).

25. The moment at the planter's door instantiates for Sutpen a virtual balance sheet of duty and revenge: because the servant never gave him a chance to state his business, he reasons, the master *"wont know [what it was] and whatever it is wont get done and he wont know it aint done until too late so he will get paid back that much for what he set that nigger to do"* (191–92). With labor incomplete (because of the nigger's failure, which is also Sutpen's failure) will the master suffer, "get paid back" in proportion to the slave's lack of industry? In this case, all things are credits and debits, and the master will only profit when the slave puts forth the appropriate energy. But, after all, the master is fundamentally detached from the work (*"he wont know it aint done"*) that he reaps the benefits from. In yet another reading, though, the *"he"* getting "paid back" becomes slippery: it could be the master, getting "paid back" in the form of revenge by Sutpen, who will rise to usurp the man who "set that nigger" to occupy a white house and turn away a white boy. Or the "he" may be Sutpen himself, who will himself get "paid back"—will pay himself back—for the indignity and debasement caused by his exclusion from the Big House.

26. This is a term used by Homi Bhabha in *The Location of Culture* (New York: Routledge, 1994), 160 and elsewhere, to describe the subaltern's predetermined status in the national narrative, always already figured as the negation of the colonizer.

27. In a connection that Matthews has recently invigorated (in "Recalling the West Indies"), Mr. Coldfield reluctantly makes an investment in Sutpen's slave-trading enterprise, his abolitionist sentiments defeated by the allure of profit.

28. Ramón Saldívar, "Looking for a Master Plan: Faulkner, Paredes, and the Colonial and Postcolonial Subject," in *The Cambridge Companion to William Faulkner*, ed. Philip M. Weinstein (New York: Cambridge University Press, 1995), 96–120; 119.

29. It deserves mention that Faulkner was facing a particularly acute financial crisis at the time of *Go Down, Moses*'s composition (1942). Richard J. Gray reports in *The Life of William Faulkner* (Cambridge: Blackwell Press, 1994) that in 1940 Faulkner was frequently writing his editor to request very specific, large amounts of money, a crisis that Gray suggests may have contributed to the "openly economic bias of the first novel in the Snopes trilogy" published that year (271). Linda Wagner-Martin also suggests in her introduction to *New Essays on "Go Down, Moses"* (New York: Cambridge University Press, 1996) that "the novel may have originated from Faulkner's financial straits" during this period, due in part to the purchase of both Rowan Oak and Greenfield Farm in the previous decade (1). In *Faulkner: A Biography* (1974; New York: Vintage, 1991), Joseph Blotner reports Faulkner's intimations (as explained in a letter to his Random House publisher) that "If he could sell some stories and get through until mid-November, when he could begin to collect on his cotton and tenant crops, he could make it" (421). Helping out in the commissary store, he was known to "neatly itemize" customer purchases "in a small ledger," a repeated activity that Blotner suggests must have made him think "that he had been doing the same thing with Random House" (417); and, in fact, Faulkner did keep an intricate ledgerlike record of his short story submissions. Such scenes underscore the kind of empathy Faulkner might have felt for Ike in his conflicted relationship to the family accounts and ledgers, lending additional support to Eric Sundquist's claim that *Go Down, Moses* was "Faulkner's most honest and personally revealing novel" (quoted in Linda Wagner-Martin, ed., *New Essays on "Go Down, Moses,"* 14).

30. William Faulkner, *Go Down, Moses* (1942; New York: Vintage, 1990), 244. Subsequent references will be cited in the text.

31. Most prominently, Ike's father Buck and uncle Buddy.

32. See Richard H. King, "Working Through: Faulkner's *Go Down, Moses*," in *Modern Critical Views: William Faulkner*, ed. Harold Bloom (New York: Chelsea House, 1986), 193–205.

33. James Early, *The Making of "Go Down, Moses"* (Dallas: Southern Methodist University Press, 1972), 55.

34. Dussere suggests similarly that Ike, in his attempt "to even things up and clear the ledger, the book which holds the record of injustice and the unrealized possibility for remuneration," ultimately discovers "that this is ultimately a false hope" (338).

35. Matthews draws on the colonial "technology" of the fetish in order to argue that throughout *Absalom*, and elsewhere in Faulkner's works, "there is a kind of knowledge that can be held while being ignored, a kind of vision that looks but does not see. Such knowledge does not disappear into the depths of its repression—the prevailing model for the work of Faulknerian evasion or deferral. Instead, such knowledge goes into open hiding on the surface of the Faulknerian text" (239).

36. As Charles Seife reports in his history *Zero: The Biography of a Dangerous Idea* (New York: Penguin, 2000), "zero was so important to the new set of numbers [in Western mathematics] that people started calling all numbers ciphers, which gave the French their term *chiffre*, digit" (73); the word gained its secondary meaning of "secret code" when Italian merchants used ciphers (for their ease of falsification and disguise) to send encrypted messages via counting boards and other instruments (80–81).

37. This sense of "ciphering" also uncannily approaches the bifurcated idea of solvency that Sutpen desires even as it threatens to dissolve him entirely.

38. Ike is appalled that "*Chinese and African and Aryan and Jew, all breed and spawn together until no man has time to say which one is which nor cares*" (364).

39. It is crucial that Faulkner comes back to define this idea of displacement as a Northern, specifically New England, antiplantation phenomenon: In *Go Down, Moses*, Ike ruminates on "the New England mechanics who didn't even own land and measured all things by the weight of water and the cost of turning wheels" (274).

On the Tragedies and Comedies of
the New World Faulkner

GEORGE B. HANDLEY

Faulkner's fiction, as studies have recently demonstrated, has relevance not only to Southern regional or U.S. national identity but to communities across the various nations affected by a shared history of slavery, civil conflict, devastation of indigenous populations, racialized social division, and the persistence of colonialism.[1] This is true not merely because of common thematic interests of authors from other American nations or because of Faulkner's notable influence on Caribbean and Latin American writers. What has emerged in the reassessment of Faulkner's relevance to New World cultures is a call for a new kind of reader that marks a departure from the reader assumed by regional and national models delineated by more strictly geopolitical borders. This paper is an attempt to take up a strand of the argument of my book, *Postslavery Literatures in the Americas*, where I outline the common anxieties the shared history of slavery has created in the literatures of the U.S. South and the Caribbean and to identify the characteristics of this new reader.[2] I specifically point to the challenges this history poses for those who seek to remember slavery's past so as to liberate New World societies from its crimes. Postslavery societies from abolition forward have tried to emancipate themselves from slavery's deeply divided and colonial past, but many of those efforts have often served to reinforce the very structures of plantation society. I insist, then, that fiction's journey into the past has certain oedipal risks, in the sense that the search for the past can easily become a redundant and perpetual recycling of slavery's trauma or of its injustices in the present. This is most often the case when individual postslavery nations pretend that the search for slavery's meaning is limited to its national borders and not to its more broadly hemispheric context. A cross-cultural approach to slavery's history has the potential to render the tragic themes of slavery more tragicomic, in the Renaissance sense of a story in which disaster is irrevocable but also potentially redemptive. Slavery does not have to determine or delimit in any inevitable way the potential for New World societies to achieve democratic health, but literary study tends to lead us to such reified conclusions when limited to single authors or strictly defined regional or national geographies.

Lest I appear to bite the hand that feeds by criticizing single author approaches to literature in a collection of essays devoted to Faulkner, let me clarify. In the pantheon of great American authors who have received close attention, there are no small number of journals and societies devoted to Mark Twain, Walt Whitman, Willa Cather, and a host of others, but few can match the astounding depth and range of Faulkner studies. These are labors of love, I believe, that give rise to journals, organizations, studies, and conferences such as this, and the fruit such love bears is a growing and widening appreciation for the world-making powers of fiction. In more properly literary terms, this is what we mean by the poetics of fiction, signified in the root Greek word *poiesis*; fiction writing, that is, is a kind of world making. The advantage of long traditions of single author studies is that in effect they broaden the created world of a writer by giving full attention to the particulars and peculiarities of the literature in question. But it is also true that the breadth and depth of our understanding of a single author's vision can become redundant and self-reaffirming if we do not vary the questions we bring to a text. The best way to enrich this process is to globalize the readership, as this conference attempts to do. As one non-local reader of Faulkner has written, Édouard Glissant from Martinique, Faulkner "needed to see whether he had been right to keep the country apart from the rest of the world in order for it to represent the world in its entirety" (53). Such an ambition cannot be realized without ever-widening circles of readers, which of course begs the question: how useful is the notion of "author" as an individual, procreative force behind the "world" that prose projects? If global means "of a world," a Global Faulkner is both Faulkner's world and the world's Faulkner, both the world he creates and the Faulkner the world has in turn created.

To examine the Global Faulkner, then, is to explore what it means to read Faulkner as much as it meant for him to write. Instead of focusing on the historical and thematic reasons for Faulkner's relevance to the broader hemisphere in this paper, though important, I would like instead to consider how for Faulkner writing and reading are twin processes that remake the world from the material of words. Reading Faulkner creatively and cross-culturally means assuming responsibility for the world we cocreate with him; we are simultaneously penetrated by the force of his worlding and enjoin our America with his and thus make ourselves answerable to a broader world. As Caribbean readers of Faulkner such as Wilson Harris, Gabriel García Márquez, and Édouard Glissant have in their turn written and transformed the meaning of incest for less tragic and often more comic ends, they have highlighted Faulkner's relevance to understanding the New World condition. One might argue that this proves Faulkner's centrality in understanding literatures of the Americas, but that would be nothing more than a tautological critical fantasy: because we place Faulkner at the center, we then conclude that he is, not surprisingly, at the center. It is closer to the truth to acknowledge that Faulkner is highly relevant for a more hemispheric approach to the meaning of "America," but that it is ultimately undecidable who the author of the Global Faulkner is: Faulkner or the world, which is another way of saying that in the end we alone are answerable to the New World we imagine.

The Tragedies of Fundamentalism

It is generally assumed (and thus the motivation for such things as standard works, canons, required reading lists, and the like) that a selected body of literature read by a selected body of people in a certain way will help to forge a communal identity among them. This "certain way" is determined by a class of scholars, priests, teachers, community leaders, or commercial powers such as Oprah, who argue in the interest of their ideal imagined community. For the purposes of my argument here, we need not distinguish between those who seek to conserve traditional notions of a canon and those who seek to reformulate the canon for the purposes of broader democratization. In both scenarios, it is generally hoped that you are what you read, that if the right books are read, the right kind of community is forged. It may be the case, of course, that some versions of this formula rely more on a fundamentalist notion of the written word than others, but I am not convinced that this fundamentalism is the unique domain of conservatives.

For the sake of my argument here, it will be useful to consider the act of reading as taking place between two extremes of a spectrum. On one end written language is revelation, given to humans from the gods or from genius itself, and the author is merely the transmitter. The reader's responsibility is passive submission to the procreative and violent force of this language, its power to make the world by fiat, just as the author herself presumably did in order to receive the word. This involves a complete suspension of disbelief that grants language its procreative power. On this end of the spectrum, language is a glass the clarity of which allows us to perceive a world previously hidden from view and hear a voice that speaks from the space of the Other. At the opposite pole, language is the means by which an active reader projects a world outward from the inner self; language does not reveal an external world but is rather the material by which the reader expresses her inner world. Meaning emerges from the procreative imagination of a reader whose imagination is stimulated by the alluring opacity of the word. Instead of a glass, language functions as a mirror, not in the sense that M. H. Abrams understands literature as mimetic of the writer's world but as reflecting an image of the reader writ large. We can think of these two extremes respectively as an encounter with the two origins of meaning, either the Other or the self. As I have argued is the case in William Faulkner and Alejo Carpentier, reading vacillates between being an prodigal journey outward into a New World or an oedipal journey back to the self.[3]

Fundamentalism can be understood as an intolerance for this inherent ambiguity. While the results of religious fundamentalism are seemingly everywhere more evident and familiar to us, fundamentalism in literary circles might be a contradiction. Perhaps no one really believes that Faulkner received his words from some novel-dictating god (there are, of course, poets such as Coleridge and Yeats who made such claims, however) but even if we admit that his novels do indeed seem to obey some impulse, some external pressure, that pressed upon him the obligation to bring a world into existence, we may not be likely to conclude that his own imagination is irrelevant to the creation of Yoknapatawpha. But critics often betray an undue impatience with the contradictions of an author's life and circumstances, such as Faulkner's strange and persistent racial ambivalence, to the degree that they wish to dismiss such quandaries as irrelevant. Or, in their obsessions with tracing the marks of error and contradiction in an author, they conclude decisively that the impure and strange mixture in literature of revelation and expression can only be readable as naked prejudice. In both approaches, readers want to make literature fundamentally revelatory or fundamentally expressive of the author's psychology writ large and remain unanswerable to the world the fiction appears to project.

William Faulkner, in "The Bear," provides his own poetics of fiction that seeks a reconciliation of these two poles, without resorting to this violent intolerance. Faulkner's prose here, as in many other instances in his fiction is always implicitly, if not explicitly, a dialogue, carrying its thoughts refracted through the perspectives, ironic interrogations, and deep-seated and sometimes unarticulated thoughts of characters fully invested in the meaning of their interpretations of Southern life. Borrowing the term from V. N. Volisinov, Richard Godden and Noel Polk call this a form of "free indirect discourse" that enables Faulkner "simultaneously to identify with and yet remain distant from a creation" (319).[4] The South's transcendent meaning is a story guessed at by multiple voices. In a significant moment in "The Bear" that provides evidence of Faulkner's deep investment in the meaning of reading, Ike and his cousin McCaslin debate the significance of human stain in the making of the Bible. Ike states: "There are some things He said in the Book, and some things reported of Him that He did not say" (249). McCaslin asks if this doesn't imply that "these men who transcribed His Book for Him were sometime liars." Ike responds:

> Yes. Because they were human men. They were trying to write down the heart's truth out of the heart's driving complexity, for all the complex and troubled hearts which would beat after them. What they were trying to tell, what He wanted said, was too simple. Those for whom they transcribed His words could not have believed them. It had to be expounded in the everyday terms which they were familiar with and could comprehend, not only those who listened but those who told it too, because if they who were near to Him as to have been elected from among all who breathed and spoke language to transcribe and relay His words, could comprehend truth only through the complexity of passion and lust and hate and fear which drives the heart, what distance back to truth must they traverse whom truth could only reach by word-of-mouth?[5]

Revelation here is deeply confused with imagination. Instead of direct and transparent transcribers of God's word, the authors of the Bible are translators, engaged in finding a new language of their own for what can only be intuited by the heart. The complexity of the confusion is evident in the fact that the authors, like novelists, must "lie" in order to speak the truth. The Bible's difficulty is in reaching those not well versed in textual exegesis, "the doomed and lowly of the earth who have nothing else to read with but the heart" who are accustomed to direct, concrete, and clear language and rely on word-of-mouth for the chance to speak with others about the meanings of what is written (249). This difficulty is really, as it turns out, an advantage, since these readers have the disposition to be astute listeners to and re-creators of the meaning of words. Written stories that get told and retold in a community, like Faulkner's own refurbishing of biblical tales, have a greater chance of approximating the truths of the heart's complexity because of their having been molded and passed across a wide spectrum of readers. The words have become part of the language of a living, suffering community. Indeed, in this version of biblical truth, the book becomes holy because it restores to memory the untold stories of quiet anguish and private suffering of those on the margins of history.

If for Faulkner the Bible is a pack of "lies," it is only in the sense that its stories, metaphors, and rhetoric are a deep reaching figurative language that is more a translation than a transcription since it uses new words to express that which the first telling could not convey. Storytelling is always a rewriting of what has been heard before, so to read the Bible faithfully, one must learn to intuit the ineffability of truth that necessitates words moving off the page and into the mouths of readers, who continue talking and seeking the right translation, reaching after truth with longing and fierce passion but without pretense to arriving at realization. The Word is made Flesh but not because it finally embodies truth but because its truths are sought after in the mouths of flesh-and-blood readers; whatever truth is has now become the property of a community of believers in words and their power to convey each speaker's individual and idiosyncratic soundings of the truth. So while the quest is a faithful yearning after what lies beyond what is written, reading results in an embrace of truth's ringing echoes in the mouths of others, a search, in other words, for humanity, for community among human others. Knowledge is not vertical, given of God to man, but found in the interstices of the stories human beings tell and re-tell. This is a kind of reading that makes the boundaries of one's community tenuous since the reader is brought out of bounds, beyond the confines of accepted knowledge and into the uncertain terrain of calls and echoes between and among communities, near and far.

Of course, such an understanding of reading also shifts the meaning of the sacred in a fundamentalist model. Rather than the word gaining its sanctity in its representation of a truth revealed by God and totally stripped of its human element, its sanctity lies in the cross-cultural and subaltern contact zones it necessitates in the search for truth. Because the truth is not transparently given, it requires dialogue and conversation, and its meaning begins to take on the form of a borderless community. If origins are never fully recoverable, they must be imagined, as if invented for the first time, from the fragments of other cultures whose pieces lie in disarray in New World soil. This is not a world created *ex nihilo*, but one organized anew of preexisting matter, which is what is implied in the Caribbean conception of creolization and what I believe Faulkner meant when he said in his Nobel Speech that he sought "to create out of the materials of the human spirit something that did not exist before" and yet he saw the award as "only mine in trust" and directed himself to writers to come who would stand in his place.[6] That the reading of great fiction can become the creation of new foundations is what the Martinican author Édouard Glissant means when he suggests in his book *Faulkner, Mississippi* that "we can accept that the sacred 'results' not only from an ineffable experience of a creation story but also, from now on, from the equally *ineffable intuition of the relationship between cultures.*"[7] Because a culture's origins are multiple, fragmented, and in effect unrecoverable in any original form, the gaps these fragments expose are a call to our imagination to make them whole. This reconstructive effort is an opportunity for the foundation of a New World culture, what Derek Walcott referred to when he wrote: "Break a vase, and the love that reassembles the fragments is stronger than the love which took its symmetry for granted when it was whole."[8] The implicit point here is that a community's origins, most notably the South's, are multiple, with competing claims from Spanish and French colonial history, Native Americans, whites and blacks, that create the conditions of what Glissant calls a "composite" culture. Ike's crisis, like Quentin's in *Absalom, Absalom!*, is having to sort fact from fiction in the storehouse of communal memory, with all of its lies, contradictions, and unreliability. The role of Faulkner's fiction in forging community in the context of a composite culture is deeply ambiguous since it exercises its world-making power at the same time that it exposes the gaps, the interstices, between communities, the deferrals that have facilitated a premature myth of unity. The tendency of recent literary criticism has been to focus on this latter consequence of fiction—that is, to critique its ability to expose the lies of national and regional myths—at the expense of the former—its powers to remake the world, that is, its poetics. And yet it is precisely this quality of Faulkner's fiction that holds the promise of shaping an identity that is tolerant of the very ambiguity of the self's boundaries.

In the context of discussing the perplexity of Faulkner's racial views, Glissant defends literature by stating: "literature matters more than making testimonies or taking sides, not because it exceeds all appreciation of the real, but because it is a more profound approach and, ultimately, the only one that matters" (64). Literary criticism no longer naively believes in literature's categorically innocent world-making powers, and this is as it should be. We need not return to the days when we imagined that a Melville, Hawthorne, Twain, or Faulkner expressed the quintessence of what it means to be an American. But in an age of increasing balkanization, we are more vulnerable than ever to the appeals of fear-mongering, commercialization of the sacred, and other means by which community is falsified and sold to the willing bidders impatient for facile healing. We don't need less but better tools of criticism and they must extend well beyond the academy into town libraries, book groups, churches, and, of course, public schools. The real challenge is reinvesting stories with the mythical power to enact such healing, a resacralization as it were, while remaining aware of the role our own wishes and imagination play in such investments. This fine line is what I believe Nietzsche meant when in *Twilight of the Idols* he insists that idols don't need to be smashed, just sounded out with the tuning fork of language so as to divulge their hollowness.[9] This is the force of Faulkner's employment of free indirect discourse because it self-consciously imitates the rhetoric of myth with the goal of sounding out its potential for forging good community. Faulkner is not merely drawing on biblical tales so as to describe modern fragmentation or to create a modernist distance from them; he is also seeking a more self-aware method of reinvesting them with power. Myths can be invested with sacred power as long as we recognize how they emerge from fragmented and incomplete memories of various peoples and have been organized anew by human hands. The most serious error of a fundamentalist reading of myth is that it insists on the blank slate of the writer's mind that passively receives the scenes that impersonal revelation passes through the mind and never accounts for the role personal imagination plays in the creation of transcendent meaning.

Antifundamentalism in "The Bear"

For Faulkner, Southern experience has rendered the quest for historical truth ironic, as evidenced in Ike's fruitless and arguably misguided search for the facts of his ancestors' interracial and incestuous contacts, but its impossibility is fertile ground for "lies," for fictions of growing complexity furbished by broader and wider ripples of interdependence. Ike's genealogical past, as for Joe Christmas, Quentin, and others in Faulkner's world, is a murky tale documented parsimoniously by an indecipherable ledger of cryptic, handwritten notes, what Faulkner calls a "yellowed procession of fading and harmless ledger-ages" (276). Godden and Polk argue that Ike is a "bad reader of the commissary documents in genre terms because he develops them in a form that begs no questions" (305). The result is that Ike reads less and less self-consciously; he is seduced by the idea that his myth of origins is not a reorganization of memory and generated by his own desire to divorce himself from a story of incest. What makes his reading tragically oedipal is his inability to see himself in the story he imagines, to consider his myth of origins as a revealed image of the sins of the past and not, ultimately, a self-portrait. This is why, as Godden and Polk note, his "thought shifts straight from closure interruptus to the conceit of self-turning ledger pages" (329). A history of self-turning pages is one in which the hand of the reader is literally absented from the story's meaning, creating the circumstances for a final tragic reencounter with oneself.

Even though the voices of the ledger are often unknown, they are particular and multiple. Ike's origins are held in the balance between these blended voices. As Godden and Polk put it, as the voices "pass into and out of one another's subject positions, the relationship between the twins and of the slave family emerges not as Isaac's 'curse' or 'doom,' but as a manifestly mutual and negotiated affection in the dreadful circumstances of 1864" (351). If we are to think of origins as reimagined at the interstices of multiple perspectives, we have a cross-cultural model of the Southern condition that permits this transformation from tragedy to comedy; or at least to tragicomedy. Again, I am referring here to the Renaissance meaning of comedy as a story that stares life boldly in the face and renders its actual circumstances with fidelity but still manages to end in resolution. While the matter of the "true" interpretation of the ledgers is ultimately undecidable, it is no doubt consistent with Faulkner's purpose to show the fictionality of Ike's rigid interpretations of his ancestors' actions, as Godden and Polk's reading has done. Since his conversation with McCaslin essentially establishes the impossibility of an unambiguously successful repudiation of the Southern past, however, it seems mistaken to insist that Ike is not at least partially aware of his own fiction-making. Indeed, it is worth wondering why Godden and Polk have used an extensive reading of the ledgers *as history* in order to make this argument, as if to suggest that Faulkner was operating on the assumption of the existence of a deep and true narrative buried deeply within the ledgers that only the most historical of exegetical readings would dislodge in order to expose Ike's fiction-making tendencies. This is a deeply problematic conclusion, since it implies that there is something inherently and perhaps morally wrong with Ike's creative answers to the ledgers. We cannot separate the truth of the ledgers from Ike's interpretation of them entirely, but this does not have to mean accepting that his version of the past becomes an inevitability. Faulkner's point is to repudiate unself-conscious interpretations of the past and to highlight the novelistic act implied in all acts of reading. The truth this language of Southern fiction conveys is not historical or revelatory but multiple, contradictory, and communal, exposing the truth of our own inevitable participation in the creation of community and meaning. This is an important distinction because unlike knowledge given to us by God or by the past, it is a form of knowledge we knowingly organize and for which we bear direct responsibility.

In Faulkner's world, human beings, nature, and history are all fundamental mysteries that cannot be facilely decoded, mapped, owned, or otherwise possessed. The tragic characters of Yoknapatawpha are those who prove intolerant of the elusiveness of historical knowledge and of their uncertain claim on others or on a sense of place in the land. They use law, tradition, property, and genealogy to help strengthen their claims of continuity from the deep past into the future, as well as strict and fundamentalist readings of the law, scripture, deeds, and genealogy in order to justify themselves. Tragedy results when the evidence needed—the records of property, slave sales, names, dates, and life events—proves insufficient. But the energy of Faulkner's fiction is essentially comic in that its substance is compensation for that absence, a new ledger of spoken deliberations about the unsatisfactory and incomplete effect of written language. As written literature itself, of course, this is a paradox. The comic resolution can only be suggested by the written representation of verbal deliberation, the tragedy compensated for by the reader's imagination. The only book large enough to contain the multiple stories and contradictions of the past would be a book of profound mystery, of incomplete truths, and inherent elusiveness, a veritable book of nature. Indeed, this is the significance of the bear and the wilderness he inhabits: "the wilderness, the big woods, bigger and older than any recorded document" is a mute witness and repository of New World violence and suffering (183). Ownership of land is a violence against these communal, interstitial, unwritten memories. In Faulkner's retelling, the Bible is an imperfect but moral refutation of this violence: "[God] made the earth first and peopled it with dumb creatures, and then He created man to be His overseer on the earth and to hold suzerainty over the earth and the animals on it in His name, not to hold for himself and his descendants inviolable title forever, generation after generation, to the oblongs and squares of the earth, but to hold the earth mutual and intact in the communal anonymity of brotherhood, and all the fee He asked was pity and humility and sufferance and endurance and the sweat of his face for bread" (246).

Like the creationist language of Sutpen's clearing of his fabled acres ("Be Sutpen's Hundred like the oldentime Be Light"), clearing land is a poor imitation of God's creation, a pretense to create the world *ex nihilo* when in fact it was always and already "mutual and intact." Ike notes the irony that despite biblical morality, "[old Carothers] . . . did own it. And not the first. Not alone and not the first. . . . Nor yet the second and still not alone, on down through the tedious and shabby chronicle of His chosen sprung from Abraham" (246). While the Bible's revelations are intended to teach humankind the "pity and humility and sufferance and endurance" necessary for good communities among diverse peoples and good and just treatment of land and its resources, it has also duplicitously provided "the shabby chronicle" of genealogical claims. The genealogical impulse of the Bible provides the sacred inspiration for liberation from slavery but it has also provided justification for violent exclusion of threatening racial others from self-designated "Holy Lands." This cyclical and contradictory pattern is modeled by Southern history. The "sometime liars" who authored the holy book, then, got it right and just wrong enough simultaneously to create or perhaps to represent the conditions of such contradictions.

Faulkner's reaction to the fundamentalist impulse within the Bible and among its readers is to insist that the Bible isn't the problem; for Faulkner, the problem has been its readers who largely miss the deeper mysteries of stories of origins and who fail to see how their interpretations of self-justification are of their own making. What if the shabbiness of the Bible's account were imagined to be the shabbiness of human readings of it? What richness might emerge from the text itself? What potential for more just communities might it portend? If shabby means threadbare, worn down by so much use, then perhaps Faulkner means to suggest that the chronicle of the Bible is comic, looking life boldly in the face and offering resolution. But if it is shabby in the sense that it offers a cheap and insufficient account, who is to blame? Penurious readers, perhaps.

Perhaps one biblical example will help to illuminate his point. While the record of the Jews was used to justify their exclusive claims to a Holy Land, the account is puzzlingly complex. After Abraham requests that his servant leave Canaan to find a wife for his son Isaac among his people who share land with the Philistines, Isaac and Rebekah return to this land, a voyage simultaneously back to the homeland and a journey out into the territory of the enemy. Prospering there, he gains the attention and envy of the Philistines. He finds that the wells dug years earlier by his father's servants have been stopped up by the Philistines, conceivably providing him genealogical justification to lay claim to the territory. However, the first two wells he digs he gives to the Philistines, and he claims the third only after he agrees to their oath: "that thou wilt do us no hurt, as we have not touched thee, and as we have done nothing to thee but good, and have sent thee away in peace" (Genesis 25:29). Isaac's claim to the land is later sanctified by sacrifice and by God's blessing but it would seem the account's morality lies in Isaac's careful recognition of the overlapping claims on the land.

If readers in Faulkner's South have followed the Bible, it is by imitating a practice of violent clearing away of the land's complex history that emerges from the shabbiest of readings of the meaning of genealogy. Clearing the land is a kind of reading, or misreading, of the mystery of the land's story. McCaslin notes to Ike: "You, the direct male descendant of him who saw the opportunity and took it, bought the land, took the land, got the land no matter how, held it to bequeath, no matter how, out of the old grant, the first patent, when it was a wilderness of wild beasts and wilder men, and cleared it, *translated* it into something to bequeath to his children, worthy of bequeathment for his descendants' ease and security and pride and to perpetuate his name and accomplishments" (245, emphasis mine). Of course, Ike recognizes that this ease of bequeathment is a lie, since the land was never his ancestor's to own, the Indians' to sell, nor his to repudiate (despite his intention to do so). The logic of Southern history is founded on the false notion that land, people, and historical origins can be owned or contained. The Thomas Sutpens and the Carotherses of Southern history have set a tragic history in cyclical motion by means of this misunderstanding, creating, and then just as quickly denying heterogeneity, leaving the Quentins and Ikes with the impossible dilemma of having to confront the heterogeneous community that is the South, without recourse to the tribunals that would sort fact from fiction. They must perform searches for origins in the past that function like exorcisms. Their chance for a comic transformation of this ever repeating story emerges when they recognize that their identity is not determined by nor answerable to the past, to the first parents as it were, but to the generative powers of relations with siblings, cousins, relations across racial and cultural lines in the present. This is a turn to the generative force of the "communal anonymity of brotherhood" of people like Sam Fathers— "childless, kinless, peopleless"—who bear histories and identities and inhabit geographies unbounded by the claims of nations, patriarchs, or singular stories of sacred origins. This uncertain genealogy is Ike's surrogate patrimony, as Sam's surname implies.

Ike's investigation begins, then, as an aspiration to the opaque status of historiography but instead becomes more transparent to the reader as the substance of fiction. In the former case, the past is thought to be given to the present, revealed as it were, whereas in the latter imagination is its creator, which is what Faulkner means in *Absalom, Absalom!* when he describes Quentin as Sutpen's father; the direction of time and the effects of tragedy can be reversed with the forceful imagination of descendants to the extent that they embrace, rather than retract in horror from, the abundance of siblings a New World history has spawned. Quentin and Ike recognize the plurality of their past but they cannot bring themselves to accept it. The tragedy of the South, Glissant explains, is that it is "a composite culture that suffers from wanting to become an atavistic one and suffers in not being able to achieve that goal" (115). The South, in other words, finds itself shaped by the mixing of fragments from many cultures but instead longs for evidence of its own continuity. As Ike's search demonstrates, even rebelling against the past would seem to require a continuity that can render meaning to repudiation of past sins. Despite their presumptive revisionary aims to reject the sins of the past, these sons of Southern history need historical truth to justify their reaction. Consequently, Ike and Quentin often fail to avoid the sins of the fathers, as exemplified in the seemingly ever present haunting specter of incest. Incest, for Faulkner, represents a tragic collapse of plantation history into itself, a perpetual return to the same, a world that cannot imagine or embrace difference or a different story than what it endlessly tells. That is, they too risk generating the same future they inherited because of their inability to accept the confusion of genealogy and the unreliability of language to determine and control meaning. Realizing this, the tragedy of suicide seems to be the only possible outcome. They excised themselves from their own acts of reading the past, so it is only logical that complete self-erasure is the outcome.

Incest as Comedy

Representations of incest in Caribbean and Latin American fiction do not often share the fully tragic dimensions of Faulkner's fiction. Arguably, these representations are instances of incest as a kind of reconciliation with the past, a comic harmonization achieved by fictionalizing the tragedies of slavery, colonialism, and violence against indigenous cultures in the New World past. Perhaps the most provocative example of this is Gabriel García Márquez's novel *One Hundred Years of Solitude*, which demonstrates a different approach to reading New World history and provides, by comparison, insight into Faulkner's understanding of reading. The way in which García Márquez's novel causes us to reconsider and further develop Faulkner's notion of reading in his fiction is not a mere coincidence of textual simultaneity. García Márquez has openly acknowledged his debt to Faulkner on several occasions, most notably in his own Nobel speech in which he praised his "master" as if to suggest he was fulfilling Faulkner's prophecy of writers to come. Moreover, it would appear that this novel is a profound interrogation of the implications of Faulkner's views. From the vantage point of a broader "America," García Márquez transforms the meaning of incest, concurring with Glissant that "in composite societies, or in those with very large families, disaffiliation does not directly generate drama and disequilibrium for the community. Perhaps that is what is meant when it is said that Oedipus—the myth and the complex—is not universal" (129–30).

One Hundred Years of Solitude begins in Colombia with the founding of a backland village called Macondo, a town isolated from the rest of the world not unlike Yoknapatawpha; consequently Macondo's story remains on the margins of the march of modern history, ignored in the larger world and unaware of its place in it. A gypsy, Melquiades, brings scientific and philosophical knowledge to Jose Arcadio Buendia, Macondo's founder, and gives him an alchemist laboratory. This room contains among other things "samples of the seven metals that corresponded to the seven planets, the formulas of Moses and Zosimus for doubling the quantity of gold, and a set of notes and sketches concerning the processes of the Great Teaching that would permit those who could interpret them to undertake the manufacture of the philosopher's stone."[10] Historically, the philosopher's stone was believed to be the supreme achievement of alchemy in that it would help to render all things transparent, to transmit knowledge and to transmute other metals into gold and silver. In the novel, the laboratory becomes a place of secret knowledge, of potential omniscience, but it is also a place where time stands still. The narrator tells us that Jose Arcadio "was the only one who had enough lucidity to sense the truth of the fact that time also stumbled and had accidents and could therefore splinter and leave an eternalized fragment in a room" (322). More specifically, then, this laboratory is a repository of Macondo's own fragmented history, splintered off from the world but rescued from oblivion on timeless parchments that Melquiades has left behind. The parchments represent those repressed memories of life on the margins of power that fiction attempts to rescue from oblivion, the mother lode of memory that every Quentin and Ike dreams of finding. They are the memories of transgression that political power seeks to conceal and of the local family history that it ignores. Without that knowledge, individuals act in ignorance of their origins, perpetually at risk of committing incest, moving through the rooms of the house where, like any Faulkner novel, "the unbearable smell of rotten memories floated" (227). Presumably this knowledge is necessary to reverse the patterns of history, but its full recuperation requires a willingness to accept the risk of incest, which is another way of stating the need to accept how those patterns have determined the present.

This paradox is evident in the nature of the parchments' translation. Whenever translation of the parchments is undertaken and recovery of lost genealogical and historical knowledge begins, the translator must race against time since the room becomes "vulnerable to dust, heat, termites, red ants, and moths, who would turn the wisdom of the parchments into sawdust" (329). If Macondo stands a chance to restore its ever-threatened memory of its own past, it will need a translator who reveals the secret knowledge of Macondo and of its genealogy in the parchments. But what will enable someone to translate? When Melquiades first donates the laboratory to the Buendia family, Jose Arcadio immediately withdraws into it. The narrator remarks: "At first Jose Arcadio had been a kind of youthful patriarch who would give instructions for planting and advice for the raising of children and animals and who collaborated with everyone, even in the physical work, for the welfare of the community" (17). The parchments' translation requires social withdrawal, and for this reason they attract several members of the family, typically in their prepubescent stage, when they do "not show the least desire to know the world that began at the street door of the house" (321). But then the parchments are abandoned once the various translators in the novel discover sexual and political desire.[11] Influenced by Octavio Paz's conception of solitude, García Márquez portrays solitude as that which brings insight, imagination, and memories of the past but which lacks communion with others. Only someone who can withdraw reflectively but simultaneously act conscientiously within history can recover the past and affect the future.

For García Márquez, incest symbolically combines these two poles since it is an act of projecting oneself simultaneously outward toward another and back into one's origins. Aureliano Babilonia is given the gift of translation at the end of the novel only after he has unwittingly committed incest with his aunt, Amaranta Úrsula. He enters the laboratory and decodes the signs, only to learn his genealogy and therefore to learn of the incestuous nature of his relations with Amaranta. The narration explains that he then begins "to decipher the instant that he was living, deciphering it as he lived it, prophesying himself in the act of deciphering the last page of the parchments, as if he were looking into a speaking mirror. Then he skipped again to anticipate the predictions and ascertain the date and circumstances of his death. Before reaching the final line, however, he had already understood that he would never leave that room, for it was foreseen that the city . . . would be wiped out by the wind and exiled from the memory of men at the precise moment when Aureliano Babilonia would finish deciphering the parchments" (383). His moment of reading himself simultaneously becomes ours since we too discover that the novel we have been reading is the parchment he has just translated. García Márquez implies that reading always involves translating ourselves, discovering how we have been participating in the making of the world every time we read. As my reading of "The Bear" has similarly suggested, reading here involves translating. Although presumably a story that moves forward through time and presumably revealed to us from an outside world, a narrative becomes an investment of the self that renders interpreted meaning an image of ourselves. Reading and writing alike seek communion with what is outside the self, but the ambiguous result is what the poet W. B. Yeats meant when he wrote: "Man makes a superhuman/ Mirror-resembling dream."[12]

It is fair to ask, then, why we should read this ending as comedic since it would seem to suggest that no New World is possible in the wake of the Old. That Aureliano is prophesying in his act of translation does nothing to stop his destiny or to heal Latin America's solitude, signified in many ways in the novel but perhaps most potently in the final disappearance of

Macondo. This would seem to be a tragic conclusion then, since all efforts to speak to others, the dead, to beings of other worlds end in soliloquy. In this sense, history can only be tragic, and tragedy only oedipal, an ever-recurring return to the self. García Márquez's point, however, is not tragic. Aureliano's incest is not a taboo or punishment for hubris but a recon-ciliation of the inward and outward impulses of the human imagination. It is a return to origins, to be sure, but with enough of a difference to be simultaneously an encounter with the Other, a difference symbolized in the fact that Aureliano's lover is not his mother, but a prodigal and world-traveled aunt. To recall the classic story, Oedipus deciphers, or translates, the riddle of the Sphinx and attempts to assign meaning to the omens and warnings of Tiresius. He tragically pretends that the meaning of his inter-pretation is divorced from his own story and from his exercise of power, however. He consistently acts in denial of the possibility that the human memory and testimony he gathers might reveal his own story as the cause of the curse on Thebes, that those fragments would form a mirror in which he finally sees his own image. That is, his tragedy is that he fails to see that he reads himself in the act of interpreting prophecy. *One Hundred Years of Solitude* suggests instead that reading brings us to a discovery of the se-cret knowledge of things past, things lost, but only if we are willing to tol-erate our ambiguously simultaneous presence in the text. The voice on the page holds the secret of the past and of our story but it has awaited an in-vestment of our own imagination for its fulfillment as a provider of a myth of origins. That is the import of his metaphor of the "speaking mirror"; reading is neither solely an encounter with oneself, nor with another but a meeting ground for both. So the result can be either tragic or comic, de-pending on our willingness to see this ambiguity as opportunity to project new futures instead of an enclosure that redundantly returns us again to the sins of the past.

If Faulkner's tragic characters hunger for anything, it is a new story, one that will not redundantly bring them back to the burdens they bear. Faced with the prospect of the end of humankind in the midst of a brewing Cold War, Faulkner's Nobel Speech insisted on the centrality of compassion to rescue reading from its tragic consequences: "when the last dingdong of doom has clanged and faded from the last worthless rock hanging tide-less in the last red and dying evening, [. . .] even then there will still be one more sound: that of [man's] puny inexhaustible voice, still talking" ("Ban-quet Speech"). The reason for hope is humankind's "compassion," which allows stories to move from the page into our imaginations and renders them mutually shared and made. As exemplified in the dialogue between

Shreve and Quentin in *Absalom, Absalom!*, storytelling is a call to listeners to share the burden of making meaning from the stories they are willing to hear and bear. This is because in listening or reading they invest their imagination so as to attribute, or more to the point, *cocreate* meaning. If it were possible for us to hear all the puny voices and to bear them together, healing of the rifts in communities could begin.

Faulkner implies that we must neither be naïve about nor discouraged by the difficulty of the task. García Márquez's novel suggests this tenuous balance in its conclusion. The narrator condemns the knowledge Aureliano gains of his solitude to oblivion, "because races condemned to one hundred years of solitude did not have a second opportunity on earth" (448). And yet because our reading coincides perfectly at that moment with Aureliano's reading of his origins, the story has nevertheless continued in the world of our own imagination and, potentially, in the future we choose to build. The fact that we get in our own way means we won't be able to transcend fully the limitations imposed on us by history, but despite fiction's secular aim of outlining this tragic failure, for García Márquez, fiction is also an expression of hope placed in the reader's compassion and thus shares the sacred ambitions of the Bible as a repository of the suffering of the human family. As if to underline this comic potential of his fiction and to highlight the comic potential of Faulkner's own tragic vision, García Márquez devoted the final moments of his Nobel Speech to the question of the end of humankind. Specifically, it is the power to invoke a New World of the imagination from the scraps of life, the power of telling, listening, and retelling, that will reverse the tragic trajectory of human history: "we, the inventors of tales, who will believe anything, feel entitled to believe that it is not yet too late to engage in the creation of the opposite utopia [opposed to the prospect of the end of man]. A new and sweeping utopia of life, where no one will be able to decide for others how they die, where love will prove true and happiness be possible, and where the races condemned to one hundred years of solitude will have, at last and forever, a second opportunity on earth."[13] History is not owned by the past, by our fathers, or by official powers, but by our imagination, which is another way of arguing that the future can be ours if we can tolerate the responsibility to imagine our own story with the ambiguous tools of fiction, instead of pretending to the transparent and one-way claims of historiography or revelation.

The simultaneity of prophecy and translation makes reading begin to resemble the writing of fiction, since it is a profound meeting point of the imagination and revelation, the present and the past, self and other. The plantation was founded on a very different principle of denial of the self's responsibility for having invented a world that permits the ownership of land and of others and a space in which progeny provide the continuity of a coherent, pure, and communicable history. This involved, as Faulkner's fiction reveals, a series of calculated lies and denials regarding the violence that such a pretense to certain borders, truths, and genealogy would require. Interpretations of the past that do not acknowledge their own myth-making dimensions commit this same violence by hiding behind the mask of objective truth. Fundamentalist readings that only see meaning given from some unspeakable, unfleshly source to which we submit our imaginations miss the sacred opportunity of participation in the meaning of the world. It is understandable why we might grow impatient with the ambiguous successes of mythmaking, but Faulkner suggests that the alternative is to act in ignorance of who we are, where we come from, or what consequences we leave behind. It is to set the stage of unwitting and tragic incest and perhaps leave suicide (which in his fiction we can understand as an instinct for social and cultural death) as the logical extension of this learned intolerance for the ambiguities and burdens of selfhood. St. Paul said that we look through a glass darkly. This might mean that reading the world allows us to see transparently, however faintly, the outlines of what lies beyond, but it also means that the glass is opaque and therefore serves as a mirror to provide us an image of ourselves reading. The ambiguity of this "speaking mirror" is what I believe Faulkner attempts to describe in his account of the Bible as the translation of the heart's complexity. If the self is effaced in the process of translation, and I have suggested that it shouldn't be, translation pretends to be revelation, as direct, undiluted, and innocent will, untainted by human hands or historical events. History, nature, and people are naturalized, stripped of their opacity and mystery, rendered perfectly legible. The lack of resolution of the South's dilemmas in Faulkner's fiction signifies for Glissant an extension "into multiplicity, into what we would call the suspension of identity. Into the inextricable, which is its boundless home" (98). If literature matters more than testimonies, legal repudiations, and other means of attempting the divorce with the past, as Glissant argues, it is because it perpetually offers new revelations as well as a new cryptic language that need more translation. This perpetual generation of stories keeps at bay the final claim of the definitive and enclosing boundaries of the self or of community, allowing an open passage of communication with the world beyond the cage of the self to which the past appears to condemn us. Faulkner's world becomes ours and ours his.

NOTES

1. Most notably, Deborah N. Cohn's *History and Memory in the Two Souths: Recent Southern and Spanish American Fiction* (Nashville: Vanderbilt University Press, 1999), the various contributors to Cohn and Smith's edited volume *Look Away! The U.S. South in New World Studies* (Duke University Press, 2004), and the work of Barbara Ladd, Hortense Spillers, Richard Godden, and John T. Matthews.

2. George B. Handley, *Postslavery Literatures in the Americas: Family Portraits in Black and White* (Charlottesville: University of Virginia Press, 2000).

3. See my chapter "Between the Insular Self and the Exotic Other" in *Postslavery Literatures*, 112–43.

4. Richard Godden and Noel Polk, "Reading the Ledgers," *Mississippi Quarterly* 55 (Summer 2002): 301–59.

5. William Faulkner, *Go Down, Moses* (New York: Vintage, 1991), 249.

6. William Faulkner, "Banquet Speech." Available online at FTP: nobelprize.org/nobel_prizes/literature/laureates/1949/faulkner-speech.html.

7. Édouard Glissant, *Faulkner, Mississippi* (New York: Farrar, Straus, and Giroux, 1998), 115.

8. Derek Walcott, *What the Twilight Says: Essays* (New York: Farrar, Straus, and Giroux, 1999), 69.

9. See *Twilight of the Idols*, with *The Antichrist* and *Ecce Homo*, trans. Antony M. Ludovici (London: Wordsworth Editions, 2007).

10. Gabriel García Márquez, *One Hundred Years of Solitude* (New York: Avon, 1970), 16.

11. A dichotomy exists, then, as Josefina Ludmer has demonstrated, between characters who are asexual, imaginative, withdrawn, mindful of history and transgression (characters who are representative of what Ludmer considers the mental axis of García Márquez's characters) and those who are driven by sexual desire, who are political, communal and interested in future knowledge and change (the body axis) Josefina Ludmer, *Cien años de soledad: una interpretación* (Buenos Aires: Tiempo Contemporáneo, 1972).

12. W. B. Yeats, *The Poems* (London: Everyman's Library, 1992), 245.

13. Gabriel García Márquez, "The Solitude of Latin America." Available online at FTP: nobelprize.org/nobel_prizes/literature/laureates/1982/Márquez-lecture.html.

Blood on the Leaves, Blood at the Root: Ritual Carriers and Sacrificial Crises of Transition in Yoknapatawpha and Oyo

KEITH CARTWRIGHT

> *Because it is possible to shift a load of wood, stones, or what not, from our own back to the back of another, the savage fancies that it is equally possible to shift the burden of his pains and sorrows to another, who will suffer them in his stead. Upon this idea he acts, and the result is an endless number of very unamiable devices for palming off upon some one else the trouble which a man shirks from bearing himself.*
> —J. G. Frazer, *The Golden Bough*

> *Ummmmmmmmmmmmmmmmmmmmmmmmmm*
> *blues falling down like hail*
> *blues falling down like hail*
> —Robert Johnson, "Hellhound on My Trail"

It is a privilege to come to Oxford to discuss a Nobel Prize–winning Southern author who has been accused of treason against his home state but has also had to defend himself against the charge of "hating Northerners." He has argued that "the root cause of the Civil War certainly was not secession" but may be found in a "scapegoat syndrome" whereby "if you have succeeded in robbing society blind you can persuade the robbed and dissatisfied sections of society that the real causes of their dissatisfaction can be traced to a particular sector of the community."[1] Along with legacies of colonial violence, slavery, civil war, North/South tension, and ecological devastations, this Southern writer navigates frontiers where religious worldviews confront secular modernity. The backward, ritual glance of his work has affinity for the purgative drama of classical tragedy. One of his favored endeavors is hunting, and his writings are filled with the lore of hunters and a vanishing wilderness. He faces that typically Southern situation of honoring ancestral rites that he knows to be as efficacious or satisfying as any anywhere while seeking to expose locally entrenched patterns of corruption and structural violence fed by (and feeding) networks of global capitalism. It makes sense that the University Press of Mississippi has become a key publisher of critical response to this author's work. I am speaking of course of the great Nigerian dramatist, poet, theorist, and activist Wole Soyinka, who was jailed during his country's bloody civil war and has braved innumerable threats upon his life.

Yoknapatawpha may be read with healthy differences when the reading is shaped by other locations in the global South, and I am thankful for how Morrison's, Márquez's, Glissant's, and Wilson Harris's Souths have helped remap a Yoknapatawpha that is, after the sermonic fires of Hell, the South's most charted mythic space. Soyinka's work may help too in our efforts to attend to hellhounded crises of racialized violence and ethnic economies of cleansing in Yoknapatawpha. Soyinka calls us to more visceral recognition of the burdens heaped upon "carriers" of ritual and quotidian cleansings. His work may then move us to cathartic responsibility for our own dirt and washing as we tend to repeating modes of violence wrought and transferred upon communities, landscapes, and psyches of Southlands local and global. And finally, Soyinka's dramatic rites and writing offer "medicinal" models of sacrificial dissociation from the universalizing conceptual violence of a neo-Platonic, Christian-colonial *Logos* that has sought to idealize, transcend, deny, and thereby strangely father the very real, bloody costs of embodied existence—costs that in denial may be deflected evermore violently upon the planet and its most vulnerable inhabitants, as Samuel Kimball's *The Infanticidal Logic of Evolution and Culture* has recently argued.[2] Faulkner himself, in public appearances as the chiefly Grandfather of Yoknapatawpha, often occluded the very sacrifices that his texts obsessively explore. When asked in Virginia of his choice of title for the story "Red Leaves," he famously explained: "The red leaves referred to the Indian. It was the deciduation of Nature which no one could stop that had suffocated and destroyed the Negro. . . . it was normal deciduation which the red leaves, whether they regretted it or not, had nothing more to say in."[3] Faulkner's statement on the "normal" Darwinian sacrifice of "the Negro" by Indians, attributed to Nature itself, would slip free of white responsibility for genocide against deciduated "red leaves" and of white supremacy's more quotidian racial suffocations. But those of us who enter Faulkner's woods and words know that the leaves of his texts always have more to say, that this has little to do with Indians or unstoppable Nature and much more to do with white Southerners' native perceptions of their own culture's deciduation and impurity, what Patricia Yaeger calls "white panic" in the face of "the unthought known"—the sacrificial blood on the leaves and at the root of every tree of Southern contact zones.[4] Soyinka too has something to say about blood rites and cultural deciduations. And it is to the ritual carriers of his plays and to his theorization of the creative/destructive cycles of the deity Ogun that we now turn for the "medicine" to read key tragic dramas of Faulkner's short fiction ("Red Leaves," "That Evening Sun," "Delta Autumn"), his works of closest formal and substantive kinship to Soyinka's staged rites.

"Where Is My Negro?"
From Oyo's Horseman to the Man's Lynchee

Death and the King's Horseman (1975), Soyinka's play engaging historical incidents from 1946 in the West African Yoruba Kingdom of Oyo, features the King's Horseman, Elesin, an important subchief over the King's cavalry stables (historically the source of Oyo's military strength and wealth) as he faces his role of committing ritual suicide following the death of the King.[5] Elesin's task of completing these rites comes at a moment of crisis, with the British established as colonial rulers, so his performance takes on a role of conserving the metaphysical world of Oyo, its self-apprehension and agency. Convergences with Faulkner's "Red Leaves" are uncanny: in both works the royal burial is delayed for the sacrifice of a retainer who will accompany the dead leader's horse and dog to serve him in the afterlife, and both seek resolution in human sacrifice at a moment of cultural crisis. A key difference, however, between the sacrifice of the King's Horseman and that of the African in Faulkner's "Red Leaves" is that the Yoruba Horseman is an important chief privileged from birth for this moment of cultural and personal power show, while Faulkner's lynched African serves another people.

Soyinka's play opens in the bustle of the Oyo market under the jurisdiction of Iyaloja, "Mother-of-the-Market." As Horseman, Elesin is the carrier of the Kingdom's ills in his transition to the ancestral dead. The drumming and praise songs of a griot goad Elesin with the efficacious honor of his forefathers: "[I]n their time the world was never tilted from its groove, it shall not be in yours."[6] Call and response patterns push Elesin to virtuoso greeting of the "Not-I-Bird," which Biodun Jeyifo describes as an elision of "'It-is-not-I-who-saw-that-bird-of-ill-omen,'" a figure of fear and panic that the Horseman, in "his ritual function as willing scapegoat," silences in dancing his/its death.[7] In colonized Oyo, "Not-I-Birds" of denial in the face of ill omen may be omnipresent; thus, the need for the Horseman's ritual art and power summons vitalizing, performance onstage— as sacrificial/medicinal dance of deliverance from a death that would fall upon all of Oyo.

Act 2 opens with District Officer Pilkings dancing a tango with his wife to a dull gramophone recording. They are dressed for a masque ball in cloth of the ancestral *egungun* cult, confiscated from the ritual embodiments of Oyo's dead. So when "Native Policeman" Amusa comes to announce Elesin's deathwatch, he is transfixed by the Pilkings' masked presence and faces jurisdictional conflict: "[S]ir, what you think you do with that dress? It belong to dead cult, not for human being. . . . [C]an man talk against death to person in uniform of death?" (*DK* 19). Since the confiscation of the egungun cloth, Elesin's rites have reached unprecedented import. Jeyifo argues that "the historic context of the ritual idioms that Soyinka employs in his dramas corresponds remarkably to what René Girard in his seminal book, *Violence and the Sacred*, has called 'the sacrificial crisis' . . . the relentless and inevitable decline of the social and metaphysical sanctions which once gave sacrificial rituals their ethical legitimacy and psychological efficacy."[8] Such a crisis, whether in Oyo, Yoknapatawpha, Washington, D.C., or Baghdad, makes for dangerous, violence-prone ground, tied to "a crisis of distinctions" and dissolving cultural "differences," often fueling the mob violence of "lynching, pogroms, etc.," and placing new demands upon "the ritualistic imagination" (in religion, politics, art) as colonial or capitalizing effort that, even as it "takes up arms against a certain type of violence . . . may well bring about another, undoubtedly more destructive type."[9]

Juxtaposed to the feast prepared for Oyo rites, the colonial residency's masque ball, with its local police band playing "Rule Britannia," creates a "left-over" taste. As the Pilkings play their egungun mask mimicry in full costume, Amusa's speechlessness in the face of their blasphemy finds counterpoint in Olunde, Elesin's son, whom we meet for the first time as he has come from medical school in England to tend to his father's funeral rites. Olunde appears as *"a young black man dressed in a sobre western suit"* (*DK* 40). When he speaks with Mrs. Pilkings in her egungun attire and engages her in spirited debate on British and Oyo rites of sacrifice, he shows himself to be one who can wear the suit of Western medicine and engage the suit of Oyo's ancestral medicine without becoming a suit or mistaking the suit for possession of its signal power. Ironically, it is Mr. Pilkings's intervention to "save" Elesin (at the last moment when the King's dog and horse have been sacrificed and await the Horseman's final death act) that makes Olunde a "walking ghost." Elesin, fallen short of fulfilling the function for which his life of privilege has been directed, is detained in a cellar "where the slaves were stored before being taken down to the coast," now a "storeroom for broken furniture" (*DK* 47). His howling from the slave storeroom resonates with the soundtrack of Yoknapatawpha: "an animal bellow from off[stage]" (*DK* 49). And

Olunde—with his father and his rites detained in the colonial storeroom of broken folklore—is stripped of patrimony: "I have no father, eater of left-overs" (*DK* 50).

Stench and decay take over a once vibrant stage and ritual actor as Elesin's failure is no merely personal matter but marks a crisis of integrity in Oyo's systems of authority. Tragic recognition comes in the slave cellar, with Elesin's confession of committing "the unspeakable blasphemy of seeing the hand of the gods in this alien rupture of his world" (*DK* 57). But Iyaloja heaps her scorn and her added charge of infanticidal behavior. At the moment when Elesin's passing should have fed the young, his appetite left nothing for the generations he was entrusted to serve. And to Elesin's and Pilkings's final horror, Iyaloja has her dirge-singing retainers unroll Olunde's corpse from a long funeral cloth: "this young shoot has poured its sap into the parent stalk, and we know this is not the way of life" (*DK* 62). After Elesin hangs himself in despair, we are left with a corpse-strewn stage and Iyaloja's words to Pilkings: "you . . . usurp the vestments of our dead, yet believe the stain of death will not cling to you. . . . There is your board, filled to overflowing. Feast on it" (*DK* 62). As Samuel Kimball's *Infanticidal Logic* helps to underscore here, Pilkings's typically Western—and fully colonial—desire to transcend moorings in violence actually "increases the risk of infanticide."[10] The leftovers of colonial violence prove poisonous. And in Yoknapatawpha, with its racializations of pollution and purity—its killing pride of white panic—all rites go awry.

So we see in Faulkner's "Red Leaves" a stunningly similar rite—staged as anti-Christian communion of white panic. Dressed for Chickasaw or Choctaw retainer sacrifice, Faulkner's Indian "play" is most grounded, as Peter Mallios argues, in anxieties of Yoknapatawpha's white natives.[11] The story opens in allegorical parallax vision: "THE TWO INDIANS crossed the plantation toward the slave quarters. Neat with whitewash, of baked soft brick, the two rows of houses in which lived the slaves belonging to the clan, faced one another across the mild shade of the lane marked and scored with naked feet and with a few home-made toys mute in the dust. There was no sign of life."[12] In native dress, Faulkner's play moves beneath plantation whitewash to ask demanding questions of his clan amidst the mute quarters of immanent lynching.

As in Soyinka's play, the dead leader's dog and horse are gathered while folk await his retainer. Oyo's Elesin, given his chiefly position, must honorably pay the price of privilege, but the house slave of the Man is expected to run, since the Africans are not integrated into the body politic of the clan: "[T]hey cannot be expected to regard usage. That is why I say that this way is a bad way" (*CS* 316). Of course, the bad way is plantation slavery—and for Faulkner's clan—the legacy of entrenchment in such a deeply riven society. Questions of legitimacy emerge. It is Moketubbe's patricide against the Man that necessitates hunting the Man's African and making him a "carrier" of the crime that confronts the community and summons its "Not-I Bird" of the unthought known:

> "Issetibbeha became dead who was not old . . . what do you think of that?"
> "I don't think about it," Basket said. "Do you?"
> "No," the second said.
> "Good," Basket said. "You are wise." (CS 317)

A key question thus arises in "Red Leaves." What is it that we/they don't think about and why? It is Moketubbe's grandfather, Doom, whose poisoning rise to power set the foundations for a plantation slave economy. Married to a West Indian quadroon "by a combination itinerant minister and slave trader" (CS 318) —showing evangelical ministry and slave trading as a joint economic venture—Doom and his investments bring the clan to "a squatting conclave over the Negro question." Here we are treated to a more wry interrogation of Faulkner's contemporary Southern "klonkaves" than we would get in more direct gaze. The question comes down to a matter of cannibalism, the assertion, "We cannot eat them," and the response "Why not?" (CS 319). Unwilling to incorporate black America into the body politic, the "native" responds that there are too many to eat, and that black flesh "has a bitter taste" (CS 314). So the decision not to cannibalize but to reeconomize along a segregationist design is quite familiar, as is the consideration of lynching: "We might kill a few of them and not eat them" (CS 319).

Two Yoknapatawpha natives musing upon their investment in the Man's crimes sound like current discussion of race, religion, and structural violence in the South:

> "What do you think"
> "What do you think?"
> "What do you think?"
> "I think nothing."
> "Nor do I." (CS 323)

While acknowledging the criminal illegitimacy of the Man's rule appears unspeakable in Yoknapatawpha, Moketubbe must still lead the hunt for his father's runaway slave so that burial may be completed and he may become the Man. The Man's funeral rites bear the weight of sacrificial crisis as the funeral has become a double rite of passage for the departed one and he who must prove himself the Man. Until Moketubbe can return things to their place and open "the door to the earth" by saying "'Here is thy dog, thy horse, thy Negro. . . . [B]egin the journey,'" he cannot be the Man (*CS* 327).

The running of the "Guinea man" (*CS* 327) enters what Soyinka calls the Ogun-infused "'chthonic realm,' the seething cauldron of the dark world will and psyche, the transitional yet inchoate matrix of death and becoming."[13] As with the rhythmic backing for Elesin, the African creek bottom rites of "Red Leaves" "let the drums talk . . . let the drums tell it" (*CS* 328). A certain drumming double consciousness splits the Guinea man's psyche (similar to Quentin Compson's reaction to the Vodou-backing of Sutpen's tale): "he could hear the two voices, himself and himself," and he admits, "'Yao, I am dead'. . . . He wished to be where the drums were" (*CS* 330).

Drum calls of transition move the African to Middle Passage memories of being a chained hunter preying on partly domesticated ship rats. The slaveship memory works up and along a rat-Negro-native Yoknapatawphan bio-economic chain of consumption, arriving topside at "the drunken New England captain intoning aloud from a book." Against powers of universalizing scripturalist consumption signified by "the single white garment which the trader, a deacon in the Unitarian church, had given him" (*CS* 330), the Guinea man has fashioned a medicine amulet from a mother of pearl opera glass and a cottonmouth skull. In its hybrid refashioning of whiteness and poison, the amulet offers remedial "flash of the spirit" to see and resist spectacles of consumptive white supremacy.[14]

Back at the big house, a congregation "in their Sunday clothes" (*CS* 331) gathers for what will be—if seen through the corrective medicine-amulet of opera glass and cottonmouth skull—a lynching as "public theatre," described by Leon Litwack as "voyeuristic spectacle" to satisfy "the emotional appetite" of a festive crowd.[15] When Issetibbeha finally gives his last breath, his horse and dog are tied to a tree, and the dog begins the howling soundtrack that permeates Yoknapatawpha. The chase begins in full. When finally entrapped, the African in "caked mud mask" embraces the white face of death and utters Faulknerian passwords to the sublime, "'Olé, grandfather,'" before allowing a cottonmouth to slash him repeatedly—to give him the poison that will be medicine for his live entry into the grave that will be slavery's afterlife (*CS* 334, 335).

Even more troubling than the Man's doom is the story's registration of the damnation of those who carry the Man's litter, "carried through swamp and brier by swinging relays of men who bore steadily all day long the crime and its object, on the business of the slain" (*CS* 335). Yoknapatawpha natives are doomed for their carrying of the crime and its object (the red slippers of political and consumer power) on the business of the slain (the need to kill an African). The Man has gotten the people to carry his crime. Indeed, "[t]o Moketubbe it must have been as though . . . he were being carried rapidly through hell by doomed spirits which, alive, had contemplated his disaster, and, dead, were oblivious partners to his damnation" (*CS* 335). Moketubbe's carriers take on a death mask themselves as they seek transference upon a black carrier of their crimes who must serve the Man in slavery's afterlife. It is unclear whether the snakebit Guinea man's sacrifice will be efficacious since "[w]e cannot send with Issetibbeha one who will be of no service to him" (*CS* 336). And since the text insists "[t]omorrow is today'" (*CS* 338), we see that hunting a carrier to open (or close) earth's door for the Man is a recurrent task: whether in response to Hurricane Katrina, in prisons that are heir to plantations, or in violent tales of chthonic boundary-crossing marketed in Dirty South rap, we sustain slavery's afterlife, its storehouses of broken furniture. Regarding the things scapegoats carry and who does the carrying, "[t]omorrow is just another name for today" (*CS* 337).

The burial scene is anticlimax. The African joins the dog, horse, and Issetibeha's corpse surrounded by Sunday-clothed clan guests. Rites of the Ku Klux Klan are enacted. Like the Confederate dead in their white egungun robes, who—famously in *Birth of a Nation*—pour a whole bucket of water down their faces to signal a thirst unquenched since Shiloh, the Guinea-man takes the gourd, "and they watched him try to drink. . . . his throat working and the bright water cascading from either side of the gourd, down his chin and breast." Faulkner repeats the scene, closing the story as the natives surround their carrier:

> Again they watched his throat working and the unswallowed water sheathing broken and myriad down his chin, channeling his caked chest. They waited, patient, grave, decorous, implacable; clansman and guest and kin. Then the water ceased, though still the empty gourd tilted higher and higher, and still his black throat aped the vain motion of his frustrated swallowing. A piece of water-loosened mud carried away from his chest and broke at his muddy feet, and in the empty gourd they could hear his breath: ah-ah-ah.
>
> "Come," Basket said, taking the gourd from the Negro and hanging it back in the well. (*CS* 341)

Part born-again altar call (or baptism played backwards), part Klan lynching, "Red Leaves," like Soyinka's play, takes up sacrificial crises in slavery's transitional afterlife. Moved by white panic—like Pilkings in his blasphemous egungun cloth for the masque ball or the Klan in the sheets of the Confederate dead—Faulkner's "natives" go atavistic in their Sunday clothes. And their rites, yearning for purity and transcendence, move in the Satanic (nigh farcical) antiritual space of the Man's christening as Doom. This may well be the state of religion in Faulkner's Yoknapatawpha and our own.[16]

"Who Will Do Our Washing Now?"
The Strong Breed of "That Evening Sun"

If I appear to do violence to Yoruba sacred space and to the memory of those traumatized by white Southern terror, I risk this only out of a call to follow Soyinka's paths to his patron hunter/blacksmith deity of iron, Ogun. It may be, as Biodun Jeyifo has observed, that "Ogun's creative-destructive axis operates like Derrida's notion of the pharmakon: artistic signification conceived in the pharmacological metaphor of the poison which could be the saving prophylactic, the disease inseparable from its cure, or the symptom which is indissociable from its prognosis."[17] Call it an Ogun-informed hair-of-the-dog prescription, but I am convinced that ritual stagings of violences at our origins can offer therapeutic vaccine, and that Southern efforts to reconfigure community must risk encounters with poisons that are also remedy. Faulkner and Soyinka both offer quite a pharmacopeia. Doom's poison powder and the presumed poison in Elesin's "charms" come to mind, and we can consider the function of cocaine in "That Evening Sun" and the drugs of preparation used on the carrier in Soyinka's *The Strong Breed*. As we know from our songs, Southerners live in locations known to call for heavy medication. For Plato (via Egyptian legends of Thoth's introduction of writing), text was a pharmakon (poison, drug, remedy, questionable medicine). We too may go to the medicine trees and sacred groves of Africa to seek and (con)textualize the strange fruit that is both poison and remedial Southern knowledge.[18]

An early play of Soyinka's, *The Strong Breed* (1967), speaks to terrors associated with Southern lynching. Set in a Niger Delta village on its New Year's Eve, the play opens with Eman, the village teacher and a stranger to the village, cleaning house with his wife, a nurse/pharmacist native to the village. Since she knows that the night calls for ritual abuse of a carrier of the year's ills—and knows that the carrier is taken from among strangers—she urges Eman to leave for the night. He refuses. A group of men creep near the house and throw a sack over a retarded boy whom Eman has befriended. Facing the village's terrorizing of a "dumb-moaning" child serving as carrier, Eman argues that "[i]n my home, we believe that a man should be willing. . . . A village which cannot produce its own carrier contains no men."[19] Oroge, the more reflective of the local leaders, recounts his prowess in bending the will to suit ritual needs: "He shall be willing. Not only willing but actually joyous. I am the one who prepares them all. . . . you will see him later tonight, the most joyous creature in the festival" (*SB* 129). This carrier, we assume, will get quite a dose of pharmaceuticals. But although Eman offers himself and serves as the boy's replacement, he soon flees the ritual abuse, and a manhunt with staged flashback scenes ensues. Eman's memories of his father, ritual carrier of his Niger Delta people, work back to the father's expectations of his son taking the position: "Other men would rot and die doing this task year after year. It is strong medicine which only we can take" (*SB* 134). But Eman left his home, having seen that its ritual structures were in corrupt hands when he had to fight his manhood tutor who caught Eman's girlfriend on a secret visit and sexually blackmailed her, ordering her to "come . . . to my hut, I shall give you some clothes to wash" (*SB* 140). In exile, Eman carries another people's dirt. His flashback-filled flight to water leads past the village's sacred grove, and because he has endangered the village's ability to heap the year's ills on a carrier and aroused sudden enmity, a trap is set. He soon hangs dead from the trees. As Ato Quayson points out, with the village teacher hanging in the grove, "emotions associated with purificatory rituals are replaced by those of guilt and self-doubt."[20] No one could raise a curse upon the carrier. Considering the scapegoating behind the Nigerian civil war, religious mob-violence in Nigeria, and the state execution by hanging of Niger Delta playwright Ken Saro-Wiwo, who carried the burden of opposing the pilfering of the Delta's environment and oil, Soyinka's early play offers a prophetic inward gaze, anticipating Saro-Wiwo's last words: *"What sort of nation is this?"*[21]

Speaking of the need for medicating redress for traumas of collective memory and chronically uneven "dynamics of human development," Soyinka asserts that we must "map . . . new directions that redress the history of societies and humanize the destiny of their peoples."[22] If "Red Leaves" maps some of Yoknapatawpha's originating contact zones, another early story, "That Evening Sun," maps sacrificial crises that drive Quentin Compson to his suicide (as willing carrier) in the Charles River. Taking its title from "St. Louis Blues," that ultimate hair-of-the-dog medicine, Quentin's narrative examines the growing divide between Jefferson and its ritual dramas and rites of purification:

MONDAY IS NO DIFFERENT from any other weekday in Jefferson now. The streets are paved now, and the telephone and electric companies are cutting down more and more of the shade trees—the water oaks, the maples and locusts and elms—to make room for iron poles bearing clusters of bloated and ghostly and bloodless grapes, and we have a city laundry which makes the rounds on Monday morning, gathering the bundles of clothes into bright-colored, specially-made motor cars: the soiled wearing of a whole week now flees apparitionlike behind alert and irritable electric horns . . . even the Negro women who still take in white people's washing after the old custom, fetch and deliver it in automobiles.[23]

Sacred groves disappear in Jefferson to make way for iron innovations. But the iron grapes, "bloated," "ghostly," and "bloodless" bespeak the sacrificial crisis described by René Girard. There is no "power of the blood" in these grapes. And what of the carriers here, the black women who carry Jefferson's dirt home and wash it? The "soiled wearing of a whole week" disappears in ghostly fashion, carried off to the "alert and irritable horns" of cars sounding like the horns of the story's blues title track. Quentin yearns for the old days of childhood, fifteen years earlier, when black women and their carrying of soiled laundry were more accessible to the spectatorial gaze, and the "dusty, shady streets would be full of Negro women with, balanced on their steady, turbaned heads, bundles of clothes tied up in sheets, almost as large as cotton bales, carried so without a touch of hand between the kitchen door of the white house and the blackened washpot beside a cabin door in Negro Hollow" (CS 289). This story, with its white house and the blacksmith deity Ogun's iron washpot, asks us to account for all that one woman, Nancy, has carried, and exposes the deciduation of white Christianity as a carrier of good faith.

It is no accident that Nancy's husband is named Jesus, and that father "told us to not have anything to do with Jesus" since Jesus "was a short black man, with a razor scar down his face" (CS 290). The story turns to investigation of faithless blues and of what brings a balance-perfect Mississippian to fall so far off-kilter. Part of the problem is that Mr. Stovall, "the cashier in the bank and a deacon in the Baptist church," is getting his jollies with Jesus's wife. Furthermore, Mr. Stovall, representative of Dixie's marriage of capitalism and churchianity, has fallen behind in his payments to Nancy. Of course it is Nancy who is jailed, and her suicide attempt leaves her jailer to say "it was cocaine and not whisky, because no nigger would try to commit suicide unless he was full of cocaine, because a nigger full of cocaine wasn't a nigger any longer" (CS 291). While these are a racist jailer's speculations, let us assume—for the pharmaceutical power of Faulkner's prose—that it is cocaine. We can be sure that the power structure will do all it can to keep its "niggers" away from cocaine and in their places as carriers of cotton, laundry, and the nasty shadows of white projections. Faulkner repeatedly uses the most poisonous word in our language as a textual drug that works a displacing shock in its prescription.

Revived by her jailer, the pregnant Nancy survives to do the Compson laundry and be their emergency cook. And Jesus speaks elliptically of the melon under Nancy's dress. Hearing Nancy say "'[i]t never came off of your vine,'" he offers a vision of end times: "'I can cut down the vine it did come off of.'" What Jesus says about the sexual workings of segregation also speaks angrily of the church: "'I cant hang around white man's kitchen,'" Jesus said, "'But white man can hang around mine'" (CS 292). The only legitimate location of Christianity in the South may well be the churches of Jesus's kin, the most inclusive carriers of the body of Christ. But "That Evening Sun" presents a Nancy who is simply finished, is tired of carrying, tired of washing, tired of fearing Jesus.

Behind the story's choral rites of transition is a "sound" that "was like singing and it wasn't like singing, like the sounds that Negroes make" (CS 296). Nancy's blues evoke a fear in Mr. Compson that leads him down the stairs with pistol in hand and unsettles the children so much that five-year-old Jason starts up the "Not-I" chants of protection, repeating, "'Jesus is a nigger. . . . Dilsey's a nigger too. . . . I ain't a nigger. . . . I ain't a nigger'" (CS 297–98). Jesus, the one who washes and carries our sins, the ultimate carrier, is "a nigger" dismissed from white households and subject to mob violence. Faulkner's insistence on the word "nigger," attached to Jesus, works a psychotropic "trip" on his readers to render religious perversions in a visceral manner. Yoknapatawpha is clearly at a sacrificial crisis of faithlessness calling for a carrier's blood. For now it is Nancy. But it *will* claim Quentin. Like the Guinea man, Nancy drinks but can't consume: "'I swallows but it won't go down me'" (CS 298). The children's naïve questions unearth buried truths: "'Why is Nancy afraid of Jesus?' Caddy said. 'Are you afraid of father, mother?'" (CS 299). Against such implied critique of patriarchy, Caddy asks, "'What have you done that made Jesus mad?'" (CS 300). While this question is directed at Nancy, it primarily addresses the reader's response to both Jesuses. It *is* an altar call.

Quentin narrates, but Nancy's blues carry a primacy, and the fury in the five-year-old voice of Jason serves authorial function as well. Jason's "'I'm going to tell. . . . Yawl made me come,'" sounds like the tattletale voice of an author forced into such positions by his older brothers and sisters (CS 306). Quentin is haunted by Nancy's dread of the bloody "root" put on her by Jesus. Nancy's claim on death gives Quentin the logic that will lead to his suicide: "'I can't do nothing. Just put it off. And that don't do no good. I reckon it belong to me. I reckon what I going to get ain't no more than mine'" (*CS* 307).[24] Something of Nancy's blood is spilled on the Compsons' childhood, traumatizing them by its presence, by their complicitous rootedness in terror. And Nancy's final words to Father read like an oracle of his son's impending self-sacrifice: "'You'll see what you'll see, I reckon. . . . But it will take the Lord to say what that will be'" (*CS* 308).

The story's closing frame insists on its two-headed oracular vision. As father and the children leave Nancy and cross the Christ-haunted ditch where "shadows tangled," Father reassures Caddy, telling her Jesus "'went away a long time ago.'" With Jason atop Father's back, "it looked like father had two heads," and in the distance Nancy sounds "the sound that was not singing and not unsinging." Here Quentin utters his only direct discourse in the story he narrates, asking, "'Who will do our washing now, Father?'" Jason makes it immediately clear that he will not do it: "'I'm not a nigger'" (*CS* 309). It will turn out to be the son of the Father, the shadow-struck, incest-obsessed Quentin, the nigger who would sleep with his sister, the tattletale of all the South would repress, who will be the carrier above the ditch grown large as the Charles River. With Jesus gone and the once balanced, queenly Nancy utterly spent, we must all do our own washing now.

"Took in What? Took in Washing?"
The Ogun Medicine of "Delta Autumn"

"Red Leaves," "That Evening Sun," and "Delta Autumn" share an autumnal, sunset sense of deciduation—ablaze in red. In Yorubaland Ogun's color is red, and it is he who "even with water present in the house, / washes himself with blood."[25] As smelter, blacksmith, hunter, and technological innovator, Ogun turns binary oppositions to fluid equations of power and potentiality: "destoyer = creator, or the obverse, creator = destroyer."[26] Responding to Ogun devotees' scarifying art of tattooing, John Pemberton points to how Ogun reminds us that "[c]ultural existence has its costs. It requires acts of violence, not only against the person who is the enemy but also against oneself and one's children, and against the forest, the land, and the animal."[27] Ogun realizations of the structural violence at the heart of society are traceable across the Niger Delta. In Idoma culture, one who has killed must undergo a ceremony of "'washing the *ògwú* [killing or pride] from the face'" administered by a blacksmith at his forge, using medicinal leaves dipped in a trough for quenching red-hot tools.[28] After immersions in Yoknapatawpha's violent pride, we might ask here and now, how wash the killing pride from our faces?

A Yoruba divination tale offers the medicine "Osa-Ogun can fight" and speaks of mystic marriages that stretch cultural frontiers as Ogun seeks divination for a wife. Making a prescribed sacrifice, he spies a buffalo cow from his stand. She shucks her skin to become a reddish-colored market woman. Stealing her skin, he follows her to market, and successfully woos her. But after he drunkenly reveals her secrets to jealous co-wives, Buffalo-woman finds her skin and kills her mocking tormentors. Her hunter-husband's sacrifices finally calm her, and she breaks off her horn to allow ritual communication, before returning to the bush: "This day I'll have gone for good / But I have left a horn with my children / You too may call / if you need me / if you know how."[29]

Intuitively, "Delta Autumn" activates this medicine via a shape-shifting doe. As Judith Gleason writes, the Osa Ogunda divination space often addresses people suffering from feelings of ineffectuality and from bounded modes of impotence that drive fear, anxiety, all the stuff of sacrificial crisis.[30] This may be the position of the aging Isaac McCaslin. The Delta hunt is Yoknapatawpha's most sacred rite. From the story's beginning we know Ike's young nephew Roth Edmonds is in pursuit of a doe "that walks on two legs—when she's standing up, that is. Pretty light-colored, too.'"[31] Ogun's iron tools have increased the distance it takes to journey past fields "scooped punily and terrifically by axe and saw and mule-drawn plow from the wilderness's flank" (*GDM* 342). But it is in entering remnant "black land, imponderable and vast, fecund," that Ike's carnal vision finds articulation as mystic marriage: "every man and woman, at the instant when it dont even matter whether they marry or not . . . whether they marry then or afterward or dont never, at that instant the two of them together were God'" (*GDM* 348).

Ike's blood initiation from Sam Fathers at age twelve is the kind of rite that is even more diminished than the "untreed land warped and wrung to mathematical squares of rank cotton" (*GDM* 354). Having tried to repudiate the burdens of the plantation past, Ike has become a carrier of banknotes by which his younger kinsman (and heir) Edmonds would wash his hands clean of the doe-woman and their child. She, whose blood "would have made a man" of Edmonds through fidelity to it, is not one of "the draggle-tailed women of the Delta peckerwoods." What she *is* suddenly dawns on Ike as she mentions her aunt's support of the family: "'Took in what?' he said. 'Took in washing?'" (*GDM* 360). Ike's outburst, "'You're a nigger!'" bespeaks frontiers he and his kin refuse to cross in marriage—mystic or otherwise—to othered kin. Isaac touches her hand, and at that touch—in fidelity to it—passes the patriarchal medicine to this "doe" as inheritance for the infant boy who bears their married blood: "The horn . . . the one which General Compson had left him in his will, covered with the unbroken skin from a buck's shank and bound with silver" (*GDM* 362–63). Ike gives the horn out of panic, guilt, and the recognition that insists on impermeability of boundaries. But Gleason writes that the Osa Ogunda "fighting medicine" in Oya's gift of her horn to Ogun "is a token of recognition" that her wild force has been married to him and passed to the children.[32] Afro-Yoknapatawphans of northern urban spaces now own the fighting medicines of Mississippi's sacred groves and blues agency. With Jesus gone in "That Evening Sun" and the patriarchs' "fighting medicine" gone too, white Yoknapatawpha's ties to legitimacy, mystic marriage, and manhood itself decay. In this "deswamped and denuded and derivered" land, there is no father to wash the killing-pride from the face, no rite but the writing of the story itself, which ends in botched sacrifice—Edmonds's killing of a doe (wilderness reproductivity) as if to avenge himself on all that has born him. In the Yoruba tale the hunter's ritual respect for his marriage allows him to receive the horn. With "Delta Autumn" the tale turns awry: the hunter loses patrimonial access to the horn that carries his gunpowder. No white Yoknapatawphan—at least until Elvis—will receive the Ogun praises Soyinka offers the King's Horseman: "Hunter who carries his powder horn on his hips and fires crouching or standing!" (*DK* 14). Do we hear something of this horn's sacred grove or grooves in Southerners like Dizzy, Bird, or Trane? Do we see something of its perceived lack in the ritualized sadoeroticism of spectacle lynching? Or photos from Abu Ghraib?

Soyinka insists on the "fundamental visceral questioning" (2) that Ogun rites, his own plays, and Faulkner's narratives open up. Speaking to the forces diminishing the big woods of "Delta Autumn," Soyinka posits that the "gradual erosion of Earth in European metaphysic scope is probably due to the growth and influence of the Platonic-Christian tradition" (3) by which "the apprehended territory of man has already begun to contract" (41). Against such contraction, he turns to Ogun's path-blazing across "the numinous . . . abyss of transition" (26).[33] The very technologies that destroy wilderness open new wild spaces. But this is dangerous ground, as Girard notes in discussing the sacred quality of metallurgy in Africa and how metal's "inestimable benefits" and "advantages are not without a reverse side; all weapons, after all, are double-edged."[34] This is recognized in Ogun's praise epithet, "A needle is sharp at both ends," and in the plain fact that our technologies of culture and transport have become weapons of our own destruction.[35] Ogun is a technological innovator and hunter-traditionalist whose smelting and reshaping, killings and skinnings, medicinal charms and poisons cut through binary thought, working—like Faulkner's sentences—as tools of entry across gaps, into ghostly groves and ditches. As Wilson Harris has observed of Faulkner's prose, his sentences serve as carriers of premises and intuitions that "are reluctant to be raised to consciousness" and are carried across (and carry the writer across) "a prickly regionalism or fortress homogeneity" in a "demanding art in which the emphasis shifts from ruling ego to intuitive layers of self or selves, and a transformed mosaic of community comes into play."[36]

In postcolonial Souths, the very idea of a transformed mosaic community tends always to be built upon the foundational violence and aspiritual shatterings of genocide, slave trade, and white supremacist political economies—the sacrifices of the unwilling and the coerced. Against the killing pride and conceptual violence of an idealizing coloniality and its reproduction, we have Ogun's pharmacopoeia—Ogun's immanence. The iron god reminds us of the inevitable, ever-present sacrificial costs of existence, costs that are increasingly inflated and that we tend to deflect unsustainably upon vulnerable others. Against colonizing politics of fear, the names of people, places, and events like Denmark Vesey, Shiloh, and Bloody Sunday resonate with the sacral power of the blood to move a fortress homogeneity into mosaic community, and the unflinching tragic dramas of Soyinka and Faulkner lead us to face a nontranscendable violence at the heart of culture.[37] They work also to turn the poisons of violence to remedial recognition of the costs of foisting ills upon unwilling, uncompensated carriers. Given America's and the South's infanticidal culture of incarceration, a culture in which the cheapness of life emits a violence fanned by disinvestments in our cities and social infrastructure, we shouldn't have needed Hurricane Katrina to show all the old mechanisms of scapegoating to be ready for high speed dial up. Familiar black carriers as well as immigrants, Arabs, and that sturdy scapegoat—gay marriage—now carry the inflated costs of sacrificial crisis. Faulkner points to some of the Man's inflating costs in the iron wash pots beside the cabins of Negro Hollow, in Jefferson's iron light poles with their decorative bloodless grapes, in Isaac McCaslin's rising from an iron cot to sacrifice the hunter's fighting medicine, and finally in Quentin's calculations calling for "two six-pound flat-irons" that will allow the "drowned man's shadow [that] was watching for him in the water all the time" to wash him clean.[38] What a waste indeed. So how do we wash the killing pride from our faces? If we take our lead from Ogun's iron repertoires, we wash it with leaves from Southern groves, dipped into the cooling systems of our weapons factories, administered by the fashioner of the weapons and words of our killing. I am not suggesting that we all go on pilgrimage to seek out Donald Rumsfeld to wash the pride from our faces. No, but I do think that Faulkner's texts are a place to start treating Southerners infected with killing pride. Other pharmaceutical sources may work better for many. But Yoknapatawpha's groves have long offered a cathartic pharmacopoeia of global reach, bringing the blues and the broken eucharistic body of Christ into the matrix of deconstruction/creationism that is Ogun:

Rich-laden is his home, yet decked in palm fronds
He ventures forth, refuge of the down-trodden.
To rescue slaves he unleashed the judgement of war
Because of the blind, plunged into the forest
Of curative herbs, Bountiful One
Who stands bulwark to offsprings of the dead in heaven
Salutations O lone being, who bathes in rivers of blood.[39]

In the dance recording *Ogun Party*, the Yoruba "juju" guitar-master King Sunny Ade sings, "Ogun Lakaye" (Ogun's fame is worldwide).[40] Yoruba diasporas of the slave trade have indeed spread Ogun's fame to ritual, musical, and literary encounters in Haiti, Cuba, Brazil, Trinidad, New Orleans, Miami, and beyond.[41] Faulkner's writing—carried and "chained" as it is by the economies and choral sounds shaping Robert Johnson and Bessie Smith and Billie Holiday—intuits the pharmacological presence of a global Ogun so fully that one need not turn to a demon Sutpen or Haitian Ogun-drumming to find a circum-Caribbean transnational presence in Yoknapatawpha. It was always already there rippling in water, in blood, molten iron and malleable "notlanguage," awaiting its mosaic community of readers. And they have come—spiritedly. In *Beloved* Toni Morrison's Stamp Paid speaks to Faulkner's ledgers with an Afro-Atlantic sense of accounting. More recently Madison Smartt Bell's Haitian trilogy features an Ogun who moves Faulkner-informed characters through rites of feeding the spirits that also feed what Michael Dash calls the Haitian Revolution's "radical application of universal human rights."[42] Indeed, it may be in the ports and backwater borderlands of global Souths—in Yorubaland, Bois Caiman, Santiago de Cuba, New Orleans, and the mythic woods of Yoknapatawpha—that Enlightenment universalism is washed of its ethnocentric pretensions and killing pride. Reason alone may prove incapable of speaking to the universal, primordial reaches of our consciousness that have been tapped artistically (and homeopathically) in ritual processes of purgative cleansing from Aeschylus, to Faulkner and Soyinka, and that get staged in global music. As Shakespeare scholar Philip Brockbank argued in an essay on Soyinka, "to encourage the slow, perplexed growth of a more adequate humanism, the ritual processes still at work in our societies urgently need to be understood and revalued."[43] What Wilson Harris asks of

Soyinka's handling of Ogun festivals should be asked of Faulkner as well: "Do the epic gods need to be unmasked within ritual establishments as self-critical buried faculties in ourselves, and in them . . . if one is to create a balance against their, and our, self-destructive orders or pageants of terror? And, if so, will divine authority at the heart of human society be reborn as bearable and re-creative even as it appears to die?"[44] Faulkner relies on a certain Ogunish primordial economy of blood and justice for balance in his ritual unmaskings of a Southern Christ's pageants of terror—in the Sunday-clothed clan lynching of "Red Leaves," in "That Evening Sun's" apocalyptic scar-faced black Jesus of the ditch, and in the foundational illegitimacies made of marriage and the hunt's sacral coupling in "Delta Autumn." The "cruel face" of Christ we've made for worship is ritually unmasked in Faulkner's prose in a manner meant to prescribe the pharmakon of cathartic terror that might begin the cleansing of fears and cheap pity bound up in our killing-pride. We might take additional stage directions from Soyinka's Iyaloja, the mother-of-the-market, and her patron Oya ("owner of the market," goddess of the whirlwind, the purifying spinning of ancestral egungun, the shape-shifting "doe" who gives her horn to Ogun). In the end, as in the beginning, it may not be simply a scar-faced Jesus and his blue-eyed double, or even Ogun's "many faces" tending the balance of our blood-costs, but also a washwoman or doe, a sister or Other mother seen in the trees, hauntingly, muddy or bloody drawered, carrying life's costs and called to caddy the game we've been making of laying life waste.[45]

NOTES

1. *Conversations with Wole Soyinka*, ed. Biodun Jeyifo (Jackson: University Press of Mississippi, 2001), 39, 51. See 132 on Soyinka's love of hunting.

2. I borrow concepts and language here from the introductory chapter of a powerful new book by my colleague, A. Samuel Kimball, *The Infanticidal Logic of Evolution and Culture* (Newark: University of Delaware Press, 2007). See in particular the section of his introduction subtitled "The Infanticidal as Cultural Limit" (21–25). In my essay's Soyinka-inspired efforts to respond to blood rites and sacrificial crises in Faulkner's work, I am also deeply indebted to the writings of Soyinka critic Biodun Jeyifo (see notes 8 and 17) for bringing me to reexamine key works by René Girard, *Violence and the Sacred*, trans. Patrick Gregory (Baltimore: Johns Hopkins University Press, 1977), and Jacques Derrida, *Dissemination*, trans. Barbara Johnson (Chicago: University of Chicago Press, 1981).

3. *Faulkner in the University*, ed. Frederick L. Gwynn and Joseph L. Blotner (1959; Charlottesville: University Press of Virginia, 1995), 39.

4. Patricia Yaeger, *Dirt and Desire: Reconstructing Southern Women's Writing, 1930–1990* (Chicago: University of Chicago Press, 2000), 88, 12.

5. In having the King's Horseman's sacrificial death rites follow the death of the King, the Oyo kingdom appears to secure stability by decreasing the threat of violent civil war or coup d'etat coming from the leader of Oyo's most powerful military arm. In this case, the

ritual violence of the Elesin's suicide may work to prevent the greater potential violence of civil war.

6. Wole Soyinka, *Death and the King's Horseman*, ed. Simon Gikandi (New York: Norton Critical Edition, 2003), 6.

7. Biodun Jeyifo, *Wole Soyinka: Politics, Poetics, and Postcolonialism* (Cambridge: Cambridge University Press, 2004), 155, 154.

8. Jeyifo, *Wole Soyinka*, 124.

9. René Girard, *Violence and the Sacred*, 49, 80, 99, 137.

10. A. Samuel Kimball, *The Infanticidal Logic of Evolution and Culture*, 22.

11. Peter Maillos, "Faulkner's Indians, or the Poetics of Cannibalism," *Faulkner Journal* 18, 1–2 (2002–2003): 154.

12. William Faulkner, "Red Leaves," in *Collected Stories* (New York: Random House, 1950), 313. Further references to *Collected Stories* are to this edition and will be cited parenthetically as *CS*.

13. Wole Soyinka, *Myth, Literature, and the African World* (1976; Cambridge: Cambridge University Press, 1995), 142.

14. I take the concept of "flash of the spirit" from Robert Farris Thompson, *Flash of the Spirit: African and Afro-American Art and Philosophy* (New York: Vintage, 1984).

15. Leon Litwack, "Hellhounds," in *Without Sanctuary: Lynching Photography in America* (Sante Fe: Twin Palms Publishers, 2000), 13–14.

16. In referring to the atavism of white panic, I am thinking of certain illegitimacies of white supremacist Christianity that—manifest as the unthought known—are coupled with the white neo-paganisms of the second Klan's reinvented "Scottish rites" and Nazi Germany's Aryan atavism, all of which appear referenced ironically in Soyinka's depiction of the egungun-clad Pilkings. Among other things, the idea of the Man rechristened as Doom suggests the Klan's own Klonkaves of Terrors, Klaliffs, Klokards, Night-Hawks, and Butt Rippers; see Patsy Sims, *The Klan* (Lexington: University of Kentucky Press, 1996, 2nd edition), 292–94; and Stetson Kennedy, *The Klan Unmasked* (1954; Gainesville: University Press of Florida, 1990). Keeping in mind Frederick Douglass's statement that "between the Christianity of this land, and the Christianity of Christ, I recognize the widest possible difference—so wide, that to receive the one as good, pure, and holy, is of necessity to reject the other as bad, corrupt, and wicked" [*Narrative of the Life of Frederick Douglass*, in *The Classic Slave Narratives*, ed. Henry Louis Gates Jr. (New York: Mentor, 1987)], 326, we can understand the desires of contemporary "Satanists" to play their religion and heavy metal backwards. Faulkner may be playing a bit of Black Sabbath backwards here himself, but beyond such binarisms there is a Third Space, best represented in Faulkner's work by Afro-Christianity in which African spirits and the Holy Spirit of Christ consciousness find marvelous incorporation.

17. Biodun Jeyifo, "Oguntoyinbo: Modernity and the Rediscovery Phase of Postcolonial Literature," *Yearbook of Comparative and General Literature* 43 (1995), 105. Jeyifo here is drawing upon Jacques Derrida's *Disseminations*.

18. In West Africa the word for tree and medicine (in its expansive sense as pharmakon) is often linked, as "medicinal" workings of "root" and "rootwork" suggest in the American South. In Senegal, the Wolof word "garab" signifies both tree and medicine.

19. Wole Soyinka, *The Strong Breed*, in *Collected Plays 1* (Oxford: Oxford University Press, 1986), 128–29.

20. Ato Quayson, "The Space of Transformations: Theory, Myth, and Ritual in the Work of Wole Soyinka," in Biodun Jeyifo, ed., *Perspectives on Wole Soyinka: Freedom and Complexity* (Jackson: University Press of Mississippi, 2001), 221.

21. Wole Soyinka, *The Open Sore of a Continent: A Personal Narrative of the Nigerian Crisis* (Oxford: Oxford University Press, 1996), 153.

22. Ibid., 143.

23. William Faulkner, "That Evening Sun," in *Collected Stories*, 289.

24. For powerful discussion of death, sacrifice, and Abraham's readiness to sacrifice his son Isaac (especially relevant to reading the character of Isaac McCaslin), see Jacques Der-

rida, *The Gift of Death*, trans. David Willis (Chicago: University of Chicago Press, 1995) and Kimball's *The Infanticidal Logic of Evolution and Culture*, 125–62.

25. Thompson, *Flash of the Spirit*, 52.

26. Sandra T. Barnes, "Introduction: The Many Faces of Ogun," in Sandra Barnes, ed., *Africa's Ogun: Old World and New* (Bloomington: Indiana University Press, 1989), 17.

27. John Pemberton III, "The Dreadful God and the Divine King," in Sandra Barnes, ed., *Africa's Ogun*, 130.

28. Robert G. Armstrong, "The Etymology of the Word 'Ogun,'" in Sandra Barnes, ed., *Africa's Ogun*, 32.

29. Judith Gleason, *Oya: In Praise of an African Goddess* (New York: HarperCollins, 1992), 183, 189. For linkage of this myth to the rather different work of another Southern writer, see Keith Cartwright, "'To Walk with the Storm': Oya as the Transformative 'I' of Zora Neale Hurston's Afro-Atlantic Callings," *American Literature* 78 (December 2006): 755–59.

30. Gleason, *Oya*, 190.

31. William Faulkner, *Go Down, Moses*, 337. Further references to "Delta Autumn" in *Go Down, Moses* are to this edition and will be cited parenthetically as *GDM*.

32. Gleason, *Oya*, 193.

33. Soyinka, *Myth, Literature, and the African World*, 2, 3, 41, 26.

34. Girard, *Violence and the Sacred*, 260.

35. Babalola, Adeboye, "A Portrait of Ogun as Reflected in Ijala Chants," in *Africa's Ogun*, Sandra Barnes, ed., 152.

36. Wilson Harris, *The Womb of Space: The Cross-Cultural Imagination* (Westport, Conn.: Greenwood Press, 1983), 5.

37. The conjuror or man-of-medicine Gullah Jack was known to be a primary leader of the Vesey insurrection plans in South Carolina (1822). The battle of Shiloh (1862), one of the bloodiest of Civil War battles, takes its name from a local church, and "Shiloh" is one of the more common names of Baptist congregations, carrying with it traces of the blood of the "grapes of wrath" and "His terrible swift sword." Finally, the march across the Edmund Pettus Bridge in Selma, Alabama (1965), that "provoked" the internationally televised mass beatings known as Bloody Sunday helped to hasten the Voting Rights Act. Again I paraphrase Kimball, who attests to the fundamental knowledge that "existence costs" (21) [see also Pemberton—note 27—on Ogun as a sacral figure pointing to the fundamental costs of existence] and would call scholars of Ogun rites, Soyinka's corpus, and Faulkner's writings to Kimball's attentiveness to "the sacrificiality of mortal existence" and "the nontranscendable infanticidism of the world" (22) in his rereading of foundational Greek, Judaic, and Christian texts that, as he argues against the grain of their usually enshrined readings, "have refused the (infanticide-provoking) dream of an escape from finitude" and have "thereby initiated a collective work of mourning through which this cultural dream might be given up" (24).

38. William Faulkner, *The Sound and the Fury* (1929; New York, Modern Library, 1956), 111.

39. Wole Soyinka, *Myth, Literature, and the African World*, 26–27.

40. King Sunny Ade, *The Best of the Classic Years*, Shanachie 66034, 2003.

41. Ogun makes his presence known in Brazil infusing candomble rites, the novels of Jorge Amado, and a range of music from Olodum to Elis Regina; in Trinidad inspiriting orisha worship, Earl Lovelace's fiction and the Ogun praise songs of Ella Andall; in Cuba giving rise to the marvelous real in Santeria worship, Alejo Carpentier's prose, and Merceditas Valdez's chants; and in Haiti riding the Vodou horses of René Depestre's poetry and the songs of Boukman Eksperyans.

42. Toni Morrison, *Beloved* (New York: Knopf, 1987). Madison Smartt Bell's *All Souls' Rising* (New York: Penguin, 1995), *Master of the Crossroads* (New York: Pantheon, 2000), and *The Stone that the Builder Refused* (New York: Pantheon, 2004) mark a formidable response to both the Haitian Revolution and Faulkner's Sutpen story, one that demands more critical attention, particularly given the current critical popularity of transnational linkages of Haiti and Yoknapatawpha in rereadings of the Sutpen story. Scenes in *All Souls' Rising*

featuring a narrator ridden by Ogun, confrontations between a mulatto son (Choufleur) and his grand blanc father (Maltrot), and the Creole erotics of Doctor Hebert and Nanon mark just some of the grounds of Madison Smartt Bell's Ogunish revision and extension of *Absalom, Absalom!* See J. Michael Dash, "Haïti Chimère" in *Reinterpreting the Haitian Revolution*, ed. Martin Munro and Elizabeth Walcott-Hackshaw (Kingston: University of the West Indies Press, 2006), 10.

43. Philip Brockbank, "Blood and Wine: Tragic Ritual from Aeschylus to Soyinka," in Biodun Jeyifo, ed., *Perspectives on Wole Soyinka: Freedom and Complexity* (Jackson: University Press of Mississippi, 2001), 78.

44. Wilson Harris, "The Complexity of Freedom," in Jeyifo, ed., *Perspectives on Wole Soyinka*, 60.

45. Bell's Ogun-ridden character Riau remarks often upon the two faces of Jesus served variously in St Domingue. On Oya as owner of the market, see Gleason, 111. For a reading of Faulkner that is moved by interests in sacrificial blood economies, but that looks into realms at least as primordial as those of the Ogun complex, see Dana Medoro's *The Bleeding of America: Menstruation as Symbolic Economy in Pynchon, Faulkner, and Morrison* (New York: Greenwood Press, 2002).

Reading Faulkner in Spain,
Reading Spain in Faulkner

MANUEL BRONCANO

While browsing one day in 1945 in a bookstore in the Madrid of the post–Civil War years, the young Spanish writer Juan Benet saw at his feet a book that had fallen off the shelves. The slim volume was open at a page that read: "VARDAMAN: Mi madre es un pez" (My mother is a fish). That day, Juan Benet avowedly "discovered Faulkner" and turned into a lifelong admirer of the Southern novelist, whose writings would play a capital role in the configuration of contemporary Spanish fiction. The anecdote, perhaps apocryphal, of the young writer and his "epiphany" when he came across the Spanish translation of *As I Lay Dying*, signals the completion of one of the most peculiar circles in literary history. That day, William Faulkner returned symbolically to the land of one of his literary ancestors, Miguel de Cervantes, and brought along a new vigor that would in time transform the way Spanish writers observed the reality of their country still bleeding from the wounds of the Civil War (1936–1939). It is my purpose to trace the route of such a voyage and to explore the kinship, or if you want, the literary complicity, between Faulkner and Spain, since I think it is a topic that fully addresses the theme of our conference, "Global Faulkner," and illustrates both the dialogic nature of literature and its universal, or global, appeal. Even though Faulkner's explicit references to Spain are not frequent, either in his writings or in his public manifestations, Spain and Spanish culture play an intriguing, even if underrated, role in his fiction.

1.

Faulkner famously admired *Don Quixote* (1605), the masterpiece of Miguel de Cervantes, who invented the novel as a modern genre suited to the needs and circumstances of the rapidly changing society inherited from the late middle ages. Renaissance Spain and the post–Civil War South of the United States share the existence of a social texture characterized by a new and unprecedented mobility, a society whose structure and values were in the process of radical and irretrievable transformation. It is little wonder that Faulkner felt attracted to Cervantes's seminal novel, since the fictional La Mancha finds many echoes in Faulkner's "postage stamp of native soil."

As is well known, William Faulkner claimed to have reread *Don Quixote* every year, "like other people read the Bible," and included the foolish Spanish hidalgo and his pragmatic companion Sancho Panza in the select group of his "favorite characters."[1] A frequent guest of the writer in his Oxford home, Thomas (Tommy) Tullos, librarian at Ole Miss, recalls how Faulkner chose a volume from the shelves, "perhaps Dickens or Cervantes, and read aloud to him and Stelle and Dot, like a Victorian paterfamilias." In fact, the visitor to Rowan Oak will find a bust of Don Quixote presiding over Faulkner's library. The bust was presented to the writer in April 1961 by the Venezuelan-American Center in Maracaibo, and Joseph Blotner suggests that it was one of the presents from his trip to Venezuela that Faulkner enjoyed the most.[2] The surviving receipt shows that the sculpture was shipped to his Oxford address, with explicit instructions to handle with care, for it belonged to a "very important person."[3] It is a carving by Venezuelan artist Marcelino Peña, in rich native wood with highly stylized lines that capture the frugal spirituality of Don Quixote, and one is tempted to think that it stands for the imaginary portrait that Faulkner may have made in his mind of the character. Faulkner's explicit references to the Spanish classic are more frequent in his mature years, as if the writer had come to realize later in life the complicity that he had established with his literary ancestor: "It is admiration and pity and amusement—that is what I get from him—and the reason is that he is a man trying to do the best he can in this ramshackle universe he's compelled to live in. He has ideals which by the pharisaical standards are nonsensical. But by my standards they are not nonsensical. His method of trying to put them into practice is tragic and comic. I can see myself in Don Quixote by reading a page or two now and then, and I would like to think that my behavior is better for having read *Don Quixote*."[4]

Faulkner's commentary at West Point becomes both recognition of and homage to Alonso Quijano, the Spanish hidalgo who invents himself as the greatest of knights, defender of honor and virtue, champion of dames, and protector of the oppressed, in a time and place where there is no room for heroes or epic deeds. Faulkner seems to value above all the dual nature of the character, his tragicomic essence, his capacity to elicit both laughter and pity in his absurd but noble attempts at restoring justice in a world of chaotic individualism. That is the greatness of Don Quixote, his stubborn rejection of the order of things and his vindication of honor and equity, a trait that many of the characters in Faulkner's universe share with him. But Faulkner also sees a redemptive, or cathartic, quality in Don Quixote, a pathetic Christ-like figure who undertakes the impossible task of promoting a better world and by so doing sets an example for a better self. Faulkner's statement indeed brings to mind Miguel de Unamuno, the Spanish thinker who urged a mystical approach to *Don Quixote*, "in the same way that the Bible is usually interpreted."[5]

Critics have explored in some detail some of the quixotic ingredients in Faulkner's fiction, such as the blurred lines between madness and sanity, or between fantasy and reality, the role that honor plays in his works, or the similarities between Yoknapatawpha and La Mancha, which prove beyond doubt the importance of the latter in Faulkner's vision. In *The Southern Inheritors of Don Quixote*, Monserrat Ginés traces a number of Cervantinian motifs in Faulkner's novels, such as the nostalgic vision of an ideal and heroic past of unshifting values, as represented for example by Quentin Compson, Gavin Stevens, or Gail Hightower (also quixotic "champions of dames"), who long for a Golden Age and reject the new order embodied by Isaac McCaslin.[6] Monserrat Ginés has made a valuable critical contribution to clarifying the presence of the Spanish classic in Faulkner's world, and his book is a useful starting point for those interested in the subject. However, I think there is still ground for further research, since there are aspects that have not been treated in enough detail such as the intertextual and metafictional dimensions in both writers, whose novels often become meditations on the nature of fiction itself and its relation to truth and history.

There are certainly close similarities between Renaissance Spain and the antebellum U.S. South. Both were societies that considered manual labor a lowly occupation, improper for gentlemen or "hidalgos," and in both, as Ginés and others have pointed out, honor played a central role in social relations. Renaissance Spain was characterized by a highly divisive social structure, marked by the purity of blood, which was articulated in religious terms: thus, individuals were either "cristianos viejos" (old Christians), or "conversos" (converts), the latter being relegated from official posts and royal privileges, and always the subject of suspicion. A by-product of the peculiar history of the Spanish Reconquest, this social categorization according to religion was in truth racial, for it was directed against both Muslims and Jews, who were forced to seek either exile or assimilation. In fact, Cervantes himself is believed to have come from a family of converts and there is increasing evidence that proves the difficulties he had to face because of such origins, despite his heroic participation in the battle of Lepanto.[7] His applications for an appointment in the administration of the American colonies, for example, were systematically turned down. We should remember that the authorship of his masterpiece is meaningfully attributed to the Arab Cide Amete Benengeli by Cervantes himself, whose manuscript the writer bought at the market in Toledo, and was translated into Spanish by a "morisco," or baptized Muslim.

By attributing the book to an Arab historian, Cervantes is not only mimicking the convention of the chivalric romance that claims a reputable source for the narrative, but he is also placing the racial problem at the core of his novel. It is indeed ironic that the memorable adventures of Don Quixote, who in many ways embodies the ideals of Christian Europe, should be recorded by an Arab who at one point is even described as a "liar." This strategy turns the novel into an apocryphal chronicle of imperial Spain, as seen through the spurious eyes of an unreliable and dubious narrator, an infidel who, however, rescues for posterity the deeds of the eccentric hidalgo. Cervantes writes, "If there is any possible objection to the truthfulness of the account, it can only be that the author was an Arab, since it's very natural for people of that race to be liars. On the other hand, since they are so very hostile to us, the author is more likely to have toned down rather than embellished his tale."[8] The irony is obvious: Cervantes is clearly, though very subtly, ridiculing these racial prejudices. It is neither casual that the writer comes into the possession of such manuscript in Toledo, nor is it surprising how easily he finds a translator from the Arabic. Toledo was the site of the most important school of translators in the Middle Ages, the place of convergence and peaceful cohabitation among the three cultures that were present on the Iberian Peninsula: Muslims, Jews, and Christians. Toledo is the icon of that other Spain, tolerant and multicultural, that was officially banished by the orthodox and intolerant Catholicism of Ferdinand and Isabella. And Cervantes's novel is the happy offspring of an intercultural marriage that would be deemed spurious by the dominant ideology of bigotry and racial discrimination of which the writer may have been himself victim.

Don Quixote distils the quintessence of Spain and Spanish history, a land of grand ideals and stark realities that becomes a fruitful soil for literature. The great empire where "the sun never set" was already beginning to show some signs of decline in Cervantes's time, as the 1588 defeat of the Armada would painfully prove. Alonso Quijano and his squire Sancho Panza embody the polar personalities of the average Spaniard, and the region of La Mancha becomes the parodic recreation of a country already in the process of long and irremediable decay. Alonso Quijano represents that petty nobility whose sustenance was provided by the rent exacted on lands that the nobles did not work. He is an inheritor of a society that for eight hundred years had been organized for warfare, living on the spoils of battle and the land grants obtained in the newly conquered territories. Alonso Quijano is a genuine product of frontier Spain, like the legendary founders of Yoknapatawpha County were of frontier America. And like so many Faulknerian characters, he is a "devoted hunter" who leads a life of ease and comfort, until his voracious habit of reading chivalric romances leads him to sell "acre by acre of good crop land in order to buy books."[9] His life is told by different narrators—Cervantes, Benengeli, the anonymous translator—and the result is a polyphonic narration that vividly resembles novels such as *Absalom, Absalom!*, a multivoiced account of Thomas Sutpen's life in which a manuscript—Quentin's letter from his father—also plays a pivotal role.

The radical distinction between old Christians versus converts forms the basis of the racial hierarchy that Spain implemented in its American colonies, establishing purity of blood as the standard for class: hence, beyond pure whiteness, there was the Negro, the Mulatto, the Quadroon, the Octoroon, and a myriad other categories that determined how much black blood the individual had. This racial categorization whose ultimate roots are to be found in the Spanish Reconquest (A.D. 711–A.D. 1492) was in its turn imported into the antebellum South, where it would become the cornerstone of its social structure, and *Absalom, Absalom!*, as I will argue in more detail, is a good illustration of this concern with racial or blood purity.[10]

2.

Faulkner's kinship with Cervantes is made explicit early in his fiction. Thus for example in *Pylon* (1935), a story in which heroism is a central motif, despite its comic and parodic tone, the protagonist is compared to the Spanish hidalgo, through an image that sheds illuminating light on the lean and generous reporter who remains unnamed throughout the novel: "The editor sat back in the swivel chair and drew a deep, full, deliberate breath while the reporter leaned above the desk like a dissolute and eager skeleton, with that air of worn and dreamy fury which Don Quixote must have had."[11] In a single brush stroke, Faulkner turns his character into a Southern recreation of the chivalric Spaniard, and his errand into a quixotic defense of a world—that of the acrobats of the air—which exists outside the conventions of society. The reporter, like Don Quixote, falls in love with an idealized woman, whom he protects and worships without any hope of reciprocation. When read from this perspective, *Pylon* becomes the chronicle of a quixotic realm where the tournaments of old are transformed into the modern-day flying races, and the knights into daring pilots that defy the limits of gravity and common sense in their arcane flying machines, all for the entertainment of an attending public that is eagerly awaiting a tragic climax in the show. A powerful meditation on modernity and its alienating effects, *Pylon* has been related, by Michael Zeitlin and other critics, to James Joyce's *Ulysses* and T. S. Eliot's *The Waste Land*,[12] as one chapter of the novel is significantly titled "The Love Song of J. Alfred Prufrock." These foundational texts of high Modernism render a multi-layered portrait of the present, in an attempt at conveying the complex texture of contemporary reality. In these texts, Joyce and Eliot intend to fill in the spiritual vacuum left by a civilization that has crumbled to its very foundations after the Great War, by recovering and instilling new meaning in the mythology that had sustained that civilization throughout the ages. And in this context, the intertextual reference to the Spanish hidalgo brings into the novel a whole new dimension that has not been pursued in depth by criticism, despite its potential relevance for understanding the character. George Monteiro is one of the few critics who point out the quixotic dimension of the reporter in *Pylon*: "The reporter becomes a modern Don Quixote—at least to the extent that he is almost impossibly isolated from reality. It is significant that the calm, ordered Quixote, who retains always his measure of dignity in the most absurd situations, becomes the neurotic reporter, whose mere presence upon the scene is the signal for a burst of derision. . . . As in the case of Don Quixote, we can decide that, although the reporter's life is unfortunate, it is, in the context of the entire work, curiously comic—ironically so, but comic nevertheless."[13] *Don Quixote* represents as much a parody of the chivalric romance as a vindication of the values that sustained that tradition. Alonso Quijano is the last knight of the middle ages, but the first hero of modernity. Through him, Cervantes rescues the chivalric myth and translates it into the present where it undergoes a revitalizing metamorphosis, giving birth to the novel as the narrative genre par excellence. Like the Spanish hidalgo, the unnamed reporter in *Pylon* emerges as a tragicomic figure embodying a sense of generosity and idealism utterly anachronistic in the world that he inhabits. Never gratuitous with his intertextual references, when Faulkner identifies his character so explicitly with Don Quixote, he is providing the reader with a clue for the interpretation of *Pylon*.

3.

It is, however, *The Wild Palms* (or *If I Forget Thee, Jerusalem*), that is probably the most Cervantinian, or quixotic, of Faulkner's works. The protagonist of the "Old Man" section is a true, though peculiar, embodiment of Don Quixote and, like his Spanish ancestor, he is the pitiable victim of excessive reading, which leads him to utterly confuse reality and fiction, reinventing himself as a hero of the pulp magazines so popular in the 1930s.

The nineteen-year-old youngster is so imbued with pulp westerns that, after careful planning, he undertakes the impossible task of a train robbery single-handedly and with a fake gun. The beginning of the "Old Man" section of *The Wild Palms* establishes beyond doubt Faulkner's intertextual bond with Cervantes:

> Once (It was in Mississippi, in May, in the flood year of 1927) there were two convicts. One of them was about twenty-five, tall, lean, flat-stomached, with a sunburned face and Indian-black hair and pale, china-colored outraged eyes— an outrage directed not at the men that had foiled his crime, not even at the lawyers and judges that had sent him there, but at the writers, the uncorporeal names attached to the stories, the paper novels—the Diamond Dicks and Jesse Jameses and such—whom he believed had led him into the present predicament . . . in accepting information on which they placed the stamp of verisimilitude and authenticity. . . . He had laid his plan in advance, he had followed his printed (and false) authority to the letter; he had saved the paper-backs for two years, reading and rereading them, memorising them, comparing story and method against story and method."[14]

As for the other convict, he is, like Sancho Panza, "short and plump," and like the tall convict, he carries a "sense of burning and impotent outrage" at his fate.[15] As ingenuous as his Spanish predecessor, the plump convict is a propitiatory victim to the chicanery of those who surround him (criminals and lawyers alike), and is forced to pay for a murder nobody believed he had ever committed. Eventually, the plump convict becomes the connection between the prison and the outer world, in which "his companions . . . could have had but little active interest," when he starts reading from the newspapers the story of the impending flood to the inmates.[16] A modern-day Sancho, this convict seems to be the bridge between the self-contained and quixotic universe of the prison and the reality outside such a monastic realm, just as the squire was the connection between his mad master and the reality of the tangible world. When the tall convict is sent on his errand to rescue the woman and the man stranded among the flooding waters, the plump convict is appointed as his assistant, despite the fact that he "cant row a boat."[17] Eventually, he deserts his companion, like Sancho Panza so often does with his master, and returns to the levee aboard a rescue steamer, where he pronounces his partner drowned.

Faulkner was probably never as satirical with popular literature as in "The Old Man." His parody of the kind of fiction published in pulp magazines, which fulfilled a role certainly similar to the chivalric romance in Cervantes's times, reveals Faulkner's Cervantinian vocation. "Old Man" contains a cluster of intertextual references that evoke those in *Pylon*, and thus acquires an interesting metafictional dimension, as a meditation on literature and truth. Here Faulkner winks an eye at Hemingway in the famous "hemingwaves" of "The Wild Palms" that evoke the waves that the convict has to fight in his heroic errand of rescuing the pregnant woman from the fury of the river. In what is at once parody and homage, Faulkner's explicit reference to Hemingway introduces a rich layer of meaning in the novel, and takes the reader in a surprising narrative twist to Spain and bullfighting, by invoking one of the most typical motifs in Hemingway's fiction. Thus, the quixotic convict eventually turns into a daring hunter of alligators who attracts spectators, "like the *matador* his *aficionados*."[18] This literary kinship between the two writers also stands, one suspects, in the background of *The Mansion*, whose female protagonist, Linda Snopes Khol, participates in the Spanish Civil War, similar to some of the most heroic characters in Hemingway's fiction.

The Cervantinian quality of *If I Forget Thee, Jerusalem* is not restricted, however, to the "Old Man" section. In fact, it is in the "The Wild Palms" where the quixotic motif is established even more explicitly, through an intertextual allusion that introduces an unexpected dimension in the novel and provides a link between the two sections of a text that Faulkner characterized as "contrapuntal."[19] Soon after their arrival in Chicago, Charlotte Rittenmayer begins to make puppets for sale: "She worked with dense and concentrated fury. . . . the actual figures almost as large as small children—a Quixote with a gaunt mad dreamy uncoordinated face, a Falstaff with the worn face of a syphilitic barber and gross with meat."[20] Faulkner provides Don Quixote with a Shakespearean Sancho Panza, Falstaff, bringing together two Renaissance masters that inspire his own work. As for Charlotte, she is, like her Manchegan predecessor, the victim of voracious reading, which instills in her a romantic notion of love and happiness that she pursues to the end. She fits into the Madame Bovary archetype of the female who loosens her grasp on reality through the excessive consumption of novels. As Thomas L. McHaney states, Charlotte is quixotic in the same way as the tall convict, "having taken her ideas about romantic love from what she has read and trying to act as if the world were like what she had learned in books."[21] Thus, *Don Quixote* provides the thread that knits together the two apparently unrelated sections of *If I Forget Thee, Jerusalem* as variations on a single theme, that of the pernicious effects of popular literature. In this respect, Wilbourne's stories for popular magazines, "which he wrote complete from the first capital to the last period in one sustained frenzied agonizing rush,"[22] add a new Cervantian twist to his metafictional parody of the dangers of reading and writing such literature.[23]

4.

Even though *Don Quixote* is universally acclaimed as the first modern novel, Cervantes is deeply indebted to the picaresque, a genuine Spanish genre that portrays the contradictions of Renaissance Spain and paves the way for the novel to become *the* genre of modernity. The foundational picaresque, *Lazarillo de Tormes* (1554), documents the social tensions that characterized the country under the reign of emperor Charles V. The novel features a dispossessed child, half-brother to a Negro, who rises in society by means of his own shrewdness and endurance, in a pattern that resembles vividly Flem's own rise "from rags to riches" in the Snopes trilogy. Lázaro de Tormes is the first anti-hero of modernity, and his narrative orchestrates the conflicting voices of a society in the process of a radical transformation. I have been unable to verify whether Faulkner ever read *Lazarillo de Tormes*, and thus I lack any first-hand evidence of the potential influence that such work, and the tradition it inaugurates, may have had in his own fiction. I have little doubt, however, that *The Hamlet* is inspired by the picaresque mode, an aspect of the novel so far quite unnoticed, except for an early critic, Florence Leaver, who identifies Flem Snopes with a pícaro and the structure of the novel as "episodic and picaresque."[24] Like Lázaro, Flem is the scion of a dispossessed family on the margins of society, and like his Spanish predecessor, he elbows his way to the center of power by means of his astuteness and lack of scruples. Lázaro is eventually appointed town crier, an official post of no little relevance at the time, and marries the maidservant and mistress of the Archpriest of San Salvador, a marriage that gains him the favor of the powerful clergyman. When Lázaro complains because of the clamorous gossip about his wife's affair with the archpriest, the latter gives him this piece of advice: "Lazaro of Tormes, anyone who pays attention to what gossips say will never get ahead."[25] The resemblance to Flem Snopes and his marriage with Eula who is already pregnant by another man and keeps a lifelong affair with still another, is quite striking. Flem consolidates his claim to economic success by being a consenter, and like Lázaro, he learns to ignore what everybody in town knows about his wife, for she is his passport to power and wealth. Therefore, I think a reevaluation of *The Hamlet* in this light may reach some interesting conclusions, though it goes beyond the scope of the present essay.

5.

Explicit references to Spain and the Spanish empire are not exactly abundant in Faulkner's fiction, and yet, it is as if the Spanish "ingredients" are fundamental constituents of the fictional universe of Yoknapatawpha, and important—even though often underrated—elements in Southern history. Thus, for example, in "Red Leaves" Faulkner makes a veiled but relevant allusion to the imperial interests that Spain had in the U.S. South, as Richard A. Milum argues in his essay "Ikkemotubbe and the Spanish Conspiracy."[26] (1974). According to Milum, the historical background of the story is the plot devised by the governor of Spanish Louisiana, the Baron Luis Hector de Carondelet (1795–97), who—with the cooperation of James Wilkinson, Major General in the army of the United States—intended to separate part of the extensive American frontier from the United States "to serve as a buffer against westward expansion and to promote trade between the new country and Spain."[27]

On the other hand, the de Spain family becomes one of the most important lineages in Yoknapatawpha, after the patriarch, Major de Spain—whose provenance is never revealed by the author—acquires his land from Thomas Sutpen, as we learn in "The Bear," and one wonders about the choice Faulkner made with the name and its potential symbolism. Faulkner was once asked whether "a few generations back" the de Spain blood or lineage "was the best in the county," to which the writer replied, quite vaguely: "It represented aristocracy, yes."[28] If the family name refers to its geographical origins, as is the case with many surnames, the de Spain family probably had Spanish roots, and they may have originated either in the colonies or the Peninsula itself. Whatever Faulkner's ultimate intention may have been, the fact is that the de Spain lineage brings into Yoknapatawpha powerful echoes of the European country and its once extensive American empire. I have suggested the similarities between Major de Spain and Alonso Quijano, both frontier landowners whose lands provide for their leisurely existence, and both expert hunters, an unmistakable sign of class. Interestingly enough, the Major's son, Manfred—Eula Varner's lover—is a veteran of the Spanish-American War, by which Spain was deprived of its last possessions overseas: Puerto Rico, Cuba, and the Philippines.

In *Absalom, Absalom!* Thomas Sutpen is horrified when he supposedly learns that his first son, Charles Bon, has inherited Negro blood from his mother, who was the daughter of a French planter and a Spaniard, or so Sutpen was told before his marriage.[29] Thomas Sutpen uses his last coin, a Spanish gold coin he had got in the West Indies,[30] to record the patent on the land he acquires from the Chickasaw. And his mulatto daughter, Clytemnestra, is described as a "Spanish duenna,"[31] who is, according to the Webster dictionary, an elderly woman serving as governess and companion to the younger ladies in a Spanish or a Portuguese family. Clytie becomes the guardian of Sutpen's household, the illegitimate progeny versus the legitimate lineage, and the Spanish duenna of mixed blood watching over the Anglo-Saxon dream of racial purity that Sutpen has deposited in his son Henry.

The Spanish ingredient in the novel emerges as synonymous with miscegenation, the "thing not named," the unspeakable truth that Sutpen tries in vain to erase from his fate. Sutpen's design is based both on exploitation and repudiation of the Spanish other: a dispossessed and exiled Southerner, Sutpen marries into the Haitian plantation, gaining thus access to class and wealth, but he repudiates wife and son on racial grounds. In exchange, he receives the slaves and the money that provide for his new beginning on the Mississippi frontier, and it is with Spanish gold that he sanctions his claim to the land. Postcolonial critics have found fertile ground in *Absalom, Absalom!*, for it reveals the profound connections between Haiti and the U.S. South. The U.S. South is like the Caribbean island whose very existence depends, in Deborah Cohn's words, on the four commodities, "sugar, cotton, tobacco, slaves," that constitute the very essence of the colonial Caribbean: "The shifting sands on which Thomas Sutpen's design was erected is the wealth that he earned in Haiti, model and precursor of the South's own racial system, of its own moral and economic edifice."[32] Haiti represents the quintessence of the Caribbean, a territory whose tormented history is embodied in Charles Bon, the repudiated son of Sutpen's racial delirium. As Melvin Backman states, Charles Bon becomes a powerful metaphor of the tragic destiny of the American Negro: "Running through his veins was the blood of the slavers and planters—the Spanish, French, English, and American—and the blood of the African Negro. But it was the blood of the Negro that would work like a strange power of fate in the lives of the planters, the slaves, and all their descendants."[33]

6.

William Faulkner publicly sympathized with the Republican cause in the Spanish Civil War. As Joseph Blotner informs us, during 1938 Faulkner responded to an appeal from the League of American Writers with this formal statement: "I most sincerely wish to go on record as being unalterably opposed to Franco and fascism, to all violations of the legal government and outrages against the people of Republican Spain."[34] When he was asked by Vincent Sheean for a contribution to a relief fund being raised for the Spanish Loyalists, Faulkner immediately sent him the manuscript of *Absalom, Absalom!*, and also offered Sheean the first-draft typescripts of *The Sound and the Fury*, *As I Lay Dying*, and *Light in August*. Faulkner wished Sheean success in the enterprise and added that he would do more if he could. As Blotner poignantly observes, "For the man who would later contemptuously recall being labeled 'a Gothic fascist' by leftist literary warriors, it was quite a contribution."[35] If the public Faulkner showed unwavering support to the Loyalist cause, revealing a profound awareness of the tragedy that was taking place in Spain, the writer would leave lasting testimony of that tragedy in Linda Snopes Kohl, a character in many senses unique in Faulkner's canon.

Even though the explicit references to the Spanish Civil War in *The Mansion* (1959) are not abundant, the fratricidal conflict on Spanish soil looms in the background of the novel as a whole. Linda Snopes Kohl introduces in the secluded world of Yoknapatawpha the echoes of a distant war that is going to affect directly the life of the Mississippi community. Linda stands for all those Americans who fought in Spain in support of the Republic, members of the Abe Lincoln Brigade that served during 1937 and 1938 against the advance of fascism. The Lincolns, as they are popularly called, fought alongside nearly 35,000 antifascists from fifty-two different nationalities who where integrated in the International Brigades. They came from all regions of the U.S. and from all kinds of jobs and, as Sam Sills states, they "established the first racially integrated military unit in U.S. history and were the first to be led by a black commander."[36] Equipped with inadequate weaponry, like the Republican forces at large, the Lincolns fought bravely and suffered nearly 750 casualties, a higher rate than the casualties sustained by the U.S. in WWII. While the official attitude of the American government was that of nonintervention and even embargo, these young Americans gave their lives for the defense of freedom and democracy against the fascist insurgency. As is well-known, the embargo imposed by the U.S. and other countries was only effective on the Republican side, since Franco received sustained support from both Germany and Italy throughout the war. No doubt, this was a decisive element in the final defeat of the Republic, and the immediate burst of WWII, for which Spain had served as training-field. This is the tragic history that Linda Snopes brings into the text of *The Mansion*.

Linda is not only the moral center of the novel, she is also the one Snopes who redeems the clan of its proverbial greed and lack of scruples. The Spanish War is parallel to the war within the Snopes family, Mink versus Flem, the dispossessed versus the capitalist, honor versus shameless ambition. Linda sides with Mink, as she sides with the Republican cause, and hers is a fight for justice, even if it requires allowing the murder of her own, putative, father, victimizing him and what he represents. Paradoxically, too, after Flem's death, Linda restores the de Spain family to its legitimate estate, the mansion that gives title to the novel. This restoration, and Mink's freedom, seems to bring to the Snopes civil war a poetic justice that history denied in the case of the Spanish Civil War. We know of Faulkner's public aversion to communists, and yet in Linda Snopes he gives life to a woman who stands by her ideals and remains faithful to them, bringing into Jefferson not only the echoes of a distant yet horrifying drama, but also a set of ideals of racial and social equality that openly defy the codes governing Yoknapatawpha.

Linda is indeed one of the most peculiar female characters in Faulkner's crowded fiction. In the past two decades, she has been the subject of a critical reevaluation that contests the traditionally negative views of her character, a view mostly based on the fact, according to Hee Kang, that unlike her mother, Eula, she "does not live up to the patriarchal 'feminine ideal' of sacrifice and silence."[37] Thus, Linda represents for Hee Kang the new, radical woman who somehow embodies Faulkner's own "changing sense of history and, with it, the need to write beyond the disempowered and marginalized women seen so abundantly in his earlier work."[38] And yet, critics seem to have paid only marginal attention to Linda's involvement in the Spanish Civil War, which is the cause of her deafness, a physical disability that has been interpreted variously, but always in "local" terms, that is, within the universe of Yoknapatawpha and its conflicts. I can't but wonder why Faulkner decided to have her involved in the fratricidal conflict in Spain, and what Linda's deafness may mean in that light. Inevitably, one is again reminded of Ernest Hemingway, who served, like Linda, as an ambulance driver and sustained severe physical injuries in WWI. Faulkner began *The Mansion* in 1956 and interrupted work on the book early in 1957 to become writer in residence at the University of Virginia. When he was asked there by a student whether he thought Hemingway's *For Whom the Bell Tolls* was a didactic novel, Faulkner replied, in what no doubt constitutes an appraisal of the novel as much as a valuable hint at his own work in progress: "Every writer is in a way writing one story. . . . there is one thing in man's condition that seems to him the most moving, the most tragic, and this time Hemingway was writing the story which still seemed to him moving and tragic, which all writers have never told well enough to please him. This one was brought about into urgency by the condition of Spain at that time. . . . He was not really writing primarily about the Spanish Civil War, but he was writing about the human condition which to him was moving and tragic in terms of that war."[39]

Faulkner knew well Hemingway's vital literary testimony of the participation of American volunteers in the Spanish Civil War. Reading *The Mansion* alongside *For Whom the Bell Tolls* is an interesting exercise postulated by the text itself, since it mentions Ernest Hemingway at least twice: in the first case, he is alluded to by Charles Mallison, who wishes to see "if the Paris of Hemingway and the Paris of Scott Fitzgerald . . . had vanished completely or not";[40] in the second case, he is invoked by Linda Snopes, in one of the rare occasions when she refers to the war in Spain and to the people who fought in it, "the people like Kohl. She told about Ernest Hemingway and Malraux, and about a Russian, a poet that was going to be better than Pushkin only he got himself killed."[41] *For Whom the Bell Tolls* provides us with the information about the reality of the war that is missing in *The Mansion*. Faulkner's novel is a reenactment of his lifelong conversation with Hemingway that reveals his perception of literature as a dialogic discourse. Faulkner's Barton Kohl evokes Hemingway's Robert Jordan quite vividly: one an instructor of Spanish in Montana, the other a Jewish sculptor in Greenwich Village, both give up their lives in pursuit of their ideals, while they attempt to prevent the advance of fascism in Europe. The reader is invited to reimagine Barton's and Linda's war experience through Hemingway's Robert Jordan and the group of Republican partisans that he joins behind the fascist lines in order to bomb a strategic bridge. Despite his absence from the narrative—we only get to know him through allusions—Barton Kohl acquires a rich symbolic dimension. The fact that he is a Jew fighting against Spanish fascism endows him with a historical significance that goes back to that Spain of the Renaissance, a place where racial intolerance dictated the expulsion of the Jewish people from what had been their homeland for many centuries, probably the first instance of ethnic purging in modern Europe. It seems as if Barton Kohl was engaged in an immemorial battle against a time-old enemy, whose latest representative was Franco, in a heroic but futile attempt to make amends with history.

7.

It is little wonder, then, that Faulkner has found in Spain an eager readership, especially among writers who were in need of new models to account for the reality of contemporary Spain beyond the narrow confines of social realism. Maria-Helena Bravo has thoroughly documented Faulkner's Spanish reception, in a seminal study that proves beyond doubt the profound impact exerted by the Southern author on Spanish literature.[42] Faulkner was known and appreciated in Spain already in the 1930s, especially after the translation of *Sanctuary* in 1934 by Lino Novás Calvo. Even though it may not have been as enthusiastic as in France, the reception of Faulkner in Spain was surprisingly early and gave way to a number of critical appraisals that match the French response in their intuition of the radical innovation that his literature represents. The Spain that emerged in the aftermath of the Civil War, however, had been depleted of its best minds, either through exile or death, and those intellectuals and artists who remained were forced to pledge allegiance to the fascist regime. In those bleak years of the early nineteen forties, Faulkner was the subject of censorship, although for religious rather than political reasons, according to the Spanish writer Pedro Lorenzo.[43] Most of Faulkner's novels entered Spain through Argentinean translations, at a time when Argentina was one of the few countries that kept commercial and diplomatic relations with the Spanish government. Such may have been in fact the origin of the translation of *As I Lay Dying*[44] that Juan Benet found by chance in the bookstore with which I opened my essay. Gradually, a young generation of writers discovered Faulkner and learned from him new techniques to cope with a country torn apart by war and shunned by the international scene, as well as a new language whose opaque indeterminacy no doubt helped to evade the scrutinizing yet rather unsophisticated gaze of official censorship. Among them, Juan Benet stands out as probably the most Faulknerian of all, and his *Return to Región*,[45] in the superb translation by Gregory Rabassa, is an excellent initiation for those readers and scholars interested in the ways Spanish writers have reinterpreted the Southern author. Faulkner's prestige in Spain has grown exponentially with the years; just witness the innumerable translations and editions of his works in Spanish.[46] After all, William Faulkner is a true descendant of Miguel de Cervantes and as such, he has found fertile soil in the country that gave birth to the adventures of the unequalled Don Quixote, where Faulkner is now universally acclaimed as one of our own masters.

NOTES

I wish to thank the Spanish Ministry of Education for the generous grant that has made my sabbatical possible at the University of Mississippi in 2005–06 and for the research project of which this essay is part.

1. James B. Meriwether and Michael Millgate, *Lion in the Garden: Interviews with William Faulkner* (New York: Random House, 1968), 251.

2. Joseph Blotner, *William Faulkner: A Biography*, 2 vols. (New York: Random House, 1974), 1738, 1785.

3. I would like to thank Bill Griffith, curator of Rowan Oak, for his help in tracking down this information.

4. Joseph L. Fant and Robert Ashley, eds., *Faulkner at West Point* (Jackson: University Press of Mississippi, 2002), 85.

5. Quoted by Jed Rasula, "When the Exception Is the Rule: *Don Quixote* as Incitement to Literature," *Comparative Literature* 51: 1 (Spring 1999): 123.

6. Montserrat Ginés, *The Southern Inheritors of Don Quixote* (Baton Rouge: Louisiana University Press, 2000).

7. The Battle of Lepanto (October 7, 1571) was a major naval engagement in Greek waters between the allied Christian forces led by Spain against the Ottoman forces of Sultan

Selim II, which had invaded Cyprus in an attempt to drive Venice from the Eastern Mediterranean. The victory had little real consequences (Venice surrendered Cyrpus to the Turks in 1573), but it meant an important boost to the European morale in their war against the Turks. Cervantes is called "El Manco de Lepanto"—the one-handed man from Lepanto—because he lost an arm as a result of the wounds received.

8. Miguel de Cervantes, *Don Quixote*, trans. Burton Raffel (New York: Norton, 1995), 46.

9. Ibid., 9.

10. The English terms "mulatto," "quadroon," and "octoroon" all come from the Spanish *(mulato, cuarterón, octorón)*. Colonial Spanish America developed a very precise terminology to discriminate the multiple racial variants that resulted in the New World from the mixing of Indians, blacks, and whites.

11. William Faulkner, *Pylon* (New York: Library of America, 1985), 807.

12. Michael Zeitlin, *"Pylon,"* in *A William Faulkner Encyclopedia*, Robert A. Hamblin and C. A. Peek, eds. (Westport, Conn.: Greenwood Press, 1999), 307.

13. George Monterio, "Bankruptcy in Time: A Reading of William Faulkner's *Pylon.*" *Twentieth-Century Literature* 4 (1958): 17–18.

14. William Faulkner, *If I Forget Thee, Jerusalem* (New York: Library of America, 1985), 509–10.

15. Ibid., 510.

16. Ibid., 512.

17. Ibid., 545.

18. Ibid., 673.

19. "I was trying to tell the story of Charlotte and Harry Wilbourne. I decided that I needed a contrapuntal quality like music. . . . I wrote the story by alternate chapters. I'd write the chapter of one and then I would write the chapter of the other just as musicians put it—puts counterpoint behind the theme he is working with." Frederick Gwinn and J. Blotner, eds., *William Faulkner in the University: Class Conferences at the University of Virginia, 1957–1958* (Charlottesville: University of Virginia Press, 1959), 171.

20. Faulkner, *If I Forget Thee, Jerusalem*, 556–57.

21. Thomas L. McHaney, *William Faulkner's "The Wild Palms": A Study* (Jackson: University Press of Mississippi, 1975), 76.

22. Faulkner, *If I Forget Thee, Jerusalem*, 577.

23. I wish to thank Theresa Towner for drawing my attention to Wilbourne's activity as a writer, a fact that reinforces the Quixotic dimension of the novel.

24. Florence Leaver, "The Structure of *The Hamlet*," *Twentieth Century Literature* 1, 2 (1955): 77.

25. Anonymous. *The Life of Lazarillo of Tormes: His Fortunes and Misfortunes as Told by Himself*, trans. Robbert Rudder. Project Gutenberg electronic text, chapter 7, www.gutenberg.org/dirs/etext96/lazro13.txt

26. Richard A. Milum, "Ikkemotubbe and the Spanish Conspiracy," *American Literature* 46: 3 (1974): 389–91.

27. Ibid., 389–90.

28. Gwinn and Blotner, 119.

29. William Faulkner, *Absalom, Absalom!* (New York: Library of America, 1990), 208.

30. Ibid., 27–28.

31. Ibid., 165.

32. Deborah Cohn, *History and Memory in the Two Souths: Recent Southern and Spanish American Fiction* (Nashville: Vanderbilt University Press, 1999), 184.

33. Melville Backman, "Sutpen and the South: A Study of *Absalom, Absalom!*" *PMLA* 80:5 (1965): 600.

34. Blotner, 1,030.

35. Ibid.

36. Sam Sills, "The Abe Lincoln Brigade of the Spanish Civil War," University of Pennsylvania Center for Programs in Contemporary Writing electronic text: www.writing.upenn.edu/~afilreis/88/abe-brigade.html. Retrieved June 22, 2006.

37. Hee Kang, "A New Configuration of Faulkner's Feminine: Linda Snopes Kohl in *The Mansion*," *Faulkner Journal* 8.1 (1992): 21.

38. Ibid., 39.

39. Gwinn and Blotner, 182–83.

40. William Faulkner, *The Mansion* (New York: Library of America, 1990), 518.

41. Ibid., 526.

42. María Helena Bravo, *Faulkner en España: perspectivas de la narrativa de posguerra* (Barcelona: Península, 1985).

43. Ibid., 46.

44. William Faulkner, *Mientras agonizo (As I Lay Dying)*, Max Dickman, trans. (Buenos Aires: Santiago Rueda, 1942).

45. Juan Benet, *Return to Region*. Gregory Rabassa, trans. (New York: Columbia University Press, 1985).

46. For a thorough compilation of Faulkner's various translations and editions in Spain, see Maria Elena Bravo and also Catalina Montes, "The Reception of William Faulkner in Spain," Notes on Mississippi Writers (1987), 41–46.

The Global/Local Nexus of Patriarchy: Japanese Writers Encounter Faulkner

Takako Tanaka

William Faulkner became world famous after he received the Nobel Prize for Literature in 1950. Though there were some Americans who thought that what Faulkner wrote was a disgrace rather than an honor for his country,[1] the American government was smarter: it sent him to Brazil in 1954 and to Japan in 1955 as a sort of cultural ambassador.[2] Faulkner was approached for political reasons domestically and internationally, and his visit to Japan also assumed some diplomatic value.[3] He came to Japan only four years after the signing of the San Francisco Peace Treaty, which had enabled Japan to regain independence from American occupation. With the People's Republic of China and communist North Korea established on the Asian continent, both Japan and the U.S. needed a good relationship with each other through the promotion of mutual understanding.

Apart from the political necessities, however, Faulkner's visit to Japan inspired Japanese writers and scholars, and helped develop wider appreciation of Faulkner's works in Japan. Faulkner was at first reluctant to go to Japan, since he was not sure if he could fulfill the duty he had been assigned by the State Department. But he enjoyed the stay more than he had expected, and even left a public message entitled "To the Youth of Japan," in which he encouraged young Japanese writers, saying that their "disaster and despair"[4] after the war would eventually lead them to accomplish highly artistic achievements. He was clearly reminded of his homeland, starting the message with a reference to the South's loss of the Civil War. But what kind of influence did Faulkner have on Japanese writers after World War II in the concurrence of local, national, and global interactions, and moreover, what common problems, if any, attract Japanese writers and scholars so much to Faulkner, well into the twenty-first century? I would like to examine how Faulkner and Japanese writers, especially Kenji Nakagami, respond to patriarchy in their respective societies, and trace how Faulkner's exploration of patriarchy, on global, national, and local levels, inspires Nakagami to pursue a critical dialogue with Faulkner through his own fiction.

At the Faulkner and Yoknapatawpha Conference in 1982, Kenzaburo Ohashi, a great scholar and the founding father of Faulkner studies in Japan, discussed in detail Faulkner's influence on individual Japanese writers.[5] In his lecture, he also mentioned some resemblances between Japan and the American South to explain Japan's particular interest in Faulkner. First, I would like to elaborate on this point a little further and review the situational similarities between Japan and Faulkner's South by mapping the U.S.A. in a transpacific perspective.

In the American hemisphere, the term "Plantation America" is often used to explain the plantation slave system common both in the American South and the Caribbean islands.[6] The slavery system necessarily brought problems of miscegenation and cultural hybridity. Japan, on the other hand, had neither a large-scale plantation economy nor African slavery. The country had never been occupied by a foreign power until the American occupation after Japan's defeat in World War II. The Japanese believe in general that they are a very homogeneous people.

In spite of the apparent contrast, however, there are in fact some uncanny resemblances between Japan and the American South, when examined more closely. Japan's loss in World War II has haunted the Japanese, just as the defeat of the Civil War haunted white Southerners. There is some difference between Japan and the South concerning their willingness to accept foreign influences, but the traumas of modernization and of the loss of traditional society and culture, caused by a foreign power or by capital, exist both in Japan and the American South. In these societies, patriarchy often depends on the legitimate succession of authentic blood to ascertain and assure the continuation of traditional culture seemingly threatened by modernization and alien powers. Moreover, the duality of being a victim and a victimizer is also discernible in Japan and the American South. In its plantation economy, the American South was a colonizer to the African American slaves, but the Southerners felt that they were virtually colonized by the predatory North after the Civil War. To their dismay, not only the Civil War but also modernization brought by Northern capitalists destroyed their traditional society, and put the South in a subjugated position in the national economy. Accordingly, Southerners easily identified themselves as victims, even though the South was itself in a colonizer's position in the American hemisphere as part of the U.S.

Much like Southern society felt Northern pressure, Japan has felt the constant pressures of Western imperial power since it opened its door to the West. As a matter of fact, the first demand from the West to open Japanese ports came from Commodore Matthew Perry of the U.S.A. in

1853. Perry anchored with his squadron off the shores of Uraga, not too far from present-day Tokyo. It was, incidentally, about the same period in which the Monroe doctrine claimed U.S. power across the American hemisphere.[7] Perry's visit caused a tremendous turmoil throughout the country, and triggered the civil war that resulted in the fall of the Tokugawa Shogunate, a feudal system that had governed Japan for more than 250 years. At roughly the same time as the Southern plantation system collapsed and the South lay in shambles after the Civil War, the Tokugawa Shogunate collapsed in 1868. The Meiji government (starting in 1868) quickly succeeded it with the restoration of the Imperial Court. The new government took the form of the ancien régime, but it was quite aware of the critical situation surrounding Japan. Western countries including Britain and France were eyeing Japan as a possible colony, and modernization was absolutely necessary to defend the country and to survive as an independent nation. The trauma of discarding traditional culture was temporarily repressed in the face of this urgent demand. In turn, the centralization of power to the Emperor and his new government reassured the Japanese of their legitimacy and helped appease people's anxiety about the continuation of the traditional culture.

The Japanese government soon came to believe that the only way to survive was to imitate and join the ranks of the Western great powers. From the Sino-Japanese War in 1894–95 through the Russo-Japanese War in 1904–5 and the Manchurian Incident in 1931 to World War II, Japan pursued a continental expansion policy with the ostensible purpose of liberating Asia from the Western imperial nations. Japan colonized Taiwan in 1895 and, as a result of the Russo-Japanese War, annexed Korea in 1910. Japan started war with China again in 1937 and moved into French Indochina in 1940. Japan was finally defeated in 1945 after the two atomic bombs at Hiroshima and Nagasaki.

This brief history shows that Japan, like the American South, has her own double consciousness of victim and victimized. But the Japanese are rather forgetful of what they did on the Asian continent during the wars. As a matter of fact, the amnesia starts at home. In Japan, there are many Koreans whose parents or grandparents were originally forced to come to Japan as laborers before and during World War II. There is also an Ainu indigenous tribe living in Hokkaido, the northern island of Japan. In the seventeenth century, the Tokugawa Shogunate claimed that Hokkaido was Japan's territory. The Ainu people subsequently suffered a lot of inequalities and sometimes resorted to minor insurrections, but on the whole, they managed to survive under the Japanese political control. When the national development project started in the middle of the nineteenth century in the Meiji era, however, and many Japanese settlers moved into Hokkaido, the Ainu population drastically declined, and the tribe's primitive way of living in accordance with nature was fundamentally destroyed.[8] There are also the Burakumin people, who descended from a social, rather than an ethnic outcast group in Japan. The outcast class was officially discriminated against until the start of the Meiji era, and it was only after World War II that both public and private efforts to eradicate the discrimination became gradually effective.[9]

The presence of Koreans, Ainu, and Burakumin proves that Japan is not as homogeneous a nation as even most Japanese believe. The Japanese government exploited and then discarded or ignored these minority groups in the name of modernization and development. But mainstream Japanese still take for granted that they, the majority, are by nature and blood the legitimate successors of homogeneous Japanese society, just as they take the Emperor system for granted.

Obviously, not all the Japanese writers attracted by Faulkner after World War II were aware of these similarities between the American South and Japan. There was little information about the American South in Japan until Faulkner's acceptance of the Nobel Prize. However, the first recognition of Faulkner in Japan had come very early. In 1932, "A Rose for Emily" was translated by Naotaro Tatsunokuchi in a quarterly literary magazine called *Bungaku*. "Bungaku" means "literature" in Japanese, and Yukio Haruyama was the poet editor in chief of the magazine. In the previous issue, Haruyama, who was interested in French symbolism and modernism in general, introduced Faulkner based mainly on the information he had obtained through French literary magazines.[10] The translations of four poems by Faulkner were also published in *Bungaku* in June 1933.[11] These publications emphasized Faulkner's cosmopolitan rather than his American nature. Unfortunately, the international situation surrounding Japan got worse, and there was no more translation of Faulkner's texts until after World War II.

The political situation in Japan in the 1930s was becoming quite tense with militarism and international isolation, but some Japanese intellectuals were eager to acquire cultural information from abroad. For instance, Junzaburo Nishiwaki translated some poems of James Joyce into Japanese in 1933, the same year that Japan withdrew from the League of Nations. Nishiwaki was an intellectual modernist poet and English linguist, and a constant contributor to *Bungaku*, the magazine that published the translation of "A Rose for Emily."[12]

In the 1930s, art was a spiritual escape from the suffocating political milieu for many Japanese writers, unless they turned to communism. Those who loved Western art, especially, felt a strong pressure. Though the art for art's sake tendency in French Symbolism and modernism served as an excuse to separate art from politics, admiring literature from hostile nations alienated the artists from their society. Japan, with her imperialist desire and increasing militarism, cannot easily be compared with the American South in the 1920s; but some Japanese artists' desire to transcend local community and chauvinistic nationalism for high art, represented mainly in France, is common to that of young Faulkner. Faulkner was not satisfied with the parochial and genteel atmosphere in Southern culture, and as a young man would rather identify himself with French symbolists, British aestheticists, or international modernists.

After World War II, the U.S. influence was overwhelming in Japan, and American popular culture rushed in. But France was still, by tradition, the first love for Japanese artists and intellectuals. It is no coincidence that some Japanese writers who appreciated Faulkner in the early period after World War II were well versed in French literature. The vigor of American culture was certainly felt, but the French existentialists' strong interest in Faulkner helped fuel his reputation.[13]

Some Japanese writers who loved Faulkner were aware of the danger of unqualified admiration for the Occident. They tried carefully to see the concrete common ground between Faulkner's texts and Japanese literature. One Japanese writer, Shin'ichiro Nakamura, analyzed the uniqueness of classic Japanese narratives in comparison not only with Western classics but with the techniques of Flaubert, Proust, and Anglo-Saxon modernists, and fully appreciated Faulkner's language experiment.[14] A few others, like Takehiko Fukunaga and Mitsuharu Inoue, made an attempt to create a fictional town like Jefferson and tried to focus there the problems of Japanese local communities.[15] Still, the French influence on Faulkner's early reputation suggests that Japanese artists appreciated Faulkner first as a cosmopolitan, modernist writer. If the separation of universal art from politics barely worked before the war, the belief in the universality of art acquired more support after World War II, now that Japan had returned to the international stage in peace.[16] The emphasis on universality, however, may have blocked some writers from recognizing the local aspects of Faulkner's texts, which, though apparently specific to the South, also suggest the common patriarchal problems with Japanese society.

Patriarchy, the rule of the Father, plays an important role both in Southern society and in Japanese society. Some people in these societies, especially men, are sensitive to any damage done to patriarchal authority, while they are rather insensitive about its harm done to different ethnic or social minority groups. We have to wait for Kenzaburo Oe, the 1994 Nobel Prize recipient for literature, to deeply appreciate Faulkner's examination of patriarchy,[17] and Kenji Nakagami, from the generation after Oe, to respond actively to Faulkner in his fundamental criticism of Japanese society. But before I proceed to discuss Faulkner's influence on Nakagami and conceptualize their critical dialogue, I would first like to trace Faulkner's artistic return from Europe to Jefferson through his recognition of the problems of patriarchal society in *These 13*. Faulkner's characters here respond to patriarchy in a variety of ways, but they also show similarities or contrapuntal relations when crossing between global, national, and local stages.

Faulkner's first collection of short stories, *These 13*, was published by Cape & Smith in 1931.[18] It is a strange combination of war stories, stories of people in Jefferson, and stories of Europe.[19] Faulkner had already created his fictional town Jefferson in his early novels from *Flags in the Dust* through *Sanctuary*. But by selecting and arranging the short stories he had written during this period, Faulkner drew a fundamental frame of the patriarchal structure of Jefferson. *Light in August*, published in 1932, is generally recognized as the first text in which Faulkner seriously explored the problem of racial discrimination in Southern society. We might locate, however, the beginning of Faulkner's critique of his society in *These 13*, where he examines patriarchy and various responses to it in a global/local nexus.

   In the first part of *These 13*, the aviators and soldiers of World War I are either trapped in the illusion of the glory of war or disillusioned into despair. The Royal Air Force pilots of "Ad Astra," for example, form a special group of chosen people that transcend the routines of common daily life as well as nationality. They are elite dare-devil aviators regardless of their different nationalities. At the Armistice, however, the R.A.F. aviators in France realize that they come from, more or less, minority positions in each of their homelands: Bayard Sartoris and Bland come from the American South with a complicated sense of loss, Monaghan is an Irish American whose father came "out of a peat bog,"[20] and Comyn is Irish. They survive the war only to find themselves bound by national or local borders after all.

   Only a captive German aviator and an Indian subadar, an aristocrat and a prince respectively in their own countries, seem calm and acquiescent to the Armistice. Simply escaping the power relationship in a local community does not liberate a person from patriarchal authority. Both the German officer and the subadar repudiate their rights of inheritance at home and become exiles. The German officer once said to his father: "You say fatherland; I, brotherland, I say, the word father iss [sic] that barbarism

which will be first swept away; it iss [sic] the symbol of that hierarchy which
hass [sic] stained the history of man with injustice of arbitrary instead of
moral; force instead of love" (*CS* 417). The Indian subadar also repeats
that "[a]ll men are brothers"(*CS* 408). The German officer and the Indian
subadar both look for the possibility of cosmopolitan fraternity in order to
resist patriarchal or imperial nationalism.[21] Their references to brotherhood suggest Faulkner's interest in fraternity versus patriarchy on a global
scale, which he expands in *A Fable*. But in "Ad Astra," the other aviators
do not pay any attention to what the German and the Indian say, and feel
it inevitable that they face their minority position at home.

Faulkner, in his apprenticeship, presumably hoped that art, like the
glory of aerial combat, delivers an artist from the boundary of local community and elevates him into cosmopolitan freedom. He wrote about geese
and hawks in his poems and associated their flight with poetic achievement and the glorious solitude of an artist.[22] However, he describes in "Ad
Astra" the dismay of would-be cosmopolitan minority aviators who fly for
Great Britain. They are forced either to acknowledge their entanglement
with their homeland and minority status, or to accept the everlasting sense
of displacement of a diaspora.

In "Victory," on the other hand, Faulkner explores the desire for identification with, as well as resistance to, patriarchal authority. In this story,
Alec Gray, the eldest son of a proud Scottish shipwright, decides to fight
in World War I. His father opposes his enlistment, saying that a Gray "has
no business at an English war" (*CS* 442), but his grandfather supports his
decision. The young Gray disobeys his father's local and Scottish authority
only to identify with a greater national and British authority. During the
war, he becomes a severe commander, repeating the abuse done to him as
a recruit. After the Armistice, Gray stays in London and still behaves like a
rigid commander who cannot forget his glory as a British soldier. Though
destitute, he does not admit that he was just a middle grade officer in the
army, appropriating military authority while he was himself exploited by
the Great Empire.

The World War I stories in the first part of *These 13* indicate a pattern of
both resistance to and identification with patriarchal power, which sometimes occurs simultaneously in a global-local nexus. When young soldiers
come from their local communities to fight in the World War, it is a chance
for them to escape from the patriarch in their families or regions. World
War I seems to promise cosmopolitan freedom and independence from filial duties, local history, and social class boundaries. Nevertheless, soldiers
cannot separate themselves from the glory of nations or the hierarchal
order and authority of the army. Faulkner's characters who flee local au-

thority so as to acquire and identify with national authority, or to aspire to transnational, cosmopolitan freedom, might encounter the same trappings of the patriarchy they try to flee. A keen sense of displacement or of being trapped, or a contrasting obsession to belong, reflects the position of minorities in these stories. These feelings are also discernible in the second part of *These 13*, where the conflict against patriarchal power is elaborated in a local setting in the stories of Jefferson.

The main characters in Jefferson are mostly minorities; the setting is claustrophobic and boundary imagery is conspicuous. Faulkner's female characters experience such boundaries especially keenly. Emily Grierson is subject to her father's tyrannical control, and though she tries to liberate herself after his death, she ends up shutting her lover and herself up as victims in his house. In "Dry September," Minnie Cooper is a victim who victimizes another minority. She is so desperate to belong to the community that, inadvertently or not, she resorts to the myth of a black rapist in order to cope with another myth of old maids.

Minnie's hysterical laughter in the dark movie theater, however, betrays her claustrophobic sense of being trapped. While Will Mayes lies silent in a bottomless kiln in the suburbs of Jefferson, Minnie's laughter bubbling out of her body expresses her cry of protest against entrapment in a heterosexual, racial, and patriarchal society. Her uncontrollable laughter ("her voice rose screaming" [*CS* 182]) is strangely reminiscent of the insensible babbling of a wounded soldier in "Crevasse" in the first part of *These 13*. A company of World War I soldiers in "Crevasse" falls underground into a large cavern, and in the darkness they stumble across the skeletons of Senegalese troops. The Senegalese were presumably gassed in the cavern in a battle in 1915. The injured soldier starts laughing and "his voice goes into a high sustained screaming" (*CS* 472) in the dark cavern. The desperate cry of the almost-demented soldier in the last story of part 1 and that of Minnie Cooper in the last story of part 2 show the unbearable pressure felt by those who help sustain the patriarchal order, either of a nation or of a small community. As a matter of fact, even McLendon, a World War I veteran and the leader of the lynching, is panting in the heat and feels suffocated at the end of "Dry September." The obsession with keeping Southern patriarchal authority intact haunts him. In the same story, Hawkshaw, the barber who is initially a party to the lynching, jumps from McLendon's car to avoid becoming an accomplice in the lynching. Hawkshaw attempts to disconnect himself from rather than belong to such a community. Hawkshaw is like the characters in the first part of *These 13*, especially the German aviator and the Indian subadar, who also repudiate their native cultures and inheritance. Hawkshaw may have chosen a nomadic life like them. The people in a small Southern town reflect some patterns of responses to patriarchy shown in the World War I stories.

In the second part of *These 13*, however, young Quentin Compson, a legitimate son, still learns and abides by the code of filial silence in Jefferson. Both in "A Justice" and "That Evening Sun," Quentin as a boy vaguely senses the injustice done to African Americans in the past and the present. Narrating retrospectively, however, Quentin does not pass any articulate judgment on the Southern white patriarchy. In "A Justice," Quentin leaves Sam Fathers as soon as his grandfather calls him and remains silent about what he was talking about with Sam. He may keep the story to himself and brood on its meaning, but while Quentin's silence suggests the beginning of secret resistance, it also indicates his reverence to General Compson's authority. In "That Evening Sun," Quentin also refrains from disclosing what happens to Nancy afterwards. If Nancy has been killed or seriously wounded, Quentin cannot reveal it because of a sense of guilt. If Nancy is safe after all, he does not reveal it because it would justify his father's callousness towards her fears. Either way, Quentin silently shares the charge of coldness and irresponsibility, since he, the eldest son, follows his father and abandons Nancy in despair.

In *These 13*, Quentin's silence both protects and indicts patriarchy. In *Absalom, Absalom!*, however, Quentin Compson is no longer a diffident, perplexed boy at the dawn of his recognition of inhumanity in the Southern patriarchy. He does not want to stay in the "strange, faintly sinister suspension of twilight" (*CS* 360). Quentin starts narrating Sutpen's story in answer to Shreve's curiosity about the South. Thomas Sutpen is regarded as a monstrous intruder into the established society of Jefferson, but he clearly follows the steps of ambitious trailblazers before him such as Quentin's great-grandfather. At Harvard, a place that signifies the North or the Nation, and in the presence of a Canadian, Quentin tries to narrate his story comprehensively and to locate Sutpen within the context of Southern society. Quentin must be able to control the "demon,"[23] as Rosa calls Sutpen, if he is to go back home and to inherit Southern society at all.

Sutpen repudiates his own biological father for an abstract cultural ideal of the patriarchal power of a plantation owner, and he refuses his mixed-blood son in order to maintain the legitimacy of white Southern patriarchal authority. Though Quentin's narration together with Shreve seems to solve the mystery of the Sutpens, Quentin is deeply shaken and repeats towards the end of the novel "Nevermore of peace" (298). Quentin and Shreve accomplish a most plausible Sutpen story in spite of gaps and unknown facts. The story, however, in a way confirms the tenacity of Southern patriarchy and creates a new myth of its persistence through its narration of Sutpen's devotion and his sons' defeat and sacrifice. Sutpen's dynasty is destroyed, and Quentin himself recognizes the inhumanity of Southern racism. But in delineating the Sutpen narrative, Quentin is not unlike Henry Sutpen, who unwillingly asserts the Southern patriarchal code by killing his half-brother. Henry is aware of its cruelty and values brotherhood instead, but he cannot help becoming an agent of what Southern patriarchy demands of him. Quentin also acknowledges the strength of the Southern belief in genuine blood lines in his narration of the Sutpen story.

Quentin does not say that Henry spoke of Bon's black blood in their dialogue at Sutpen's mansion, but Quentin has a long history of understanding the significance of silence for a legitimate son. Nevertheless, if Quentin attempts to destroy Southern patriarchy by breaking silence and narrating, there is also the danger of renewing the legend. Besides, Quentin cannot even finish the narrative with any aesthetic or tragic sense of ending. The aesthetic, if claustrophobic, closure of Southern patriarchy is an illusion: Shreve adds, as a joke, that the western hemisphere will be occupied by Jim Bond's posterity, which Quentin, like Henry, cannot yet accept. In *These 13*, a cry of protest and despair pierces through the patriarchal enclosure. In *Absalom, Absalom!* the collapse of Southern legitimacy results in the permeation of hybridity beyond the South, while the legitimate son himself is entrapped within the patriarchal spell of a white narrative.

If Faulkner's Quentin Compson is to confront patriarchal power as a legitimate son, Kenji Nakagami challenges the patriarchy in Japan more from an illegitimate son's point of view. Kenji Nakagami is the most important contemporary writer in Japan.[24] It is surprising that his novels remain untranslated into English. He was born in 1946 in a small castle town called Shingu, located in the mid-southeast of the largest island in Japan, Honshu. In his novels, he created *"Roji"* ("an alley" or "alleyway" in English), as a background where several families and many individuals repeatedly present themselves. He was inspired by Faulkner's use of maps, genealogy, and rumors, and constructed his imaginary community based on his own hometown.[25] But born illegitimate, and also born in the old social outcast class of Burakumin, Japanese pariahs or untouchables, the discrimination against which is supposedly now eradicated in Japan,[26] Nakagami regards himself basically as an illegitimate son in conflict with the established system of Japanese society. Most of his characters come as well from the Burakumin class, and *Roji* represents the district where the Burakumin people live.

In *Karekinada* (*The Sea of Kareki*), published in 1977, Nakagami writes about a young man's conflict with his father. Akiyuki Takehara, the protagonist, comes from *Roji*, an old community constructed on kinship and rumors. His real father, Ryuzo Hamamura, is a newly rich timber dealer and land broker with his own family, and is called the "King of Flies"[27] in *Roji*, Akiyuki's poor neighborhood. Ryuzo came from nowhere and acquired much of the land in the *Roji* area through cheating, arson, and other sinister means. In defiance of his father, who pursues his egoistic end without any sense of morality, Akiyuki makes love to Satoko, a young prostitute who he suspects is Ryuzo's daughter by another woman. Finally, Akiyuki fights with Ryuzo's second son, Hideo, and beats him to death, half through self-defense and half through anger and hatred.

Kenji Nakagami started Akiyuki's narrative in *Misaki (The Cape)* in 1976[28] and developed it into *The Sea of Kareki* in 1977. These two texts are often mentioned in comparison to Faulkner's *The Sound and the Fury*, since the incest theme in the family is apparent. Nakagami's next novel about Akiyuki is *Chi no Hate, Shijo no Toki (The Ends of the Earth, the Supreme Time)* published in 1983, and the three stories about Akiyuki are often called the "Akiyuki trilogy" by critics. *The Ends of the Earth* is associated with *Absalom, Absalom!*, since in this novel Akiyuki's struggle with his father is examined in a larger social context than in *The Sea of Kareki*. Akiyuki goes to work for his father, Ryuzo, after he has served his three-year sentence for the death of his half-brother, Hideo. But in this novel, *Roji* is destroyed for commercial development, Ryuzo abruptly commits suicide, and Akiyuki disappears from the region for good.

In the Akiyuki trilogy there are many points of resemblance between Ryuzo Hamamura and Thomas Sutpen. They are despised and feared by the community as outsiders and demons. Both of them are determined to establish a dynasty in the community to avenge themselves. They want their sons to inherit their family and land, but cause fratricide and/or incest among their children. On the other hand, Akiyuki plays the complicated role of Quentin Compson and Charles Bon put together. When Akiyuki remembers all the rumors about Ryuzo and broods on what Ryuzo has really done to *Roji*, he is like Quentin Compson of *Absalom, Absalom!*, who must clarify Sutpen's life to understand the South. But when Akiyuki commits incest, he is closer to Charles Bon, who pressures Sutpen by approaching Judith. And when Akiyuki confesses the incest to Ryuzo, we also have to think about Quentin Compson of *The Sound and the Fury*.

Admittedly, Akiyuki's motive for confession is different from Quentin's. Quentin's incest is only imaginary, and he wants his father to represent patriarchal authority and to cast him out with Caddy. Akiyuki, for his part, wants to shock Ryuzo and to make his father suffer and repent. But Quentin and Akiyuki are both disappointed at their fathers' reactions. Mr. Compson advises his son to take his sister's loss of virginity as a natural phenomenon, and refuses to exercise patriarchal power. Akiyuki on the other hand is shocked that Ryuzo does not look bothered at all by his confession. Ryuzo only says curtly, "It can't be helped. It's just one of those things that happen anywhere" (*The Sea of Kareki* 145), and gives a low laugh. In the same scene, Satoko, Akiyuki's half-sister, declares in anger at Ryuzo that she is going to give birth to an idiot as the result of this incest. Satoko's mention of "idiot" evokes the groundless discrimination that the Burakumin people, the social outcast class, suffered in the past. But Ryuzo retorts that there is plenty of land for an idiot or two of his grandchildren to inherit.

Ryuzo Hamamura is also a contrastive figure to Thomas Sutpen.[29] In spite of the fratricide (Akiyuki's murder of Hideo), Ryuzo seems to be satisfied if Akiyuki, the eldest son, despite his illegitimacy, compensates for the death of his second and legitimate son by replacing him. Legitimate or not, Ryuzo is content as long as his paternal line continues. By contrast, Sutpen is faithful to the racial code of Southern society and wrestles with the dilemma that forces him to choose between the continuation of his dynasty and its authenticity and racial purity. Ryuzo, on the other hand, thinks nothing of social rules or prohibitions. As a matter of fact, in pursuit of his ultimate goal of dynasty, Ryuzo's ambition countervails Charles Bon's threat of miscegenation to society: Ryuzo dares to accept Akiyuki's incest and the imaginary idiot inheritors, who are analogically parallel to Jim Bond's posterity, which so horrifies Quentin. Ryuzo's audacious defiance of society surpasses that of Akiyuki or of Charles Bon.

Ryuzo becomes a more complicated figure as the Akiyuki trilogy moves from *The Sea of Kareki* to *The Ends of the Earth*. Ryuzo sometimes stands totally defenseless in front of Akiyuki, as if he expects to be killed by his son. In the second text of the Akiyuki trilogy, *The Sea of Kareki*, it is Ryuzo's second son, Hideo, who starts quarreling with Akiyuki and blindly courts death by the hand of his illegitimate half-brother. Ryuzo repeats Hideo's unconscious courtship of death to Akiyuki, presumably to merge with his second son, Hideo, and with Akiyuki at the same time. Ryuzo often calls Akiyuki "Aniyan," which means "brother" or "the eldest" in English. It is not so strange in Japanese custom for a father to use this appellation when referring to his eldest son. But certainly, it is more commonly used by brothers or friends. Ryuzo on the surface enjoys his paternal authority to call his son what he likes. We might suspect, however, that Ryuzo unconsciously wants to take the place of Hideo and associates with Akiyuki as a rebellious sibling, or even that Ryuzo desires to turn into Akiyuki himself. While Ryuzo is a demanding father, he is also a prototype of a defiant, illegitimate son for Japanese society. Though he emphatically wants to establish a paternal dynasty, Ryuzo sometimes deliberately warps the father-son relationship into that of fraternity.

Ryuzo finally commits suicide, and the reason for his suicide is unknown. Akiyuki loses the opportunity to repudiate Ryuzo to his face as a father. Akiyuki is a refractory, illegitimate son to Ryuzo. It would have been easier for him to reject Ryuzo, if Ryuzo were a tyrannical father faithful to the authentic patriarchal society like Sutpen; but Ryuzo himself is an outrageous rebel who threatens such an establishment and disrupts social order. In spite of his acquisition of much of the *Roji* area for commercial development, Ryuzo keeps the core of his land as a vacant lot to the end of the novel. Ryuzo destroys *Roji* and forces Akiyuki to come out of the maternal community of memory and kinship. But the empty grass patch in the developed area also contradicts and mocks modernization. For all the speculations about the land, the vacant lot flouts economic efficiency.

As a matter of fact, Ryuzo let Yoshi, his old buddy and accomplice in the heinous crimes of his past, occupy his vacant lot illegally. Yoshi is an old bum and drug addict, a counterpart of Ryuzo, the winner. But in a sense, the outcast bum, Yoshi, who is shot to death by his teenage son, is the incorrigible, out-and-out rebel Ryuzo wanted to be. Unlike Yoshi, who in his delirium regards himself as a descendant of the nomadic hero "Genghis Khan,"[30] Ryuzo remains the "King of Flies" in *Roji*. Presumably, Ryuzo feels the snare of the establishment that catches even the king of flies. To compete with Yoshi, his old buddy, and to return to his original position as a destroyer and a rebel, Ryuzo must commit suicide and makes everything null at the height of his prosperity.

After Ryuzo's suicide, Akiyuki disappears from *Roji* when a fire breaks out in the vacant lot. Most likely, Akiyuki started the fire. But Akiyuki's act is more a refusal of his father's legacy than a repetition of his father's arson in the past. The vacant lot comes to suggest Ryuzo's entrapment in an authoritarian society. The vacant lot is an empty center where Ryuzo's defiance against Japanese society is suspended in paralysis, because at the same time, Ryuzo unwittingly represents the patriarchal establishment which appropriates rebellious sons. Yoshi once dreamed that the empty grass patch would finally lead to Genghis Khan's vast, boundless prairie. Akiyuki cannot be so optimistic a derelict, but he burns Ryuzo's lot as a symbolical refusal of all Ryuzo tries to hold on to, and of all that holds Ryuzo. Akiyuki finally repudiates the patriarchal space, which seems to have conquered *Roji*, and crosses beyond the boundary of *Roji* as a displaced person, a nomad.

Nakagami attempts to destroy patriarchy from the illegitimate son's position. But even the rebellious power of Charles Bon as an illegitimate son, shared both by Ryuzo and Akiyuki, becomes ambiguous, so far as illegitimacy is a part of the binary opposite within patriarchy. The establishment corrupts and appropriates the rebel, and the victim becomes the victimizer. In battle with a subversive father, the illegitimate son might become the legitimate, either for the father or for society. And as Quentin Compson in *Absalom, Absalom!* proves, the legendary narrative of patriarchy returns in spite of the indictment of it, so far as one remains and narrates, however resistantly, inside its system.

Nakagami is quite sensitive to the influence of patriarchy in the ancient Japanese narratives and legends. In the old folklore stories of Japan, a noble prince in exile, deserted and wandering throughout the country, will eventually be found by his father and recognized as a legitimate son. Nakagami, an illegitimate son, and coming from the old outcast class, is quite attracted to the traditional narrative pattern. Such a narrative appreciates the hardships and sufferings of a deprived prince and promises him grace and legitimacy in the future. But Nakagami is also quite aware of its dangerous allure and declares that all novels are to be written from a deserted child's point of view. According to Nakagami, a novelist's duty is to persecute and indict the father who killed or deserted the sibling.[31] Nakagami in this assertion is quite conscious of Japanese patriarchal society and the Emperor, because the Emperor took a leading role in ancient times not only in politics but also in literature. The Emperor was active both as a poet and as a protagonist in the legends. The Emperor also ordered the official compilations of the old chronicles of the nation, and of the Japanese poems, to construct the foundation of the imagined community. Ryuzo, on the other hand, is the "King of Flies," a dark prince who plays the double role of a demanding as well as a conciliating father, and a deserted child in rebellion against society.

Nakagami must have discerned another entrapment in Quentin's narrative, the legitimate son's indictment in *Absalom, Absalom!* While Faulkner leaves the puzzles and indecisive elements open, Quentin and Shreve gradually aim for a dramatic, comprehensive conclusion for their grand narrative. Nakagami does not let Akiyuki start a new revision or an ambitious retelling of Ryuzo's story. In *The Ends of the Earth*, Akiyuki makes some new discoveries about Ryuzo's life. He visits the village where Ryuzo passed his boyhood in extreme poverty and finds that Ryuzo as a boy was constantly despised and persecuted. Akiyuki also confirms that Ryuzo's former boss is alive and well, contrary to the rumor that Ryuzo killed him. With such new information, however, Akiyuki does not correct or revise all

his memories or the rumors of the town. He broods on the new information, but in contrast to Quentin, he often lets rumors about Ryuzo stand as
they are. In the Faulkner International Symposium held in Japan in 1985,
Nakagami talked about the common denominator of the luxuriating power
of the South in Faulkner's texts and in his own.[32] Nakagami is determined
to retain his subversiveness in the running on, permeative style, which goes
over or through any boundary of patriarchy, or through the well-wrought
structure of patriarchal narratives.

After *The Ends of the Earth*, Nakagami deliberately seals up *Roji*, though
many people roaming through wider space in his texts are still related to
the *Roji* of the past. Nakagami sometimes warps the perpendicular line of
patriarchy to the horizontal line of fraternity in *The Ends of the Earth*. He
continues this attempt in his later works in the theme of nomadic brothers
or buddies drifting in the world. In a sense, they represent the dissemination of Ryuzo's subversive spirit, but they refuse to be obsessed with land
as Ryuzo is. In *The Ends of the Earth*, Nakagami has Ryuzo refer to his land
as "a postage stamp of land" (121, 291) a couple of times. The expression,
originating in Faulkner's reference to his Yoknapatawpha, is Nakagami's
challenge, as well as his homage, to Faulkner. He acknowledges his great
literary debt to Faulkner, who inspired him to create his own Jefferson and
Yoknapatawpha saga, but he has Akiyuki burn the vacant lot of Ryuzo's
"postage stamp of land" and tries to go beyond it to overcome the patriarchal control of Japanese society.

It may be too hasty to connect Nakagami's nomadic brethren with
Faulkner's Corporal and World War I soldiers in *A Fable*. But Nakagami
follows Faulkner's intuition in *These 13*; he believes with Faulkner that fraternity is important to fight against patriarchy. Even Ryuzo in *The Ends of
the Earth* secretly desires to flee from treacherous patriarchy and return
to fraternity. Suffice it to say now, however, that Nakagami had great difficulty in narrating the nomadic protagonists without flattening and atten-
uating them into abstract cosmopolitans.[33] Nakagami does not want to follow the fate of Faulkner's would-be cosmopolitan aviators in *These 13*, who
find themselves serving the imperial nation after all. At his death, Nakagami was still in the process of creating a convincing narrative in which nomadic people transcend local or national boundaries and which shuns the
traditional return of the sons to their fathers.

Faulkner, for his part, steadily continues his critique of patriarchy in a
legitimate son's repudiation of inheritance. Isaac McCaslin in *Go Down,
Moses* repudiates his inheritance represented by his grandfather and
chooses Sam Fathers as his spiritual father. As a matter of fact, in "A Justice" Sam Fathers has already indicated to Quentin the possibility of re-

pudiating the patriarchal line: when Doom sold his mother to Quentin's great-grandfather, Sam chose to go with his slave mother rather than to stay with his Choctaw father. Actually, Sam's choice further suggests the future development of Faulkner's interest in black matriarchy in *Go Down, Moses*. We may relate it to Kenji Nakagami's concern with matriarchy and the narrative power of old women in *Roji*. Nakagami explored the narrative power of an old midwife in *Sennen No Yuraku* (*Millennium of Joy*), published in 1982, less than a year before *The Ends of the Earth* came out. Nakagami is a giant who resorts to as many resources as Faulkner does in his creative imagination, but the power of women in Faulkner and Nakagami is another subject.

NOTES

I would like to thank Anne Goodwyn Jones for reading my paper before I presented it at the Faulkner and Yoknapatawpha Conference in July 2006.

1. From a *New York Times* editorial about the awarding of the Nobel Prize to Faulkner: "Incest and rape may be common pastimes in Faulkner's 'Jefferson, Miss.' but they are not elsewhere in the United States" (*New York Times*, 11 November 1950, 14), quoted in Michael Millgate, *The Achievement of William Faulkner* (New York: Vintage, 1966), 48.

2. Faulkner attended an international writers' conference at São Paulo, and in Japan he had many interviews and attended a series of sessions at Nagano Seminar for the U.S. Information Service's Program. He continued his trip to the Philippines after the visit to Japan before he headed for Europe. See Joseph Blotner, *Faulkner: A Biography* (New York: Random House, 1974), 1504–6, 1543–67.

3. For the political explanation of why Faulkner became so famous after the Second World War, see Lawrence H. Schwarz, *Creating Faulkner's Reputation: The Politics of Modern Literary Criticism* (Knoxville: University of Tennessee Press, 1988). Helen Oakley's discussion on the timing of Faulkner's visit to Latin America, carried on in a politically sensitive situation, is also suggestive. See Oakley, "William Faulkner and the Cold War: The Politics of Cultural Marketing," in *Look Away!*, ed. Jon Smith and Deborah Cohn (Durham: Duke University Press, 2004), 405–18.

4. *Essays, Speeches, and Public Letters*, ed. James B. Meriwether (1965; New York: Modern Library, 2004), 83.

5. Kenzaburo Ohashi, "'Native Soil' and the World Beyond: William Faulkner and Japanese Novelists," in *Faulkner: International Perspectives: Faulkner and Yoknapatawpha, 1982*, ed. Doreen Fowler and Ann J. Abadie (Jackson: University Press of Mississippi, 1984), 257–75. See also Ohashi, "A Japanese View," in *Faulkner: After the Nobel Prize*, ed. Michel Gresset and Kenzaburo Ohashi (Kyoto: Yamaguchi Publishing House, 1987), 3–12.

6. George B. Handley, "A New World Poetics of Oblivion," in *Look Away!*, 25. See also Vera Lawrence Hyatt and Rex Nettleford, eds., *Race, Discourse, and the Origins of the Americas: A New World View* (Washington: Smithsonian Institution Press, 1995).

7. The move to the Pacific was related to the U.S.A.'s expansionism over the American hemisphere. See Gretchen Murphy, *Hemispheric Imaginings: The Monroe Doctrine and Narratives of U.S. Empire* (Durham: Duke University Press, 2005), 62–64.

8. In contrast to the battles between Native Americans and U.S. troops, no bloody battles were fought between the Ainu and the Japanese except for a few Ainu riots at the end of the

18th century. But roughly about the same period, what happened to the Native Americans in the U.S. happened to the Ainu in the northern island of Hokkaido. A very small population of the Ainu people still survives, but their cultural tradition is preserved mainly for tourism.

9. No theory has yet confirmed the Burakumin's origin, and some scholars think the discrimination began as early as the fourteenth or fifteenth century. At the start of the Edo era in the seventeenth to the eighteenth century, when classes were firmly established to solidify the feudal society of the Tokugawa Shogunate, these people were treated publicly as the outcast class of society. There were four classes of plebeians (warriors, farmers, artisans, and merchants), but the Burakumin was excluded from each category. Their occupations were limited to such jobs as gravedigging, the slaughter of animals, or handling of raw hides or furs, jobs which were quite despised in Buddhist society. They were called *"hinin"* (*"hinin"* means "nonhuman"). In the Meiji era in 1871, the law of discrimination was abolished, but their class remained at the bottom of society as before. See George De Vos and Hiroshi Wagatsuma, *Japan's Invisible Race: Caste in Culture and Personality* (Berkeley: University of California Press, 1966).

10. See Ohashi, 1984, 259–60. Haruyama consulted such magazines as *n.r.f.* and *commerce*. Haruyama, "Faulkner in the Early Days" (in Japanese); *William Faulkner: Materials, Studies, and Criticism* 2:1 (June 1979): 34–35, "William Faulkner" (in Japanese), 36–37. Haruyama's "William Faulkner" is translated by Toshio Koyama into English as "William Faulkner (1932)," *Faulkner Studies in Japan*, compiled by Kenzaburo Ohashi and Kiyoyuki Ono, ed. Thomas L. McHaney (Athens: University of Georgia Press, 1985), 177–80.

11. Appendix G, "Faulkner in Japanese" provided by Ohashi, *Faulkner: International Perspectives*, 341. The titles of the poems indicate they were selected from *A Green Bough*, published in April 1933.

12. Nishiwaki studied at Oxford University in the early 1920s, and he was in London at the time of the publications of *Ulysses* and *The Waste Land*. Junzaburo Nishiwaki, *Poems of Junzaburo Nishiwaki* (Tokyo: Iwanami-Bunko, 1991), 472–74.

13. See Ohashi, 1984, 260–61; Hajime Shinoda, "Faulkner Once Again" (in Japanese), afterword of *Niso eno Chingonka* (*Requiem for a Nun*), *Fokuna Zenshu* 19 (Tokyo: Fuzanbo, 1978), 305–18. Takehiko Fukunaga read some of Faulkner's texts in French before World War II. Fukunaga, "Faulkner and Myself" (in Japanese), *William Faulkner: Materials, Studies, and Criticism*, 2:1 (June 1979), 69–74. Fukunaga's article is translated into English by Toshio Koyama in *Faulkner Studies in Japan*, 181–86. As for the publication years of the translations of Faulkner's texts into Japanese, see Appendix G, "Faulkner in Japanese," *Faulkner: International Perspectives*, 339–42.

14. Shin'ichiro Nakamura, "My Encounter with Faulkner" (in Japanese), afterword of *Abusaromu, Abusaromu!* (*Absalom, Absalom!*), *Fokuna Zenshu* 12 (Tokyo: Fuzanbo, 1980), 361–71; Nakamura, *On Court Literature* (in Japanese) (Tokyo: Shincho-Bunko, 1978).

15. Mitsuharu Inoue described a coal-mining area in Kyushu (Ohashi 1984, 264–65), and Fukunaga created two fictional towns in Hokkaido (Fukunaga, 1985, 186).

16. See Shinoda, 314–15; Ohashi, 1984, 261. *1946: Literary Reflections* (in Japanese) (Tokyo: Kodansha Bungei-Bunko, 2006), a collection of literary essays and criticism written by Shuichi Kato, Shin'ichiro Nakamura, and Takehiko Fukunaga, shows how the ambitious young Japanese writers after World War II aspired to be as universal and competitive as Western literature. The book was first published by Shinzenbi-sha in Tokyo, 1947.

17. Oe's *Man'en Gannen no Futtoboru* (*The Silent Cry*) clearly shows Faulkner's influence. Kenzaburo Oe emphasizes "the feminine" in Faulkner in "Reading Faulkner from a Writer's Point of View," *Faulkner Studies in Japan*, 62–75. Oe's essay was first published in Japanese in *Bungakukai* 35 (July 1981). See also Ikuko Fujihira, "The Image of Hell, the Myth of Family, and the Paradox of Narrative in William Faulkner, Toni Morrison, and Oe Kenzaburo," *The Faulkner Journal of Japan* (May 1999), 24 August 2006, www.isc.senshu-u.ac.jp/~thb0559/fjournal.htm.

18. In 1927, Faulkner had already suggested the idea of "a collection of short stories of [his] townspeople" in a letter to Horace Liveright. See *Selected Letters of William Faulkner*,

ed. Joseph Blotner (New York: Vintage, 1978), 34 (18 February 1927). As for the discussion of the period of Faulkner's writing the short stories collected in *These 13*, see Hans H. Skei, *William Faulkner: The Short Story Career* (Oslo: Universitetsforlaget, 1981); Edmond L. Volpe, *A Reader's Guide to William Faulkner: The Short Stories* (Syracuse: Syracuse University Press, 2004); James Ferguson, *Faulkner's Short Fiction* (Knoxville, University of Tennessee Press, 1991), 1–38; Diane Brown Jones, *A Reader's Guide to the Short Stories of William Faulkner* (New York: G. K. Hall, 1994); Lisa Paddock, *Contrapuntal in Integration: A Study of Three Faulkner Short Story Volumes* (Lanham, New York, Oxford: International Scholars Publications, 2000).

19. Millgate and Polk respectively discuss persuasively the well-organized structure of *These 13*. Millgate, *The Achievement of William Faulkner*, 259–75; Noel Polk, "William Faulkner's 'Carcassonne,'" *Studies in American Fiction* 12 (1984): 29–43.

20. *Collected Stories of William Faulkner* (New York: Vintage International, 1995), 416.

21. In his examination of the incest theme in Faulkner, Karl F. Zender points to the contrast between brotherhood and fatherhood in "Ad Astra" and continues to examine the cultural and political importance of brotherhood in *Absalom, Absalom!* and *Go Down, Moses*. Zender, *Faulkner and the Politics of Reading* (Baton Rouge: Louisiana State University Press, 2002), 1–31.

22. See, for instance, Poem XIII of "Helen: A Courtship" and Poem IV ("Wild Geese") of "Mississippi Poems" in *Helen: A Courtship and Mississippi Poems* (New Orleans and Oxford: Tulane University and Yoknapatawpha Press, 1981), 124, 152.

23. *Absalom, Absalom!* (New York: Vintage International, 1990), 8.

24. Nakagami was born in 1946 and died of kidney cancer at the age of forty-six in 1992. Apart from some short stories, most of his novels have not yet been translated into English. Ohashi introduced Nakagami first in *Faulkner: International Perspectives*, 270–71.

25. Nakagami in his nonfiction essay on the Kishu Peninsula, his homeland, says that the way he describes the peninsula in his essay resembles the way Faulkner describes Yoknapatawpha in his texts. Nakagami, *Kishu: Ki no Kuni, Ne no Kuni Monogatari* (*Kishu: A Tale of the Land of Trees, Land of Roots*) (Tokyo: Shogakkan-Bunko, 1999), 12. For the importance of community and rumors for Nakagami, see also Nakagami, "Faulkner's Impact" (in Japanese), *Nakagami Kenji Essei Senshu: Bungaku, Geino Hen* (Tokyo: Kobunsha21, 2002), 214–16.

26. See note 9. Timewise, the liberation of the Burakumin approximately parallels with that of African Americans in the U.S.A.

27. *Karekinada* (Tokyo: Kawadeshobo Shinsha, 1985), 106.

28. *Misaki* in *Nakagami Kenji Zenshu 3* (Tokyo: Shueisha, 1995), 167–242. *Misaki* is translated into English in *The Cape and Other Stories from the Japanese Getto*, trans. with a preface and afterword by Eve Zimmerman (Berkeley: Stone Bridge Press, 1999).

29. See Michiko Yoshida, "Kenji Nakagami as Faulkner's Rebellious Heir," *Faulkner, His Contemporaries, and His Posterity*, ed. Waldemar Zacharasiewicz (Tübingen: Francke, 1993), 350–60; Mats Karlsson, "Nakagami and Faulkner," *The Kumano Saga of Nakagami Kenji* (Edsbruk: Akademitryck AB, 2001), 60–74; Yuji Kato, "'The Luxuriating South,' William Faulkner, and Gabriel García Márquez: Voices, Narrations, and the Place of Existence," *The Faulkner Journal of Japan* (May 1999); 24 August 2006, www.isc.senshu-u.ac.jp/~thb0559/fjournal.htm; Anne McKnight, "Crypticism, or Nakagami Kenji's Transplanted Faulkner: Plants, Saga and *Sabetsu*," Kato paradoxically sees the original absence of the Father in the texts of Faulkner and Nakagami through Sutpen and Ryuzo. His reading can be partly supported by Nina Cornyetz who points out "gendered ambivalences" both in Nakagami's *Roji* and the male characters. Cornyetz, *Dangerous Women, Deadly Words: Phallic Fantasy and Modernity in Three Japanese Writers* (Stanford: Stanford University Press, 1999), 219. Also see "Faulkner and Kenji Nakagami," Symposium (in Japanese), Akira Asada, Seiko Ito, Mats Karlsson, Kojin Karatani, Shuji Takazawa, Fumiaki Noya, and Naomi Watanabe, *Waseda Bungaku* 28 (November 2003), 4–39.

30. *Chi no Hate, Shijo no Toki* (Tokyo: Shincho-Bunko, 2004), 38.

31. Nakagami, *Fukei no Muko e, Monogatari no Keifu* (*Beyond Landscapes: A Genealogy of the Narrative*) (Tokyo: Kodansha Bungei-Bunko, 2004). See Yoshida, 350–51, for a tight, condensed explication of Nakagami's argument here.

32. Nakagami, "Hammo suru Minami," first published in *Subaru* 7 (August 1985), reprinted in *Nakagami Kenji Essei Senshu: Bungaku, Geino Hen*, 203–10; translated into English as "Faulkner: The Luxuriating South," *Faulkner: After the Nobel Prize*, 326–36. With an artist's intuition, Nakagami sensed the importance of the dynamic imagery of the South, which means not only the American South but also the South of any place, and saw the common background between his hometown Shingu city in the southeast of the Kishu peninsula and Faulkner's Jefferson.

33. One of Nakagami's novels that deal with nomadic characters, *Izoku* (*The Tribe*) (Tokyo: Shogakkan-Bunko, 1991), is unfinished, though he started writing it in 1984 and continued publishing parts of the text until 1991.

Artificial Women, the Pygmalion Paradigm, and Faulkner's Gordon in *Mosquitoes*

Mario Materassi

The account of a comically ill-fated three-day excursion on Lake Pontchartrain involving more than a dozen intellectuals, artists, hangers-on, and members of the New Orleans underworld, *Mosquitoes* is largely a *roman à clef*. Most of the characters are thinly disguised portraits of people whom Faulkner had come to know during his formative sojourn in New Orleans from 1925 to 1926. This motley coterie is treated with pervasive irony that often turns the various likenesses into downright caricatures. Not even Gordon, the aloof sculptor who stands out from the crowd of futile professional conversationalists on board the *Nausikaa*, is spared this treatment. The present paper, however, is not concerned with the question of *Mosquitoes* as a *roman à clef*. As a premise to the discussion that will follow, it is nevertheless important to bear in mind that Gordon is usually understood to be a combination of the writer's self-portrait and a likeness of the artist William Spratling, Faulkner's friend and roommate in New Orleans as well as his collaborator in the joint venture of *Salmagundi*, the slim volume of graphic and prose caricatures of French Quarter characters.[1] At the beginning of the novel, Gordon is presented as the only real artist, totally devoted to his work, given to creativity rather than to talking about creativity, and ready to sacrifice everything to his calling.[2] The opening scene, which focuses on the gruff sculptor besieged by the annoying socialites who come to visit his studio, forcefully defines this opposition: the stern upholder of artistic integrity on the one hand and, on the other, the frivolous, sterile representatives of intellectual superficiality. Thus, notwithstanding his description as the stereotypically unkempt artist lacking in social grace, Gordon is immediately imprinted in the reader's mind as the novel's positive pole, in emblematic contrast to the negative pole of mundane, parasitic society.

This paper synthesizes a nearly 100-page chapter focused on Gordon and the Pygmalion paradigm in my latest book-length study of Faulkner; the chapter, in turn, is the development of a suggestion I made elsewhere that Gordon may owe something to Démétrios, the protagonist of Pierre Louÿs immensely popular novel *Aphrodite, moeurs antiques*, published in 1896.[3] This earlier, passing suggestion was prompted by the observation that, at the beginning of *Mosquitoes*, Gordon makes a declaration that appears, strikingly, to encapsulate Démétrios's attitude towards women. That his words also appear to be an echo of a passage in Maupassant's *Notre coeur* further strengthens paradigmatic affinities.[4] As Gordon's pronouncement constitutes the starting point of the present discussion, it will be useful to quote it here.

Before his routinely admiring visitors, Gordon thus introduces his marble torso: "This is my feminine ideal: a virgin with no legs to leave me, no arms to hold me, no head to talk to me."[5] At first these shocking words can be perceived in the light of the traditional stance of an artist intending to *épater le bourgeois*, or, to shock the Yahoos. Progressively, however, they reveal themselves to be faithful indicators of Gordon's personality. Indeed, there is no irony in the sculptor's utterance. As paradoxical as his words are, they disclose some deep truths about Faulkner's artist.

Gordon's pompous stance is countered by Pat Robyn, the girl of eighteen to whom he is reluctantly attracted and who functions as his opposite in the dynamics of the overall organization of meaning in the novel. An almost androgynous teenager often described as sexless, Pat forcefully refuses to succumb to Gordon's rhetoric. With youthful, carping spontaneity, she unleashes barbs that ruthlessly deflate his high-handed tone: "'Hadn't you rather have a live one?'" she asks, referring to the marble torso; and then: "'No woman is going to waste time on a man that's satisfied with a piece of wood or something.'. . . Thirty-six years old, and living in a hole with a piece of rock, like a dog with a dry bone. . . . Why don't you get rid of it?'" (270).

Gordon's pronouncement and Pat Robyn's barbs announce the structural opposition art versus life, central in the novel, that makes of *Mosquitoes* the umpteenth variation of the myth of Pygmalion. For, as Claus Daufenbach writes, this is a myth that "through the combination of erotic and artistic creation . . . and its transgression of the boundaries between life and art, . . . has time and again supplied a fascinating motif for both literature and the fine arts."[6]

In the early variants of the myth, Pygmalion was the king of Cyprus; later, he was downgraded by Ovid to simply a renowned sculptor. Pygmalion fashioned an ivory statue of a woman whom he named Galatea, and immediately fell in love with it. He then asked Aphrodite to give life to his artwork; the goddess granted his wish and turned the statue into a woman. Then, as it were, literary history began; and for the past two thousand years, Ovid's masterful rendering of this tale, the most celebrated variation of the Greek legend, has continued to influence the entire western culture. The phenomenological basis of the myth of Pygmalion and of the paradigm into which it developed is the erotic attraction for a statue, known as *agalmato-philia*. By extension, I will refer to *agalmatophilia* also when the object of the attraction is a painting, as is the case, among many others, of Balzac's *Gillette or The Unknown Masterpiece* (1831), E. T. A. Hoffmann's *The Devil's Elixir* (1814), Théophile Gautier's "La toison d'or" (1839), or Emile Zola's *The Masterpiece* (1886).

Pierre Louÿs's *Aphrodite* is a typical product of the enduringly success-ful "pagan school" against which Baudelaire had inveighed half a century earlier. In *Aphrodite* Bérénice, Queen of Alexandria, commissions from Démétrios a marble statue representing herself to be adored in the temple of Aphrodite-Astarte.[7] The queen poses for the statue, and the artist and the model become lovers; once the statue is finished, however, Démétrios is so enraptured with his creation that he coldly rejects the model in favor of her likeness. Soon after he becomes attracted to Chrysis, a courtesan who promises to give herself to him on three conditions: that he filch a pre-cious mirror from Bacchis, a rival courtesan; steal a precious comb from a high priestess, whom he then kills while making love to her; and rob the statue of the queen of its necklace.[8] After complying with the woman's re-quests, however, Démétrios refuses to lie with her, explaining that since he had a marvelous erotic dream of her, he will not run the risk of being dis-illusioned by reality. He then sends Chrysis to her death for having stolen, killed, and committed the sacrilegious act of wearing the queen's necklace. In the end, he enters the dungeon, places the woman's corpse in an erotic pose, and creates a clay model of it. This he later develops into a marble statue which he calls *La Vie Immortelle*, the Immortal Life. Démétrios's final act epitomizes the paradox inherent in the very act of artistic creation. In order to eternalize the woman, the artist forces his model to suspend movement, the primary signal of life. Implicitly, he exchanges life for its il-lusion, which, insofar as it pertains to the realm of ideas, ensures perma-nence. The "pose" (that is to say, the condition for the image to be fixed, whether in clay, in marble, on canvas, or on the plate) takes on the state of apparent death. In order to subtract the woman from death, the artist, if only temporarily, deprives her of life.[9]

Louÿs was more interested in sensationalism than in aesthetics, a fact that is nowhere more evident than in the novel's concluding scene. This lurid passage, which literalizes the oxymoron inherent to art without touch-ing on its potential for symbolic interpretation, shows no attempt on the part of the author to present *The Immortal Life* as the result of a long, per-haps tormented process of creative development, much less as its success-ful culmination. Indeed, none of the key moments in Démétrios's story are presented as stages in his artistic growth: not his choice of the artifact over the model;[10] not the preference given to the woman in his dream over the real woman; not his venture into the world of Thanatos, where, somewhat ambiguously and certainly in line with the necrophilic taste of the Decadents, he makes solitary use of the still limp corpse of his mistress manqué and victim. In fact, Démétrios is only nominally an artist. He is, first and foremost, a rake, a jaded *tombeur de femmes* turned into a rogue who indulges in pedophilia, experiments in thieving, and thinks nothing of murdering his mistresses. In short, Louÿs has filled his stage with a number of props suited to a dramatization of the age-old question at the center of all discussions about art, that is, the art versus reality debate; but instead of following through on his premises and thereby offering his variation on the paradigm of the artist torn between art and life, Louÿs, contented with mere sensationalism, reduces his artist to a shallow, insensitive débauché.

Excepting Gordon's initial declaration, Faulkner's *Mosquitoes* manifests none of the Grand Guignol morbidity of Louÿs's *fin-de-siècle* potboiler. On the paradigmatic level, however, Démétrios and Gordon are quite similar. Both reject the real woman in favor of the artificial one, choosing cold matter, resistant to deterioration, over the living flesh that is subject to the action of time. Both give preference to their abstract constructs, which change cannot affect. Ideally, both choose death over life. Although a number of further textual elements connect the two sculptors, we shall not linger on the hypothesis that Faulkner may have had Louÿs's *Aphrodite* in mind when he created his Gordon. What needs to be emphasized here is that both artists are to be seen as part of a cultural universe they share with many other literary characters of the 1800s. It is in this context that one must search for the epistemological roots of the hideous treatment of the woman evident in both *Aphrodite* and Gordon's personal manifesto.

One example of the prevailing nineteenth-century attitude suffices to indicate the cultural background shared by the two sculptors. In *Mademoiselle de Maupin*, Chevalier d'Albert declares: "'there is something grand and beautiful in loving a statue. Here love is perfectly disinterested in that one does not need fearing either surfeit or disgust following victory, nor cannot reasonably hope for a second prodigy analogous to that in Pygmalion's story.'"[11] By established convention, it is not the author but the individual character who must be held accountable for his actions and attitudes. However, in consideration of the amplitude, both diachronic and synchronic, of the phenomenon under discussion, the responsibility may fall also on the writer himself as an individual immersed in the cultural climate of his time. The inadvertent but by no means less weighty complicity of the epochal context provides the general framework within which

values, positive or negative, go largely unchallenged. The question, therefore, arises whether Gordon should be understood as Faulkner's mouth-
piece as regards petrification, the ultimate degree of the conventional attitude toward women that the sculptor shares with Démétrios.

Quite definitely, the answer can only be negative. Although Faulkner
participated in a traditional system of visualization of women, he was far
from the necrophiliac orientation that Pierre Louÿs had in common with
many of his contemporaries. He was immune to the morbid extremes of
Decadent aestheticism that colored literature and the visual arts in the
second half of the nineteenth century and after, from Gautier ("la morte
chez elle semblait une coquetterie de plus")[12] to Albert Samain ("la beauté
sublime qu'ont les morts"),[13] from Walter Pater to Igino Tarchetti to John
George Huysmans to Gabriele D'Annunzio, from John Everett Millais to
Paul Delaroche to Anne Louis Girodet-Trioson, to name just some of the
major writers and artists who succumbed to the fascination with death. At
the same time, Faulkner, however, did ascribe at least a measure of this extreme strain of Decadent aesthetic ideal to his sculptor by making Gordon
into a sort of residual representative of the cultural climate that had long
reigned in western Europe.

Both Démétrios's macabre inclinations and Gordon's paradoxical feminine ideal result from the accruing of epistemes and of cultural models
and fashions, including the Pygmalion paradigm, that literature and the
fine arts had disseminated and universalized throughout the 1800s. Behind
Démétrios and Gordon there is much Fernand Khnopff and much Gustave
Moreau—the Moreau in whose *Salomé* Jean des Esseintes, the protagonist of Huysmans's *À rebours*, saw "the symbolical deity of indestructible
Luxury, the goddess of immortal Hysteria—the accursed Beauty."[14] This
is the typical rhetoric of nineteenth-century intellectual misogyny grafted
onto an ancient and deep aversion to and fear of the Belle Dame sans
Mercy. It was a form of misogyny that projected a wishful self-image of
man as heroically impervious to the Temptress's snares, an image of the
ideal *fin-de-siècle* male.

This ideal of manhood, which is strictly tied to the ideal of the artificial woman, goes back to Ovid's Pygmalion and to a number of Greek
and Roman authors, from third century B.C. Philostephanus of Cyrene
(Ovid's probable source) to Euripides, from Iginus to Pliny the Elder to
the Pseudo Lucian. In the works of these authors we find either the earliest
known variations of the Pygmalion theme, or certain elements pertaining
to it that were destined to be incorporated into later variations. For instance, in Euripides's eponymous play, the image of Helen "breathed" (that
is to say, fashioned) by Hera for the purpose of foiling Paris is a stratagem

that Shakespeare was to adopt in *Measure for Measure* in his only explicit reference to the Pygmalion paradigm.[15]

The present occasion does not call for a detailed analysis of this paradigm in its numberless avatars through the centuries. Suffice it to say that after the classical era, the story of Pygmalion reappears at the end of the thirteenth century in Jean de Meun's portion of *Le roman de la rose*, where we are presented with an extraordinarily modern view of Galatea's transformation into a human being not as a miracle, not as the effect of a transcendental intervention, but as a mental construct, that is to say, through the unexpected irruption of psychology in the Middle Ages. Subsequently, during and after the Renaissance, thanks mostly to Arthur Golding's translation of the *Metamorphoses* (1567), Pygmalion's story became a favorite subject with both playwrights and poets—including John Marston, George Pettie, Thomas Middleton, and Jean Jacques Rousseau. Ultimately, it became a major *locus classicus* of both literature and the fine arts in the nineteenth and the early twentieth centuries. A purely cursory list of the writers who variously made use of the Pygmalion paradigm during this period will give a sense of the extent of the phenomenon. In France, we have Alfred de Vigny, Alfred de Musset, André Chénier, Alphonse de Lamartine, Balzac, Flaubert, Gautier, Maupassant, Prosper Mérimée, Alphonse Daudet, Anatole France, Zola, Pierre Louÿs, George Charles Huysmans, Villiers de l'Ile-Adam, Proust, Marcel Prévost, and Jacques Prévert as the screenwriter of *Les enfants du paradis* (1945). In England, we have Thomas Lovell Beddoes, Lord Lytton, William Morris, Oscar Wilde, Walter Pater, William S. Gilbert, Norman Douglas, G. B. Shaw, and, surprisingly, also Agatha Christie. In America, in addition to Faulkner, we have Poe, Hawthorne, Louisa May Alcott, Oliver Wendell Holmes, Henry James, Edith Wharton, Joseph Hergesheimer, Sherwood Anderson, Vernon Lee, John Gardner, Rudolfo Anaya. In the German speaking world, it will be enough to mention Hoffmann, Nietzsche, Wilhelm Jensen, and Freud; in Italy, Michelangelo, Giovanni di Carlo Strozzi, Giorgio Vasari, Igino Ugo Tarchetti, Gabriele D'Annunzio, Alberto Savinio, Arturo Loria. Variations of the Pygmalion paradigm are present as well in the works of Russian, Scandinavian, and Spanish writers. Although far from exhaustive, this list, which includes so many of the most important authors of the last two centuries, indicates the extent, both geographical and linguistic, to which the Pygmalion paradigm continues to influence modern culture.[16]

In the course of two thousand years, the story of Pygmalion and Galatea naturally acquired elements that are extraneous to the prototype. This process of accretion was particularly intense in the last two centuries, and the changes wrought on the prototype proved quite significant. As a result, when Faulkner began writing *Mosquitoes* in 1926, the general notion of Pygmalion had indeed little in common with the original model, except for the key factor of the artist developing a passion for his creation. Basically, only the agalmatophiliac syndrome had survived. A typological investigation of the changes to the Pygmalion paradigm through the centuries evinces that, with some notable exceptions, until the 1700s included, the "plot" tended to maintain the three fundamental elements of Ovid's model: the artist, the artificial woman who is the object of his passion, and the metamorphosis.[17] We find this is the traditional pattern in *Le roman de la rose*, in Marston's "The Metamorphosis of Pigmalions Image" (1598), in Pettie's "Petite Palace of Pettie His Pleasure" (1576), in Rousseau's "Pygmalion, scene lyrique" (1762). For several centuries, the fact that the artificial woman is born out of the artist's imagination is an unquestioned given, as no live woman provides the model for the marble or the ivory Galateas.

With the 1800s, substantial changes in the structure of the story emerge. We still have the artist and his artwork but the metamorphosis begins to be either eliminated or limited to the artist's wishful thinking. When the miracle occurs, it often happens behind a veil that enhances the necromantic nature of the event.[18] Most important, a real woman appears as the model for the artificial one. Still, it is always the latter that originates the artist's agalmatophiliac syndrome. Often the story ends in tragedy: the artist kills himself as in Zola's *The Masterpiece*, burns his canvas and commits suicide as in Balzac's *Gillette or The Unknown Masterpiece* (1831), kills himself and the woman as in Poe's "The Assignation" (1834), is slain or simply dies, respectively, in Balzac's "Sarrasine" (1831) and in Maupassant's *Fort comme la mort* (1890), or is murdered by the model as in Agatha Christie's *Five Little Pigs* (1943), known in the United States as *Murder in Retrospect*. In Poe's "The Oval Portrait" (1842), where there is neither the metamorphosis nor any trace of *agalmatophilia*, it is the wife, and the model for her portrait, who passes away. In Hoffmann's *The Devil's Desire* we still have the metamorphosis but the model dies.

A happy ending that legitimizes the unnatural passion is the almost imperative conclusion of the 19th-century American texts that distance themselves from the often perverted inclination of coeval French works by stressing, instead, family or social values. In the end these values always prevail, as in Hawthorne's *The Marble Faun* (1860), Louisa May Alcott's *A Marble Woman* (1865), and Oliver Wendell Holmes's *The Guardian Angel* (1867).[19]

On both sides of the Atlantic, the place of the artist may be taken by a different character: a lover (as in "The Assignation"), a hysterical young man (in Oscar Wilde's "Charmides," 1881), a scholar (in Wilhelm Jensen's "Gradiva," 1903), an artist manqué (in Gautier's "Le Roi Candaule," 1844) or a madman (in Norman Douglas's *Nerinda*, 1901). In such cases, the creation of the artificial woman antedates the beginning of the plot, and it is the discovery of the artifact that triggers the man's erotic response.

Whereas in the nineteenth century the occasional metamorphosis tended to be presented in a negative light (see Gautier's "Arria Marcella," 1852 or Mérimée's "La Venus d'Ille," 1837), in the twentieth century it was usually stripped of moral connotations. At times, the metamorphosis is treated ironically. For instance, in "L'Andalou" (The Man from Andalusia, 1985), a short story by the Spanish writer Gregorio Manzur, the Venus of Milos is impregnated by a night watchman and the director of the Louvre Museum arranges for an abortion.[20] Another ironic twist is found in "La vera storia di Galatea" (The True Story of Galatea, 1962), by Gino Supino. Here is the story: After several years of progressively less exciting matrimonial life owing to Pygmalion's having become impotent both sexually and creatively, and to Galatea's unhappiness at noticing the tell-tale traces of the passing of time, the couple asks the goddess for a second miracle; and, obligingly, Aphrodite reverses the metamorphosis.[21]

When both the artist and the metamorphosis are absent and only the artificial woman is left of the original structure, the surviving element can be a false statue, as in *The Winter Tale*; a statue (in "The Last of the Valerii" by Henry James, 1874); a doll (in *Cytherea* by Joseph Hergesheimer, 1922); or a mannequin (in "Rose-Agathe," again by Henry James, 1878), and in "La parrucca" [The Wig], 1932) by Arturo Loria). It can also be a young girl whom her tutor, bent on concealing his latent pedophilia, transforms into a legitimately marriageable woman (in *Watch and Ward* by James, 1878) or, as an emotionally sterile martinet, turns into the object of a professional experiment, as in George Bernard Shaw's *Pygmalion* (1912).

Issues concerning artistic creativity, social pressures, psychological tensions, and aberrations of the unconscious—that is to say, issues of high relevance in the modern context—were grafted by legions of writers and artists unto the myth of Pygmalion and Galatea. But rather than trying to ascertain which of the innumerable texts pertaining to the Pygmalion paradigm were known to Faulkner, the question to address here is: How much did Faulkner bring of his own to the paradigm? In art, and especially in modern art, it is the divergence that makes a difference. As a contemporary of Ezra Pound and a keen, albeit peripheral observer of Modernism, Faulkner was certainly aware of Pound's injunction to his fellow artists and writers to "Make it new!" By 1925, in the sophomoric tone he indulged at the time, Faulkner had reviewed Hergesheimer's *Cytherea* as

well as *Linda Condon* (1919), two novels strongly indebted to the Pygmalion paradigm; and he may very well have had Louÿs's Démétrios in mind
when he created his Gordon. As an ambitious young writer imbued with
Modernist ideas, however, he strove for originality; he strove, in fact, to
"make it new." We know what Gordon has in common with the various
Démétrioses who precede him. Our task is to ascertain where our sculptor
stands in the multimillenial gallery of statues metamorphosed into flesh-
and-blood women, of women literally petrified, of artists and nonartists
who yearn, become mad, reach momentary elation, kill themselves, or
are physically or spiritually destroyed as the result of the encounter with
these entities characterized by an enigmatical, polyvalent, and ultimately
inaccessible nature. For these are entities (they can hardly be classified as
"beings") fathered by men who are also their lovers or would-be lovers, as
the result of that which Huysmans called a "cerebral onanism," a "worse
than normal incest . . . because here the father violates his spiritual daughter, the only one totally pure and totally his own, the only daughter whom
he engendered without the concourse of a different blood."[22]

What is different about Gordon? In *Mosquitoes* we have the sculptor,
the artificial woman (the legless, armless, and headless marble bust), and an
ambiguous form of *agalmatophilia*. The novel, however, lacks the model;
instead, with an interesting inversion of time levels, it is the real woman
who, upon seeing the artifact, recognizes it as her own likeness: " 'It's like
me,' " Pat Robyn says, referring to the marble bust's lack of any appre-
ciable sexual markers (24). As in most modern variations of the paradigm,
there is no metamorphosis in *Mosquitoes*. Neither is there the happy ending that Gordon is tempted to pursue. The structural nucleus of Faulkner's
variation, therefore, rests on that exclusively intellectual form of *agalmatophilia*, which manifests itself in the sculptor's initial proclamation. Gordon
is last seen entering a brothel in the French Quarter and lifting a prostitute to himself—a clear indication of the split between his ideal of femi-
ninity and the feminine reality available to him. Proof of this is his attraction to Pat Robyn. Eight times the girl is said by the narrating voice to be
"sexless"; she is "almost breastless" (82), like the marble bust; three times
she is associated with children, six times with a boy; three times, either
directly or indirectly, with masculinity. Both physically and psychologi-
cally, Pat seems to be under the age of puberty, and often acts accordingly.
A sort of androgynous being, she initiates, without bringing to completion, a lesbian encounter. The nearest physical contact that Gordon establishes with her is a dubious moment of intimacy when he places her on his
knees and spanks her "good" (271) for having uttered a vulgar expression.
Caught between the two extremes of his ideal virgin and the prostitute, he

is both tempted and frightened by this sexually borderline being, a teaser who thwarts his sexuality by tantalizingly presenting herself as an object of pedophilic attraction. Unlike his ideal and his marble torso, however, Pat has a head—a constantly talking head whose function is to challenge and ridicule his certainties. Gordon's *agalmatophilia*, therefore, is totally intellectual. He has none of the original Pygmalion's explicit sensuality, as oddly directed as it was prior to Aphrodite's miraculous intervention; he has none of the sexual prowess with which so many of Pygmalion's later avatars are endowed. Only through the agency of a nameless prostitute can he give vent to his repressed sexuality.

During the nineteenth century, the conflict between the ideal and the real, particularly in the sphere of sexuality, had been honed to behavioral and social perfection. Reflecting the general trend, the literature and the arts of the period exalted this conflict, with both writers and artists developing a universal metaphorical language to express it. This, too, was part of our author's legacy. In fact, young Faulkner consistently resorted to the epochal repertoire that associated women either with the coldness of ice or the heat of fire, viewed her as either a nun or a harlot, an innocent girl or a femme fatale, an angel, or an animal such as a snake, bird, kitten, tiger, lioness, or leopard. All these stereotypical labels can be found in Faulkner's early works and, to a lesser degree, in his later ones as well.

These markers give eidetic support to the conventional view of "woman," strengthening the legitimacy of a hierarchical rapport with the "weaker sex," the "other" par excellence. Literally an ideologic construct in that it is based on an idea and, therefore, is unassailable by reality, this rapport makes the individual woman hopelessly inadequate vis-à-vis the ideal type. The latter becomes the yardstick by which the woman is judged and, inevitably, it is the ideal that prevails. In Balzac's "Sarrasine," the woman cries to her lover: "'Oh! you are making me over according to your own taste! . . . You don't want me to be me!'"[23] Maupassant understood that in man's eyes the woman is "born for the role of fetish," whereas man is "born to believe in absolute ideas" (*Notre coeur*, 177). In *La vie errante* (1890) he wrote, "[poets] look to women for something beyond what is there, because women seem to comprise and express a little of the unreachable ideal. . . . The woman they embrace is transformed, completed, and disfigured by their art."[24] The artificial woman, then, is not simply the likeness sculpted in marble or stone, carved in wood, cast in bronze, molded in wax or filled with straw and sewn, as is Vernon Lee's life-size doll of a dead wife. It is not only Hoffmann's automaton, the inflatable rubber doll of the porno shop, the silicone inflated Playboy Bunny, or the latest technologic creation, the virtual woman. "My sweet rock—my only wife," sighs

Beddoes's Pygmalion.[25] Upstream of all this, she is (but we should say, *it* is) the *thought* of the woman, the *dream* of the woman. She is, in short, man's cerebral invention. This is what Jean de Meun intuited at the end of the thirteenth century in *Le roman de la rose*: "Whence did this thought come into me, / How was this love ever conceived?" asked his disconcerted Pygmalion, freed for a moment from the traditional reliance upon preternatural mechanisms, and unexpectedly launched toward the inscrutable universe of interiority.[26]

Young Faulkner's dependence upon certain conventions in the visualization of women, both conceptual and linguistic, indicates that this future giant of Modernism was yet to renounce his turn-of-the-century cultural legacy. What saved him from the deadly solemnity of many of his models was his use of irony. Through irony, Faulkner at least partially distanced himself from the inherited constructs, deflating their founding assumptions. In *Mosquitoes* he established this distance chiefly by means of Pat Robyn's merciless, systematic puncturing of Gordon's absolutes, beginning with her response to Gordon's solemn, graven words about his ideal of womanhood.

This process of debunking, begun early in the novel and consistently sustained, vindicates the reader's immediate reservation toward Gordon's pronouncement. What, indeed, is the reason for these appalling words, sure to impress a roomful of idle chit-chatters but suggestive of values that are inappropriate for a character seemingly meant to represent the rejection of conventionality? Are these words indicative of the author's cultural make-up, or are they functional to the configuration of Gordon as a convincing character?

In the works prior to his major phase, Faulkner frequently entrusted the expression of certain personal opinions to one or more of his characters. He did not obliterate himself within the text, as he was to do in *The Sound and the Fury*, *As I Lay Dying*, or *Absalom, Absalom!*, his greatest achievements in the modernist mode. At this stage in his career, young Faulkner was indifferent to the risk of burdening his characters with elements extraneous to their configuration and liable to undermine their consistency. Gordon's pronouncement is typical of the cultural and ideological context of which Faulkner was part, and therefore the question rises whether the author automatically appropriated its implications or was in control of their damning impact instead.

Arguably, Faulkner was fully in command. This is made evident by the contradictory treatment of Gordon. Gordon functions as a foil to the inane prattlers filling the grounded ship of fools on which he has embarked in his own foolish pursuit of the elusive, sexless young woman. His incriminating words, however, undermine his credibility as the ideal artist who, in the Romantic tradition, rejects all cultural and behavioral conventions. The ambivalent treatment of Gordon shows that Faulkner did not intend to present him as a thoroughly positive model. Admittedly, the sculptor is a more genuine artist than the various intellectual quacks aboard the *Nausikaa*. But at the same time, he is also burdened with emotional inadequacies, cultural shortcomings, and ideological misconstructions. In short, he is a French Quarter version of the typical *poète maudit*: socially disagreeable, personally offensive, erratic in his behavior, and indifferent to intellectual rigor.

Two characters provide a double mirror in which Gordon's deficiencies are reflected, so that the reader is presented with an alternative perspective. One of these characters is Fairchild, the pontificating writer—quite transparently, a caricature of Sherwood Anderson. "'He ought to get out of himself more,'" Fairchild says of Gordon: "'you can't be an artist all the time. You'll go crazy'" (51). The other, as we have seen, is the teenager who, for all her grating peevishness, is a sharp dispenser of paradoxical common sense: "'No woman is going to waste time on a man that's satisfied with a piece of wood or something'" (270).

A modern Pygmalion sealed into an emotionally sterile contemplation of his impossible feminine ideal, Gordon forever freezes his amputated Galatea into silence, immobility, and sexlessness. He is, indeed, thousands of years distant from the joyously sensual Pygmalion of yore. Unlike his prototype, he never bends down to kiss and caress the icy forms, never dreams of praying for these forms to be metamorphosed into warm, pulsating flesh. Of course, the historical context is quite different: in twentieth century New Orleans there is no goddess of love to invoke and to ingratiate through the sacrifice of a white heifer. Universal compulsions, however, never die. *Agalmatophilia*, for one, has survived the gods' disappearance from Mount Olympus—witness the unequivocally polished breast of a female marble bust on the first landing of the Uffizi staircase.[27] The fact is, in obeisance to one of the major motifs operating in the novel ("Talk, talk, talk: the utter and heartbreaking stupidity of words," 186), Gordon merely *talks* about *agalmatophilia*. Those past followers of Pygmalion who left their shameful marks on the marble forms would not recognize poor, stiff Gordon as one of their own.[28]

Like Démétrios, Frenhofer, Tiburce, Claude Lantier, and all the other modern-age Pygmalions before him who strove to establish their individuality vis-à-vis their remote model, Gordon struggles within the constricting confines of his allotted space, crowded as he is by the overwhelming presence of the original on the one hand and by the impositions of his own context on the other. He must be both recognizable as a variation, and as un-Pygmalion-like as permitted by the net cast toward the future by the prototype over two thousand years ago. Because, as we know, a paradigmatic character achieves its success when the writer neither locks it within the strictures of the type, nor allows it too much free range at the risk of losing sight of the intended direction.

It is precisely as the result of this struggle that the character of Gordon achieves its success. Enough of the original elements are present. First, of course, he is a sculptor; second, he creates a statue that fully expresses his ideal of womanhood; and, third, he entertains an ambiguous rapport with his creation. At the same time, he is clearly endowed with a specific individuality. He is unkempt, gruff, inept in his social exchanges; he drinks his whisky from a cup intended for the shaving cream—a vivid, realistic touch. When suddenly attracted to Pat, in a burst of inconsistency he forgets about his work to run after her; yet he can see the unattainable girl only as a danger to himself: "'She is dark, darker than fire. She is more terrible and beautiful than fire,'" he says and feels powerless before the Gordian knot of his constrained emotions (329).[29] He then gets drunk, momentarily lets himself go in the safety of a brothel, and finally retires to his disorderly loft to hammer away at yet another piece of marble—"or something," as the girl dismissively puts it. None of this, of course, has any relation to the prototype.

Faulkner, however, did not overplay Gordon as the picturesque *artiste maudit*, the admirable depository of creativity under the aegis of rebellious behavior such as the nineteenth century delighted in presenting. Thanks to the pincer movement whereby Pat Robyn and Fairchild introduce a no-nonsense perspective upon the sculptor, Gordon's proclamation is stripped of any smokescreen of conceptual dignity it might have hoped to raise, and is thrown back into the intellectual fog of "talk, talk, talk" that reigns aboard the *Nausikaa*, this symbolic vessel of all foolishness. The ironic light suffusing Faulkner's supposed partial self-portrait discloses the writer's perception of his creation—and, perhaps, of himself. Ultimately, Gordon's pronouncement is not to be swallowed whole as, in their uncritical snobbery, his visitors passively do. It must be understood as a symptom of his fear of woman, a cultural and ideological disease that from time immemorial man has vainly attempted to conceal from himself through escape, violence, impotence, and fantasies of emotional independence. In other words, through the systematic relegation of the woman to one or the other of two imaginary worlds: hell or heaven.

And, more prosaically, through the furtive caresses that, century after century, thousands of anonymous visitors to the Uffizi have been bestowing upon the icy breast of the poor, defenseless Roman matron, unwittingly giving proof of that universal temptation—*agalmatophilia*.

NOTES

1. See Michel Gresset, "Faulkner's Self-Portraits," *Faulkner Journal* 2.1 (Fall 1986): 2–13. According to Hyatt H. Waggoner, "we may discern [Faulkner's voice and sentiments] in the words of . . . Gordon," in *William Faulkner: From Jefferson to the World* (Lexington: University of Kentucky Press, 1959), 16. For Edmund L. Volpe, "on several levels" Gordon and Faulkner "merged successfully," the former representing "one aspect of Faulkner's image of the artist"; cf. *A Reader's Guide to William Faulkner* (London: Thames and Hudson, 1964), 62, 58. See George H. Wolfe: "The bearded sculptor . . . looked something like Faulkner's friend, Bill Spratling," in *Faulkner: Fifty Years after "The Marble Faun,"* ed. George H. Wolfe (Tuscaloosa: University of Alabama Press, 1976), 5. Forty years after the events he related, Spratling wrote: "Bill . . . had just mailed off his text for *Soldiers' Pay*, the novel in which he depicted some of my own traits in one of his characters"; cf. "Chronicle of a Friendship: William Faulkner in New Orleans," in William Spratling and William Faulkner, *Sherwood Anderson and Other Famous Creoles* (Austin: University of Texas Press, 1966), 13; clearly, Spratling was confusing the two novels.

2. See, among others, John T. Matthews: "[Gordon's] sculpting pretends to an ideal of perfect representation and self-expression," in *The Play of Faulkner's Language* (Ithaca: Cornell University Press, 1982), 45; David Minter: "[Gordon] practices deliberate sublimation," in *William Faulkner: His Life and Work* (Baltimore: Johns Hopkins University Press, 1980), 60; Olga W. Vickery: "[Gordon,] the only genuine artist in the group, . . . exists naturally and easily in a state where disguises and fetishes are both impossible and unnecessary," in *The Novels of William Faulkner: A Critical Interpretation* (Baton Rouge: Louisiana State University Press, 1959), 9, 12; André Bleikasten: "perhaps the only authentic artist in the group," in *The Ink of Melancholy: Faulkner's Novels from "The Sound and the Fury" to "Light in August"* (Bloomington: Indiana University Press, 1990), 24. See also Cleanth Brooks, *William Faulkner: Toward Yoknapatawpha and Beyond* (New Haven: Yale University Press, 1978), 134–40; Max Putzel, *Genius of Place: William Faulkner's Triumphant Beginnings* (Baton Rouge: Louisiana State University Press, 1985), 79–90; Lothar Hönnighausen, *Faulkner: Masks and Metaphors* (Jackson: University Press of Mississippi, 1997), 100–02.

3. Cf. "Agalmatofilia, la donna artificiale e la sindrome di Pigmalione," in *Faulkner, ancora* (Bari: Palomar, 2004), 47–144; cf. also "Faulkner's Use of The Song of Solomon in Quentin's Section of *The Sound and the Fury*," in *Études Faulknériennes II: Naissances de Faulkner*, ed. André Bleikasten et al. (Rennes: Presses Universitaires de Rennes, 2000), 55–62 (55). All quotations from Louÿs's novel refer to *Aphrodite. Moeurs antiques* (Paris: Albin Michel, 1986), and will be included parenthetically in the text. Louÿs's novel was translated into English as *Aphrodite: Ancient Manners*.

4. Mme de Burne is "armée de beaux bras faits pour attirer, pour enlacer, pour etreindre, et de jambes . . . faites pour fuir"; Guy de Maupassant, *Notre coeur*, ed. Marie-Claire Banquart (1890; Paris: Gallimard, 1993), 91. Unless otherwise indicated, all translations from French are mine.

5. William Faulkner, *Mosquitoes* (New York: Liveright, 1927), 26. All quotations from the novel refer to this edition. Page references will be given parenthetically in the text.

6. Claus Daüfenbach, "The Aesthetics of Form: Sculpture and Sculptor in *Mosquitoes*," in *The Artist and His Masks: William Faulkner's Metafiction*, ed. Agostino Lombardo (Roma: Bulzoni, 1991), 81.

7. Charles Baudelaire, "L'école païenne" (1852), in *Oeuvres*, ed. Y.-G. Le Dantec (Paris: Bibliothéque de la Pléiade-Gallimard, 1954), 979; for Baudelaire, the prevailing antiquarian taste could produce only "un pastiche inutile et dégoûtant." Henry James followed suit,

branding Flaubert's *Salammbô* (1862) as "an archeological novel of the highest pretensions," *French Poets and Novelists* (London: Macmillan, 1884), 199.

8. Louÿs delighted in intertextual allusions. In *Aphrodite*, two such diversions are heralded by proper names lest the allusion go unnoticed. Démétrios, who is "beau comme Apollon" (43), destroys Chrysis; in the Iliad, Apollon saves Chryseis, the daughter of his priest Chryses. The name of Chrysis's rival from whom Démétrios must steal the precious object is Bacchis; in Gautier's "La châine d'or" (1837), a courtesan's would-be lover must steal a precious object from her rival, whose name is Bacchide. Significantly, Maupassant, who despised the current archeological taste, had his Olivier Bertin reach success by meeting the demand for this "art démodé" with a painting of Cleopatra, a favorite subject throughout the 1800s (cf. *Fort comme la mort* [1889; Paris: Gallimard, 1983] 269, 33). Deploring "all the elaborate Orientalism with which," as he put it, "we are deluged nowadays in painting" (*The Painter's Eye. Notes and Essays on the Pictorial Arts by Henry James*, ed. John L. Sweeney [London: Hart-Davis, 1956], 188), James placed the statue of Cleopatra by his friend W. W. Story in the context of the epochal taste for "the romantic, the anecdotic, the supposedly historic, the explicitly pathetic," and could not bring himself to speak of it in more positive terms than as "admirable" and "living"; cf. *William Wetmore Story and His Friends* (Boston: Houghton, Mifflin, 1903), vol. 2, 77, 217, 216. Cleopatra also appears in *Aphrodite* as Bérénice's perverse younger sister. For the fortune of Cleopatra as an artistic subject, see *Cléopâtre dans le miroir de l'art occidental* (Geneva: Musée Rath, 2004).

9. This paradox is not present in Ovid, as his Pygmalion has no model for Galatea. In Pliny's account of Apelles, instead, the artist has a model, Pancaspe, whom he then chooses over his portrait. The shift of interest in the Pygmalion's story from a paradigm focused on sexuality to one focused on the conflict between life and artistic creation seems to be the result of a modern grafting of Pliny's story onto Ovid's.

10. The only explanation that Louÿs offers for Démétrios's rejection of the live model is a sudden impotence: as acknowledged by the sculptor, it is the queen's "beauté *vivante*" (italics added) that now renders him impotent (104). Neither the character nor the narrating voice seems aware that this impotence may be creative rather than erotic.

11. Théophile Gautier, *Mademoiselle de Maupin*, ed. Geneviève van der Bogaert (1835; Paris: Flammarion, 1999), 155. ". . . surfeit or disgust, following victory": *Psyche*, Louÿs's final novel, published posthumously in 1927, confirms the difficulty of his protagonists to develop an enduring relationship even with the most desirable woman.

12. Théophile Gautier, *La morte amoureuse, Avatar et autre récits fantastiques*, ed. Jean Gaudon (Paris: Gallimard, 1981), 97.

13. "Ilda," in *Oeuvres de Albert Samain* (Paris: Mercure de France, 1924), vol. 2, 81. See Walter Pater on the "Medusa of the Uffizii": "Leonardo alone . . . realizes it as the head of a corpse. . . . What may be called the fascination of corruption penetrates in every touch of its exquisitely finished beauty," in "Leonardo da Vinci: Homo minister et interpres naturae," in *Three Major Texts (The Renaissance, Appreciations, and Imaginary Portraits)*, ed. William E. Buckler (New York: New York University Press, 1986), 138–39.

14. Joris-Karl Huysmans, *À rebours*, ed. Marco Fumaroli (1884; Paris: Gallimard, 1977), 145–46.

15. Euripides, "Helen," in *Helen, Phoenician* (Cambridge: Harvard University Press, 2002), 31–36. William Shakespeare, *Measure for Measure* III.ii.42–46.

16. Among the innumerable painters, sculptors, and engravers who through the centuries created representations of Pygmalion, we may mention Angiolo Bronzino, Louis Gauffier, Louis-Jean-François Lagrenée, Jean-Léon Gérome, Giulio Bargellini. In 1971, Hungarian artist and photographer Gyula Halász, known as Brassaï, sculpted in Carrara marble a Galatée that, like Gordon's torso, is headless, armless, and legless; unlike it, and unlike Pat Robyn, this Galatea is endowed with very prominent breasts. (In the beginning of October 2006, at the Drout Montaigne auction, Halàsz's *Galatée* was sold for the record figure of €58,000.) Another example of the persistence of this model is a painting by Adolf Hartmann, dated [19]56, now in a private gallery in Padua, which shows sculptor Bernhard Heiliger staring at the marble bust of a woman similarly headless, armless, and legless.

17. Among these exceptions, cf. Giovanni di Carlo Strozzi's epigram about Michelange-lo's *Notte* and that of Buonarroti in answer to it, in both of which the statue comes alive but there is no overt trace of *agalmatophilia* nor of a real-life model. Cf. Michelangelo Buonar-roti, *Rime*, ed. Ettore Barelli, introd. Giovanni Testori (Milan: Rizzoli, 1975), 281.

18. Sergio Perosa, "Galatea distrugge Pigmalione," *Atti dell'Istituto Veneto di Scienze, Lettere ed Arti*, 162 (2002–2003), 1–18.

19. Oliver Wendell Holmes's novel is partly a rework of the anecdote, related by Pliny the Elder, concerning Apelles and Alexander the Great. Apelles was commissioned by Alexander to paint a portrait of Pancaspe, the emperor's favorite, but exchanged his artwork for the woman. Pliny omitted to record whether Pancaspe was consulted.

20. Gregorio Manzur, "L'Andalou," *Contre-Ciel* (February 1985): 50–53.

21. Luigi Supino, *La vera storia di Galatea*, introd. Dino Buzzati (Milan: Ceschina, 1962). For a discussion of *Pygmalion and Galatea. A Mythological Comedy* by Sir William S. Gilbert (1871), an early comic variation including the artist, his wife, and a statue first turned into a live woman and then transformed back into a statue, cf. Perosa, 16–18.

22. Joris-Karl, *Là-bas* (1891; Paris: Stock, 1904), 258.

23. Honoré de Balzac, "Sarrasine," *La comédie humaine*, ed. Marcel Bouteron (Paris: Bib-liothèque de la Pléiade-Gallimard, 1950), vol. 6, 96.

24. Guy de Maupassant, *La vie errante* (1890; Paris: Conard, 1926), 124.

25. Thomas Lovell Beddoes, "Pygmalion. The Cyprian Statuary," in *Plays and Poems of Thomas Lovell Beddoes*, ed. H. W. Donner (London: Routledge and Kegan Paul, 1963), 192–96, v. 176.

26. Jean de Meun, *Le roman de la rose*, ed. Francisque-Michel (Paris: Librairie de Firmin Didot, 1864), vol. 2, vv. 21837–38.

27. By their own admission, analogous attentions were paid by Ugo Foscolo to the Me-dici Venus in the Uffizi, by Flaubert to the copy of Canova's "Psyche" in Villa Sommariva in Como and to a "tronçon de torse" at the Acropolis, and by Maupassant and Comisso to the Venus in the Archeological Museum in Siracusa. Cf. Ugo Foscolo, *Epistolario*, ed. Plinio Carli (Florence: Le Monnier, 1954), vol. 4 (1812–1813), 177–78; Gustave Flaubert, "Voyage en Italie," in *Oeuvre de jeunesse. Oeuvres complètes*, ed. Claudine Gothot-Mersch and Guy Sagnes (Paris: Bibliothèque de la Pléiade-Gallimard, 2001), vol. 1, 1011, and letter to Louis Bouilhet of February 10, 1851, in *Oeuvres complètes de Gustave Flaubert, Correspondance*, deuxiéme série (1847–1852), Paris: Conard, 1926, 298–99; Guy de Maupassant, *La vie er-rante*, 119, 121, 122; Giovanni Comisso, *Il grande ozio* (Milan: Longanesi, 1964), 246. In 1819, after just two months of being on display in the collection of the Prince Regent (George IV, a year later), Canova's *The Fountain Nymph* (now in the Queen's Collection) had to be protected from similar attentions by means of a spiked brass fence.

28. Plinio, *Storia naturale, Mineralogia e storia dell'arte. Libri xxxiii-xxxvii*, ed. and trans. Antonio Corso et al. (Turin: Einaudi, 1988), vol. 5, 21.546–49; Lucian, "Affairs of the Heart," in *Lucian*, trans. M. D. MacLeod (London: Heinemann, 1967), vol. 8, 13–16, 171–75. André Chénier subsumed this motif in his "Jeune homme fou par amour," in *Oeuvres complètes*, ed. Gérard Walter (Paris: Bibliothèque de la Pléiade-Gallimard, 1959), 521.

29. The present occasion does not permit extending this discussion to fire, the comple-mentary traditional metaphor applied to the woman. See my *Faulkner, ancora*, 112–14, passim.

Almost Feminine, Almost Brother, Almost Southern: The Transnational Queer Figure of Charles Bon in Faulkner's *Absalom, Absalom!*

ELIZABETH STEEBY

Perhaps more than any of his other works, William Faulkner's 1936 plantation novel *Absalom, Absalom!* is a global tale mapped onto scenes of intimacy. In this novel, Faulkner's penchant for blurring lines of longitude and latitude, for merging stories with histories, has far-reaching implications. My focus here is on that tension between the intimate and the worldly, the local and the foreign, which structures how and where characters come to be locatable within this text. Desire and narrative work to produce one another, both within the novel and in the larger historical context that frames it. This dialectical relationship between desire and the discursive has particular implications for two of the novel's most crucial elements: Haiti and Charles Bon. Through Haiti and Bon, Faulkner constructs narratives of desire that work to queer the relationship between the local and the foreign(er). Like the novel's narrators, I will return to Bon throughout as the cosmopolitan queer who continually evades an easy reading and who explodes this sutured body of stories throughout.[1] In performing a queer reading of Bon and the symbolic meaning of his ties to Haiti, I stress the value of mining the texts of Faulkner and other members of the Southern canon for their representations of the multiplicity and intersectionality of identity, for thinking of ways in which the "almost" quality that so characterizes Charles Bon might continue to invigorate debates about identity and language.

My discussion of Charles Bon necessarily begins with a recontextualization: the significant, but not often considered historical events involving Haiti that surrounded the publishing date of this novel. *Absalom, Absalom!* was published in 1936, on the heels of the United States' nearly twenty-year military occupation of Haiti, which began in 1915 and ended in 1934. Mary Renda characterizes this as a time when "U.S. Americans who presided over, visited, or read about Haiti found opportunities to reimagine their own nation and their own lives as they appeared to be reflected by and

refracted through Haitian history and culture."[2] Faulkner's novel then joined
the ranks of popular cultural and literary texts whose narratives mapped
imaginary sites of burgeoning U.S. imperialism. Mary Renda claims that
the occupation of Haiti was an event that would not only determine the
fate of Haiti in the twentieth century but would palpably alter the ways in
which race, gender, sexuality, and nation were reformulated and deployed
within the U.S.

I situate the novel's nineteenth-century slave-era transplantation and incorporation of Haitians into a U.S. national framework (and in particular,
into a Southern regional framework) in relation to the twentieth-century
U.S. imperialism, which attempted to "ingest a territory, or another nation
in the case of Haiti, without allowing it to become too obviously a part of
the nation or the national culture."[3] In *Absalom, Absalom!* Faulkner depicts Haiti as the site where the "ur-planter" Thomas Sutpen goes to make
his fortune, and more importantly where he goes to learn to manage a
plantation supported by violently policed slave labor.[4] Rather than locating
Supten's training and his imperial plantation design in the nineteenth century, I argue that he may be read as a twentieth-century U.S. marine, an
ambassador of U.S. military and culture, who looks to Haiti to provide resources and raw materials in the service of U.S. empire-building. A wife,
Eulalia, and a son, Charles Bon, are to work in the service of that project
as the foundations of a family dynasty. Instead of fulfilling their roles, however, Bon and his mother ultimately complicate Sutpen's project as a result
of a "misrepresentation of such a crass nature as to have not only voided
and frustrated without his knowing it the central motivation of the entire
design" (211).[5] Bon, rather than becoming a legitimate heir, becomes the
symbolic product of imperial desire whose ambiguous identity works toward the dissolution of the very building blocks of empire itself.

As Renda acknowledges, two central discourses dominated depictions
and imaginings of Haiti during the occupation: the discourses of paternalism and exoticism. These twentieth-century imperialist discourses involved both disavowal of Haitian independence and right to self-rule and
misrecognition of racial, sexual, and gendered identities that defied normative white American heterosexual constructs. As this novel reminds us,
these imperialist practices of disavowal and misrecognition had historical roots in the system of slavery in the South. Within the polarized racial constructions of the antebellum U.S. South, slaves were discursively
rendered as children in need of white paternalism while the paternity of
"mulatto" slave children was systematically disavowed by white planters.
By the time of *Absalom*'s publication in the 1930s, Jim Crow segregation
policies elided histories of miscegenation and the institutionalized rape of

black women, histories that would have disrupted dominant constructions of race, in favor of artificial notions of "pure" and "impure" blood. Additionally, in the early decades of the twentieth century, emergent discourses of sexuality and race were increasingly co-constitutive. Consequently, the policing of whiteness was often most virulent in scenarios coded as sexually charged.[6] The white Southern family, which appeared as a monolith, was, in actuality, a well-guarded myth. Faulkner's novel then engages with both the larger national/imperial depictions of black Haitians and with the U.S. regional political and social constructions of race and sexuality.[7]

This essay aims to address two central questions regarding Faulkner's take on Haiti: How does Faulkner's reworking of these paternalist and exoticist discourses under the rubric of the Southern regional specificities complicate the inclusion of the Haitian "other" in the national framework? How do Haitians become (contested) "Americans" and "Southerners" in *Absalom*? In order to address these questions, I begin with the genesis of Sutpen's family and fortune. As a result of Sutpen's successful conquest of black Haitians, his infamous "design" is set into motion in two important ways: his conquest of black Haitians garners him a wife, Eulalia, the daughter of the afflicted planter, and eventually he procures black Caribbean slaves who will construct his own plantation on Mississippi soil. Faulkner's intricately layered modernist novel centers around Bon, the product of Sutpen's abbreviated marriage to Eulalia, who embodies the symbolic instability "racial mixing" brings to rigid notions of color lines and who transgresses heavily policed markers of gender, sexuality, race, and nation. Bon, who is *only* ever discursively rendered and never "seen" or "heard" by the narrators, is figured as both racially and sexually exotic and is therefore contested as child/son under white Southern paternalism. But even as Bon then is written as outsider, as "other," he is a Sutpen and therefore, in part, a Southerner. In his various incarnations, Bon is coded as exoticized French Creole, black Haitian male, seducer of men and women, but he is also son/brother Sutpen and therefore inextricably part of a Southern family genealogy whose obsession with racial "purity" is based on misrecognition, misrepresentation, and violent exclusion. As a transnational subject of the Americas whose racial status potentially defies strict black/white binaries and who can be read as queer, Bon poses the ultimate threat to the reproduction of a "white" Sutpen line, the "white" Southern family *writ large*. Bon is simultaneously the outsider subaltern who, by virtue of Sutpen's "occupation" of a Haitian plantation, has been violently *ingested* but not wholly *included* in the larger U.S. American family.

In this novel, which is intrinsically and unavoidably revisionist with its overlapping narratives and narrators who ceaselessly add onto, retract, and

repeat their own words and the words of others, Bon is the character who
seems to be most impacted by this revision as he undergoes a kind of re-
incarnation as each narrative unfolds. The novel's historian character, Rosa
Coldfield, first distinguishes Bon as an outsider by constructing him as
cosmopolitan subject, ambiguously identified with Creole Louisiana and
with the *world*. Though the novel is narrated primarily from a dorm room
at Harvard University in Cambridge, Massachusetts, by Quentin Compson and his Canadian roommate Shreve McCannon, the figure of Bon has
not only topographical mobility but social mobility as well. His "foreign"
origin and worldly experiences are unintelligible within the white Southern framework of rural Mississippi. In Rosa Coldfield's early narration to
Quentin, Bon emerges as "Charles Bon of New Orleans, . . . —a young
man of a worldly elegance and assurance beyond his years, handsome, apparently wealthy and with for background the shadowy figure of a legal
guardian rather than any parents—a personage who in the remote Mississippi of that time must have appeared almost phoenix-like, fullsprung
from no childhood, born of no woman and impervious to time" (58). Narrators throughout the novel continually attempt to locate Bon, but, like
Rosa here, they often find Bon to be a paradoxical figure. In this passage,
Rosa first identifies Bon with the creolized, transnational port city New Orleans, a destination for many post-Revolution white Haitians and creoles
of color.[8] New Orleans is representative of the stratified codes of race and
gender prevalent under French colonial culture and the European colonization of the extended Caribbean South. Rosa prefigures Bon as someone
too old, too cosmopolitan to be in this "New World," whose status in the
world will be determined not by birthparents but by the law. That a man
of no known origin or parentage must be guarded by the law is indicative
of the ways that U.S. and Southern laws appropriate racial taxonomies in
order to delineate those who will have access to legal rights and citizenship
and those who will not. By aging Bon, then, Rosa is articulating multiple
anxieties: that those more elastic conceptualizations of race still linger and
are traveling via Bon outside New Orleans into "remote Mississippi"; and
further, that Bon, parentless and motherless, seems not to have been produced by normative heterosexual union. Instead, Bon's origins here are
queer and mythic.

Though Bon is initially associated with New Orleans, his origins eventually shift and retrace transnational migrations from the West Indies to
the U.S. South. The extended South is made to include Haiti, which, like
Bon, is depicted as "too old" in some sense to fit neatly into a U.S. national
framework and so its imperial ingestion is marked by violence.[9] Quentin's
grandfather depicts Haiti (via Mr. Compson and later Quentin) as un-

moored and mobile, as "of the Americas" then as "a little lost island in a latitude which would require ten thousand years of equatorial heritage to bear its climate, a soil manured with black blood from two hundred years of oppression and exploitation" (202).[10] Charles Bon, as part-Haitian, part-Southern progeny, is similarly unlocatable in time or space. Rosa's depiction of him as "phoenix-like" ultimately aligns him with the mythical legacy of the burnt ashes of postplantation Haiti, which "impervious to time," continues to challenge U.S. imperialism in the twentieth century, just as it resisted nineteenth-century French colonial rule. Through the miscegenated, queered, transnational figure of Bon, racial paradigms that undergirded imperial designs are destabilized and disrupted by histories of contestation. In *Absalom*, New Orleans then becomes a kind of surrogate for an unmoored, mobile Haiti, as it is geographically (if dubiously) intelligible within U.S. American borders. The city serves as a link between U.S. South and the extended South.

Bon's notions of race and gender are constructed in direct relation to French colonial sex practices in this New Orleans context. In a scene in which Henry and Bon visit a New Orleans brothel, a symbolic impenetrable wall is opened for Bon by a "swarthy man resembling a creature out of an old woodcut of the French Revolution" with whom Bon speaks French, a language incomprehensible to Henry, who is designated as "an American" distinctly foreign in this New Orleans space (89). Bon considers Henry to be a guest rather than a native of this place, and so negates the assumption that this territory has been, or is being, Americanized, placed within U.S. national borders. According to our narrators, Henry as the American Southerner struggles when confronted with these differences, with experiences that are outside of his limited cultural knowledge, while Bon moves about the world with relative ease. For example, Henry is unable to fathom Bon's relationship with a quadroon woman. Consequently, Henry and Bon's experience together in New Orleans results in apprehension and a crisis of logic: "You give me two and two and you tell me it makes five and it does make five," says Henry (94). Bon has shown Henry a space in which relationships and constructions of identity are ordered quite differently from Jefferson, Mississippi, and Henry assumes that something is missing from that equation. The narrators will ultimately suggest that what is missing is the black surrogation of Bon in his construction of New Orleans and his West Indian, or more specifically, Haitian Creole identity. Shreve in particular concludes that, without "blackness," Henry's South is without order or logic. However, the sameness of the homosocial bond between the two men presents no such crisis for Henry. Therefore, we might also consider that the one piece missing from the two plus two equals five equation is the place that might be occupied, if unnamed, by the love between Henry and Bon.

In the case of the U.S.'s twentieth-century discourse on Haiti, Renda argues: "With regard to sexuality, the discourse of exoticism, so essential to resolving the tension between nation and empire, contributed to the reshaping of sexual norms and representations."[11] As the desired Other in the novel, Bon exemplifies this discursive tension between the domestic and the foreign. He functions as the magnetic, influential figure whose difference is acknowledged and (initially) welcomed. He becomes objectified and feminized by the Sutpen family and by the students at the University of Mississippi, who seem dangerously drawn to him. Rosa tells Quentin that Ellen Sutpen "spoke of Bon as if he were three inanimate objects in one or perhaps one inanimate object for which she and her family would find three concordant uses: a garment which Judith might wear as she would a riding habit or a ball gown, a piece of furniture which would complement and complete the furnishing of her house and position, and a mentor and example to correct Henry's provincial manners and speech and clothing" (59). If Bon is a garment, a dress, for Judith, then he is a feminized object, transgressing normative gender roles, while significantly being positioned as Henry's mentor and role model. As a piece of furniture that would insure Judith's class status, Bon might be read as both exoticized and racialized other: as property, he functions to buttress white plantation culture as did slave labor; as fetishized object, he becomes sexualized adornment to white culture as did "mulattos" and "quadroons" in the colonial Caribbean and New Orleans. Beyond Sutpen's Hundred, at Ole Miss, he is likewise described as "reclining in a flowered, almost feminised gown," object of wonderment for the "entire undergraduate body of that small new provincial college" (76).[12] "Almost feminine" throughout much of the novel, Bon challenges constructions of masculinity held by the untraveled "country boys," and so becomes dangerous, not simply because of his presence beyond the boundaries of New Orleans, but because the "hinterlands" are impressionable. He is literally traveling from the metropole to the marginal space of the newly developed white South. If New Orleans represents colonial decadence, it also represents a space where the theatricality of gender is called attention to in festivals that celebrate masking and cross-dressing.[13] The extravagance and wealth implicit in Bon's feminization seems to be a component of the influence he wields, but significantly he also challenges normative constructions of Southern masculinity.

Though Bon's heterosexuality and masculinity would potentially be reassured and stabilized via his engagement to Judith Sutpen, his ties to

Judith are called into question even as they are established. Though Rosa tells Quentin that she and Ellen Sutpen had an assumption of Bon and Judith's engagement, "Ellen did not once mention love between Judith and Bon" (59). This heterosexual union is precluded by an unknown, unspoken event, an unnamed "something" that "happened": "Nobody knew what: whether something between Henry and Bon on one hand and Judith on the other, or between the three young people on one hand and the parents on the other" (62). The supposition that the unknown event may have actually occurred between Henry and Bon, not between Judith and Bon, is reinforced by the homoerotic intimacy between the two men. From the start, the storytellers remind the listeners that Henry ultimately sacrificed all his inheritance and privilege for Bon, and this is paired with assurances that the monumental seduction occurred between Bon and Henry: "Yes, he loved Bon, who seduced him as surely as he seduced Judith—the country boy born and bred who, with the five or six others of that small undergraduate body composed of other planters' sons whom Bon permitted to become intimate with him" (76). Though as we have seen, the love and seduction between Judith and Bon has already been called into question, the love between Bon and Henry (at least Bon's seduction of Henry, and Henry's resultant love for Bon) is reinforced by multiple layerings of narration while Judith's role is effectively evacuated.

As Eve Sedgwick argues, male homoerotic components of nineteenth-century British literature collapsed into competition for the love of a woman.[14] Accordingly the relationship between Bon and Henry is transposed onto the abstraction of Judith. Mr. Compson relays to Quentin: "She was just the blank shape, the empty vessel in which each of them strove to preserve, not the illusion of himself nor his illusion of the other but what each conceived the other to believe him to be—the man and the youth, seducer and seduced, who had known one another, seduced and been seduced, victimised in turn each by the other, conquerer vanquished by his own strength, vanquished conquering by his own weakness, before Judith came into their joint lives even by so much as girlname" (95). We may consider this as a moment in which the roles of "Bon" and "Henry" are destabilized. Judith Butler's reading of Nella Larsen's *Passing* provides an important context for the role of queering in literature "as the exposure within language—an exposure that disrupts the repressive surface of language—of both sexuality and race."[15] Much of the laborious writing and rewriting, telling and retelling in this novel calls attention to the inadequacies of language, to the epistemological fissures that occur when attempting to render identities and relationships that signify illusory rather than solid boundaries. Judith, who could be any "girlname," becomes the space where Henry and Bon preserve their union, the seduction that necessarily is as much a struggle as the words that try to convey that union.

Because Bon is ultimately racialized as a black character who has "passed," we have to reread (as the novel is constantly requiring the reader to do) the desire that Judith and Henry project onto Bon as racialized as well. As a modernist text, Faulkner's novel is very much concerned with ocular centrism and the ways in which desire is racialized and gendered. Henry's vision is transposed onto Judith's and together they create an image of Bon: "She must have seen him in fact with exactly the same eyes that Henry saw him with. And it would be hard to say to which of them he appeared the more splendid—to the one with hope, even though unconscious, of making the image hers through possession; to the other with the knowledge, even though subconscious to the desire, of the insurmountable barrier which the similarity of gender hopelessly intervened" (75, 76). This typically disjointed Faulknerian syntax disallows for a "straight," or linear, reading of Judith's or Henry's desire for Bon. Again, Butler's reading of passing in Larsen's novel is useful in examining the relationship among race, sexuality, and language: "Queering is what upsets and exposes passing; it is the act by which the racially and sexually repressive surface of conversation is exploded, by rage, by sexuality, by the insistence on color."[16] In many ways "knowledge" seems to be the "other" in this passage, constituted by an unnamed "insurmountable barrier" that may or may not be defied by or constitutive of "the similarity of gender." If Henry's desire for Bon is subconscious, then he has in some way access to knowledge of that desire, but compulsory heterosexuality would disallow for the conscious realization of that desire. Because Bon is "that black son of a bitch" at the conclusion of the novel, we reread this passage as queering the familial and engaging in the quite typical sexualization and eroticization of many "mulatto" characters in nineteenth- and twentieth-century literature. Bon as "almost (mulatto) feminine" then is figured as "whore," as the New Orleans quadroons are deemed degenerate by Henry. What we "know" at the conclusion of the novel is that the insurmountable barrier between Henry and Bon is potentially built upon familial, racial, sexual, and national boundaries. What "queering" upsets in this passage is the "repressive surface of conversation" that prevents speaking directly of those who challenge normative constructions of identity; queering exposes Bon's multiple "passings" and calls attention to the instability and fallibility of those boundaries.

Bon as outsider or "other" is narrated as forebodingly fatalistic throughout. But the lingering central question of the novel still remains difficult to answer: why did Charles Bon have to die? More specifically, why did Henry Sutpen have to kill him? As John Howard reminds us: "historically the notion of brotherhood often stood in for, or alongside, queer desire."[17] However, even when coded as "brotherhood," representations of queer desire often ended in the death of characters who acted upon those desires. Faulkner's novel, while it complicates this conventionally tragic narrative, also employs its central conventions. Henry and Bon find themselves in an emotional and physical duel upon their return to Sutpen'sHundred at the close of the Civil War.[18] The potential marriage between Bon and Judith, now presumably signifies miscegenation and incest to Henry, but also a repudiation of the beyond-brotherly love between the two men. "*Think of her. Not of me: of her,*" Henry urges Bon.[19] Bon replies: "*I have. For four years. Of you and her. Now I am thinking of myself*" (285). If heteronormativity relies on the assertion of gender difference, this scene reveals a certain defiance of that. Henry seems to require Bon to separate his concern for him (Henry) from his concern for Judith, but Bon sees them as intrinsically linked. Henry reasserts their fraternity and consequently their "similarity of gender": "*You are my brother,*" but Bon responds: "*No I'm not. I'm the nigger that's going to sleep with your sister. Unless you stop me, Henry*" (286). In Shreve and Quentin's telling, as Henry affirms his possession of Bon, Bon disavows their bond and instead acknowledges his status as twin threat to Henry: he will be guilty of miscegenation and he will be intimate with her who is ultimately *not-Henry*. Up until this point, Henry has sacrificed all to keep Bon close and has cultivated their homofamilial intimacy of brother/lover. However, when Henry kills Bon, he prevents Bon's inclusion into the Sutpen line as brother/husband, and what follows is the dissolution of Sutpen's imperialistic dynasty.

Many fascinating readings of this novel have explored the causes for Bon's exclusion. I have aimed to supplement those readings and to further recontextualize Bon as a transgressive figure through whom competing and complimentary discourses are filtered. In this novel, the Sutpen family, which I have suggested we consider in light of U.S. empire building, acts as a symbolic institution within which gender and racial difference structure power. As Butler asserts, "the symbolic domain, the domain of socially instituted norms, is composed of racializing norms, and . . . they exist not merely alongside gender norms, but are articulated through one another. Hence it is no longer possible to make sexual difference prior to racial difference or, for that matter, to make them into fully separable axes of social regulation and power."[20] Faulkner uses Charles Bon's character to interrogate those intersecting axes of social regulation and power. As Bon alternately signifies French colonialism/revolution, New Orleans Creole, black Haitian, feminized man, seducer of men/women/sister/brother, he crosses the various boundaries imagined by the community of the white South of the nineteenth and twentieth centuries. In some sense then, his mobility across borders is stopped to prevent his double inclusion into a Southern family that denied his right to recognition and privilege. As in Faulkner's novel, the ongoing relationship between the U.S. and Haiti in the nineteenth and twentieth centuries, and between the U.S. South and this extended South, is undergirded and contested through constant re-imaginings and reformulations of Haiti as child, as threat, and as seducer.

Bon's status as "mysterious stranger" must ultimately be positioned in relation to both nineteenth-century norms as well as twentieth-century discourses of the Haitian imperial subject, as representations of race increasingly hinged upon notions of gender and sexuality. In the novel, Bon's nonnormative performance of gender is then compounded with a queer sexual performance, rendering his radical alterity unassimilable into the regional or national family. Bon seduces the Southern Sutpen family, but then is construed as a national outsider and ultimately a racial outsider. As the layered narrations progress from Bon's nonnormative gender to his sexuality to his national origins and finally to his racial status, all of these classifications are ultimately collapsed into Shreve's pronouncement of Bon's "blackness." However, the presumed finality of this racial alterity by no means erases the previous constructions of Bon as outside of the national or the heteronormative, and so these various transgressions must be reread as interrelated and intersecting, rather than as explanations consistently offered and then abandoned in favor of the "real" reason for Bon's exclusion. The various narrators' desire to know and to locate Bon continually necessitates a retelling. Bon's dangerous position as the intimate outsider ultimately works to queer an emergent twentieth-century U.S. imperial discourse that was anything but stable.

NOTES

1. Other recent generative queer readings of this novel include Norman Jones's "Coming Out through History's Hidden Love Letters in *Absalom, Absalom!*," *American Literature* 76.2 (2004): 339–66.

2. Mary Renda, *Taking Haiti: Military Occupation and the Culture of U.S. Imperialism, 1915–1940* (Chapel Hill: University of North Carolina Press, 2001), 20.

3. Ibid., 22.

4. Much insightful scholarship has been done by Richard Godden and others on the nineteenth-century legacy of the Haitian Revolution in this novel, as Faulkner contentiously and anachronistically positions Sutpen's quelling of a Haitian plantation slave rebellion in 1827, at a time when historically there were no Haitian "slaves," as such. I am taking Faulkner's "mistake" as a cue then to consider the recurring histories of exploitation and imperialism in

Haiti as extending beyond 1804 or 1827, well into the twentieth century. Bon's transnational identity becomes particularly threatening for the reproduction of the white Southern family and nation as it carries the memory of the defeat of white colonialism.

5. All citations from *Absalom, Absalom!*, Vintage International Edition, New York, 1990.

6. See Siobhan Somerville's *Queering the Color Line: Race and the Invention of Homosexuality in American Culture* (Durham: Duke University Press, 2000).

7. I argue that Faulkner's *Absalom* confronts the articulation of these paternalistic and exoticizing discourses in the context of early twentieth-century U.S. occupation of Haiti as well as in the nineteenth-century context in which it is traditionally read.

8. In her reading of *Absalom*, Barbara Ladd situates New Orleans as the pivotal locus for white Southern (and U.S. national) contestation of strategies of assimilation versus segregation of colonized populations of color. The structures of political, economic, and social power under French colonialism allowed for more diversified constructions of race and gender than the strict black/white binaries of U.S. and Southern codified systems of power. See *"The Direction of the Howling": Nationalism and the Color Line in "Absalom, Absalom!"* (345–72) and *Subjects and Citizens: Nation, Race, and Gender from Oroonoko to Anita Hill*, ed. Michael Moon and Cathy Davidson (Durham: Duke University Press, 1995).

9. As Vera Kutzinski states, "New Orleans has functioned historically and imaginatively as link between the United States and the West Indies, that problematic territory even more south," *The New Centennial Review* 1.2 (2001): 55–88.

10. Kutzinski asserts, "Haiti, unable to be contained geographically and temporally, becomes an archetype grafted onto those other spaces where it leaves traces of Jacobean rebellion and spreads cultural Africanisms of various kinds that, surreptitiously but persistently, call into doubt paradigms that encode and disseminate beliefs in racial purity, as well as attempts to separate the edifice of white culture from its foundation of slave labor" (66).

11. Renda, 22.

12. Consider here the double entendre of his influencing both the collective "undergraduate body" and the literally male bodies of its students.

13. Joseph Roach, *Cities of the Dead: Circum-Atlantic Performance*. (New York: Columbia University Press, 1996).

14. *Epistemology of the Closet* (Berkeley: University of California Press, 1990).

15. Judith Butler, "Passing, Queering: Nella Larsen's Psychoanalytic Challenge," in *Bodies that Matter: On the Discursive Limits of "Sex"* (New York: Routledge, 1993), 176.

16. Ibid., 177.

17. *Men Like That: A Southern Queer History* (Chicago: University of Chicago Press, 1999), 190.

18. The Civil War did not resolve the conflict for them, as perhaps the fatalist Bon imagined that it might. We might also think about Bon's war service in relation to the proliferation of "conscription" and militaristic discourses surrounding the twentieth-century U.S. occupation of Haiti. See Renda.

19. I would argue that the implicit plea is a repetition of Henry's earlier plea to Bon: "*I did that for love of you; do this for love of me*" (92).

20. Butler, 182.

Fear of a Black Atlantic? African Passages in *Absalom, Absalom!* and *The Last Slaver*

JEFF KAREM

From anxieties about slave revolts in San Domingo, to plans for a sphere of influence, to schemes for outright colonization, the United States has looked to its southern neighbor, the Caribbean, with both horror and desire, attributing to the region fecundity and refinement to be envied, but also miscegenation, primitivism, and violence to be feared. In William Faulkner's work, this connection is similarly conflicted, as the Caribbean (particularly the Latin Caribbean) resonates both as a register of difference and as an uncanny double for the South. In recent years, with the rise of globally directed American studies, many excellent critics, among them Éduoard Glissant, Vera Kutzinski, and John T. Matthews, have directed substantial attention to unraveling the role that the Caribbean and the Black Atlantic, more generally, plays in Faulkner's work.[1] Such scholarship usually claims that Faulkner offers a critique of hemispheric imperialism in the islands (both European and American) comparable to his searing examination of racial politics within his home region of Mississippi. Maritza Stanchich finds that "Faulkner's portrayal of Haiti . . . solidly links the curse of Southern slavery with the curse of American imperialism."[2] John T. Matthews argues that the Haitian connection in *Absalom, Absalom!* "signals a persistence of historical knowledge that survives even the effort to shut one's eyes to it."[3] While I agree that Faulkner's Caribbean and Atlantic glances do "recall," in Matthews's words, hemispheric connections that are often ignored, I assert that Faulkner's vision of the Caribbean and Africa simultaneously evades such specific "historical knowledge," in favor of a mythic projection of guilt that is symbolically rich but historically impoverished. I present archival findings from the manuscript history of *Absalom, Absalom!* (1936) and the screenplay *The Last Slaver* (1936) to show how Faulkner's handling of the Caribbean and the Black Atlantic both recalls and obscures these regions.

In *Absalom, Absalom!* the Caribbean is both overdetermined and under-represented at the same time. The dangerous and fertile Caribbean is both Sutpen's mentor and his nemesis, a source of wealth and a source of contamination: there he learns the slave trade and passes into manhood, and there he fathers the (possibly) mulatto son who will later ruin his plans for a Southern dynasty. At the same time, the Caribbean past within the text is disembodied, abstract, and unvoiced—not a single unmediated word is transmitted from those episodes; rather it descends through many layers of Compson family narrators.[4] The attenuated origin of the West Indian story cautions us against treating these passages as Faulkner's attempt to evoke a reliable historical reclamation of that regional connection. Similarly, critics should resist the temptation to use Sutpen as a figure intended to represent the South as a whole. Although Stanchich and Matthews situate Sutpen's Haitian past as emblematic of the conflicted relationship between the U.S. and the Caribbean,[5] Sutpen is presented as an outsider and arriviste in *Absalom, Absalom!* Using a marginal white figure like Sutpen to establish this West Indies connection confirms a connection between the wealth of the U.S. and that region, while evading the direct historical juxtaposition of Caribbean and Southern slavery that might result from comparing a Haitian plantation to that of the Compsons, the Stevenses, or some other first family of the region.

At first glance, there may seem to be a distinct tension here between Faulkner's use of Haiti as both an overdetermined proving ground and an underrepresented, or even unrepresentable, Other, but these two qualities are actually complimentary: it is precisely because the region is not locatable as a historical space within the novel (indeed, it is a historical impossibility—Sutpen could not have been serving as a plantation master in Haiti, where slavery had been outlawed in the Haitian Constitution of 1804[6]) that it can serve as such a capacious symbolic reserve. Faulkner's process of revision surrounding these Caribbean passages confirms a design to use the region as a kind of New World unconscious, a place that is resonant but unvoiced. His revisions of the West Indies section form a set of precise subtractions that make the region and Sutpen's time there more shadowy and underrepresented. One might say that Faulkner revised not for clarity in his handling of the Caribbean, but for carefully orchestrated obscurity.

Most of these key revisions center on the "siege" scene of Sutpen barricaded in the sugar planter's house, where he performs the vigorous defense of the family that earns him his fortune, his bride, and, perhaps, his curse. In the original manuscript, Faulkner treats the actions of the black Haitians as a political revolt. For example, when Sutpen shoots his musket, in the original he does so "into the Haitian darkness where the insurrecting niggers crept and hid and howled and sang."[7] The manuscript shows that Faulkner crossed out that passage, and, in the first published version of *Absalom, Absalom!* (1936), all references to "insurrection" disappear. Sutpen simply "fired through the windows" and there is no mention of the Haitians outside or their sounds.[8] In a similar vein, the period of waiting is described in the original as a war scene: "during the 7 or 8 nights while they were besieged" (Langford 257). In the published version, it is rendered as "the seven or eight nights while they huddled in the dark" (249). The effect of these subtle changes is to remove the conflict between the planter and his slaves from the realm of a political insurgency, to a primal confrontation between Sutpen and an impersonal, disembodied "darkness" outside the house.

The sense of historical guilt located in Haiti is also rendered more obscure and depersonalized by Faulkner's revisions. In a bravura section that touches on displacement and the Middle Passage, Faulkner wrote, in his original manuscript of "that land, earth, which would require 10,000 years of equatorial heritage to bear it—a little island which was not even the halfway point between the jungle they came from and the civilization they were doomed for, which the black blood, the black arms, and hands and bones and thinking and remembering and hopes and desires" (258). This passage was crossed out in the manuscript by Faulkner and he represents it in almost exactly the same form in the final version of the novel, but the arms and hands have disappeared, in favor of "the black blood, the black bones, and flesh" and the island is reframed as "the halfway point" between jungle and civilization (250). In neither version is the black body embraced as a whole entity, but in the second, it is not even differentiated into limbs (which have power to act—arms and hands), but into raw tissues—blood, bone, and flesh. These revisions depoliticize Haiti, paradoxically, even as they locate it as an original site of historical guilt. The descriptions of the Haitians render them as entirely abject victims, without agency or voice. Faulkner represents the island as a "theater for violence" (250) in this section of the novel, but, in theatrical terms, the blacks have no roles or parts. Such passages, particularly the revised versions of them, show Faulkner to be offering a paradoxically ahistorical anti-imperialist critique, one that is as evasive as it condemning. The stereotyped abstraction (jungle versus civilization), and the misleading symbolic resonance of Haiti as a "halfway" point between Africa and America serve to position the Caribbean and the Middle Passage not in the realm of recovered history but in transcendent myth, where responsibility is abstracted rather than historicized. The hyperbolic time frame (10,000 years) escalates the scope and resonance of the slave trade so that it becomes an epic enormity outside of modern history, rather a specific economic and political system with recent connections to the hemisphere's development. Especially given Sutpen's role as an outsider within Yoknapatawpha, the Haitian passages seem less an apotheosis of the Southern system, or a chronotope of hemispheric imperial exchanges, and more a screen for evoking a system of slavery that is fecund, primal, and dangerous, but reassuringly distinct from the "civilization" in the United States.[9]

Faulkner evokes and evades the Black Atlantic even more powerfully in one of his most unusual film projects, *The Last Slaver*,[10] which he helped write in 1936, the same year that *Absalom, Absalom!* was published. *The Last Slaver* forms a fine parallel to *Absalom, Absalom!*, and it provides us with the only Faulknerian enterprise that depicts African scenes and the Middle Passage itself. In addition, this melodrama, especially in its early drafts, offers probably Faulkner's most powerful vision of slavery as a *national* institution in his body of work. Much as the story of Sutpen is the product of multiple narrators, *The Last Slaver* has a similarly tortuous narrative history. The screenplay's origin is traceable to an obscure novel from 1933 by George S. King. Faulkner was brought in by Darryl Zanuck and Nunnally Johnson to adapt the novel into a screenplay, with help from Sam Hellman and Gladys Lehman.[11] King's novel *The Last Slaver* is based on a historical episode in which a member of a New York yacht club converted a pleasure/racing yacht for the purpose of slave running in disguise. King builds a maritime adventure novel out of this episode, with a geographic range from North America, to Africa, to the Caribbean, and eventually to London. The primary dramatic tension in the novel arises from the fact that the third mate, Kane, is a Yankee sailor of "old revolutionary stock" but is tricked into serving on the *Wanderer*, a slave ship.[12] The ship is captained by the superficially charismatic, but ultimately dissipated and tyrannical Pierre LaRoche, a native of New Orleans, who works for the shadowy African Trading Company.

The bulk of the plot stays above deck and at sea, where Kane struggles, along with a large and loyal African cook, Kalva, and a right-minded group of northern European sailors, to defeat LaRoche and his Latin partisans. King includes infrequent, but detailed scenes of the slave trade—the irons, the purchasing, visits to the slave fort at the Congo, and a trip into the belly of the ship, where the slaves are held. By the end of the novel, Kane, in contrast to his biblical namesake, acts as his black brothers' keeper and repatriates the slaves to Congo with the help of the British navy. The denouement of the novel is essentially a sunny revision of *Heart of Darkness*. Kane and his British allies overthrow the Portuguese slave fort and, in gratitude, the Africans lead them to a cache of ivory upriver, bearing them on royal litters most of the way. At the end, Kane sails in triumph back to London, with the *Wanderer* now his ship, a load of ivory in the hold, and the lord's daughter as his intended.

Faulkner's two screenplay adaptations of the novel are essentially whole-sale rewritings. In terms of overall focus, Faulkner and his co-writers kept *The Last Slaver* largely a melodramatic sea tale of love, mutiny, and smuggling. A key difference from the novel, however, is the underrepresentation of the Africans themselves. While Kalva in the novel *The Last Slaver* is essentially a stock character—the simple, loyal African—he has a large speaking role and figures significantly in the righteous revolt on board, even saving the life of the hero, Kane. In each screenplay of *The Last Slaver*, by contrast, there is only one speaking part for a black actor; a "negro boy" delivers a letter to the mate and tells him, "White man gimme this to give you."[13] Furthermore, the slaves themselves are reduced to a mere backdrop for the action: they are seen only when being loaded or unloaded into the ship. In this respect, the role of the slaves is parallel to that of the Haitians in *Absalom, Absalom!*—a source of horror and victimhood in the background, with white masculine struggle in the foreground. An even greater change is that the slaver captain (renamed Lovett) becomes the primary character in Faulkner's adaptation, rather than the Yankee sailor (renamed Duncan in the first two screenplays). Captain Lovett bears more than a passing resemblance to Thomas Sutpen. He is strong, charismatic, and straightforward, but rough around the edges. Nevertheless, he is represented as basically a decent man trapped in a system, with perhaps a dose of the original Sutpen "innocence." In both versions, he explains to Nancy, his wife, that he got into the business as a boy and found it was "too late" to get out: "I went into when I was a boy. All it meant to me then was excitement. Boys have no sense. Then it was just my life—like farming is somebody else's life. I never thought any more of it than that—and then I was older, before I knew it, and I met you. That told me what I—what I was—and what I was doing. I knew then that I was dirty . . . filthy . . . I was ashamed. But I loved you so much—that I thought I could escape from it, so you'd never know—and that's what I tried to do. But it was too late."[14]

In Faulkner's adaptations, Lovett tries to end his career as a slaver after falling in love with and marrying a young Virginia woman named Nancy. He surprises the crew with Nancy and indicates that he is going to Jamaica to retire as a sugar planter with his wife. The crew, led by the violent first mate, Thompson, mutinies and forces Lovett back to Africa for another slave run. After taking on a load of slaves, Duncan steers the ship to a safe colonial port, and the screenplay reaches its dramatic climax. Duncan spirits Nancy away on a boat while Lovett unchains the Africans and has a final gunfight with Thompson. Lovett finishes as a tragic hero who has finally done the right thing, but must die for his sins. Each version ends with the ship exploding after a lantern fire reaches the powder magazine. Lovett's ship and legacy, the *Wanderer*, meets the same spectacular end as Sutpen's home.

This romantic handling of a slave captain may be galling to contemporary readers, but nevertheless there are complexities of politics and plot that hint at a more challenging understanding of the history of slave trade, and a broader sense of the Black Atlantic, than in *Absalom, Absalom!* While King's novel basically follows the historical routes of nineteenth-century slave trade, Faulkner makes some key revisions. First, he eliminates the West Indies altogether, except as a hoped-for place of retirement for Lovett. In doing so, he sidesteps both the geography of the novel, as well as much of the history of the trade routes themselves. Why would Faulkner make this choice, especially given his interest in the Caribbean in portions of *Absalom, Absalom!*, published that same year? Faulkner's revision of the plot mapping within *The Last Slaver* shows a design to depict an enlarged geography of the slave trade in North America, in effect expanding the vision of a Black Atlantic that he touched on in the Haitian passages in *Absalom, Absalom!* Both screenplay versions begin with a launching not in New York City but in Salem, Massachusetts. A young girl, explicitly Nancy in the second version, christens the yacht, but as soon as she breaks the champagne on it and it launches into the water, it crushes a sailor. An old sea salt watching the scene proclaims it is "launched in blood!" "She's evil. She's begun evil and she'll end evil" (24 September 1936, 4–5). The ship passes to Captain Lovett at an auction, where he is the sole bidder, as mishaps have given it a reputation as a cursed ship. In both screenplays, the *Wanderer* will never go farther South in the U.S. than Virginia. In choosing to stay so close to the North and the mid-Atlantic, Faulkner relocates the focus of slave trade away from the Deep South and the Caribbean towards the heart of the Eastern seaboard. In giving the ship a Massachusetts origin, he also creates a symbolic connection that unites the slave trade with a region that is the cradle of Puritanism, liberty, and witch hunts. One might call this sectionalist evasion, but Faulkner achieves in this revision a Hawthornian evocation of the deep, guilty dependence that *all* of the United States had on slavery for its wealth and development.

Faulkner makes this confrontation even more polemical in the first version of the screenplay. When Lovett purchases the ship, it most recently was owned by someone from the "Potomac Yacht Club," the premier boating club in Washington, D.C., to which the admiral of the U.S. Navy himself belongs. Lovett keeps the Potomac's insignia and uses its

elite provenance as a disguise: no one will pull over a ship thought to belong to the club, even navy cruisers, as the captains fear offending the admiral and the Washington elite. As Lovett brags to his mate, "With this
yacht and that pennant up there, I've practically got a license from the
government to import slaves" (24 September 1936, 19). Although this is a
rather flimsy plot device (which may be why it was eliminated in the second
version), it evokes the sense of national complicity, even as the Webster-
Ashburton treaty of 1842 mandated that Britain and the U.S. patrol elimi-
nate slave ships. By placing a slave ship in the heart of the nation—at its
very capital—Faulkner suggests the inextricable connections between the
nation and the illicit trade. Faulkner's depiction of United States enforce-
ment of the treaty in the first draft is deeply cynical. When the exploits of
the slaver come to light, the British ambassador confronts the secretary of
state: "To put it bluntly, Mr. Secretary, our English government simply
cannot understand how this running of African slaves can continue in the
face of our treaty to fight it with both our navies." The American secretary
"suavely" offers a lukewarm reply: "You may rest assured, sir, that the matter will not be allowed to pass without the fullest inquiry" (24 September
1936, 8). This same exchange is then parroted down the bureaucratic chain
of command: to the Secretary of War, to Admiral of the Navy, to a Commodore, to his lieutenants. The effect of this repetition (the dialog repeats
exactly) is to suggest a rote exchange of official pronouncements, with the
promises ultimately hollow. In the first version, an idealistic young lieu-
tenant, Tom Duncan, suspects that the *Wanderer* is a slaver and speaks
with the Secretary of War about his suspicions, but he is promptly fired
for his allegations: "Are you implying that a member of the Potomac Yacht
Club is running slaves?" intones the secretary (24 September 1936, 54).
After his discharge, Duncan goes to work in a tavern, where he ends up being recruited by Thompson, to serve, unwittingly, on the very ship he had
almost caught.

    Producers Zanuck and Johnson were not enthusiastic about these gov-
ernmental scenes, and they were all excised in the second version of the
script. There is no focus on the navy's failure to catch the slaver, and
Duncan is rewritten as a disgraced British seaman who signs on in Africa
when the *Wanderer* is taking in slaves during its first voyage. The screenplay offers a series of Senate speeches, where senators from Massachusetts and Georgia deplore the slave trade, culminating in a senator shout-
ing "Slaving ships must be driven from the sea!" and receiving "applause
from the galleries and the floor" in great "waves." (10 October 1936, 12).
To enhance the melodramatic effect of discovering that her husband is a
slaver later in the film, Faulkner has Nancy in the gallery, watching these

speeches about the slave trade. The need to emphasize an American commitment to ending the trade appears to have been very strong, because in
the second version, justice emerges not from a final confrontation near the
British naval base of St. Helena, but at a fictitious American antislavery
outpost in the Atlantic named Maricoba.

The elimination of the cynical political backdrop effectively reduced the
sense of national complicity at the level of official government, but Faulkner and his co-writers tweaked some details in the second version to locate another kind of responsibility—uncanny and personal, and it centered in the role of Nancy. In the second version, the fatal christening of
the ship, named *Silver Queen*, was accomplished by Nancy as a young girl,
so that she, from the start, has figurative blood on her hands and a direct
connection to this ship, although she does not realize it until much later
in the screenplay. When Nancy confides to Lovett her traumatic memory
of the episode, which gives her a fear of sailing, she relates, "It was awful!
But now that I'm with you, darling, nothing matters—I'm going to love the
Wanderer because it's yours" (10 October 1936, 73). Lovett replies to her
with a line that will soon take on a chilling resonance: "Ours, sweetheart.
Let's never say 'yours' or 'mine'—always 'ours.'" In the second version,
Nancy makes a shocking discovery (for her) that proves Lovett's claim of
their shared ownership, although with a different connotation. Right after
Lovett confesses his occupation to her, she flees him and "goes to a port-
hole for air," where she discovers, "engraved in the copper are the words:
SILVER QUEEN." The stage directions read: "Her eyes widen in horror.
This is the yacht she christened as a little girl—the yacht that was launched
in blood" (10 October 1936, 100). This discovery of her personal tie to the
ship, combined with the revelation of her husband's profession as a slaver,
links her intimately, in both girlhood and womanhood, to the destiny of the
slave ship. The honeymoon cruise, launched with the blessings of the domestic union and personal renewal, becomes a site of contamination by illicit commerce and guilt.

Nancy later makes a surprising discovery on the African shore that establishes a more personal, embodied link to the slave trade. In both screenplays, shortly after they embark, Lovett offers her "his dowry"—a casket
of jewelry. Nancy rifles through the jewelry, finds the "loveliest bracelet,"
puts it on, and exclaims, "It's so exciting it's, it's sinful" (24 September
1936, 79). When the ship reaches Africa, Nancy discovers the origin of
the bracelet, and it provides a horrific scene of gothic revelation—perhaps the most worthily Faulknerian scene in the screenplay. As the *Wanderer* takes on its last load of slaves, Nancy watches. A scene without dialog
ensues, with the following stage directions: "Approaching her are several

female slaves. As they draw nearer, Nancy's eyes are caught by the bracelet on a woman's arm. She gasps. It is a duplicate of the one on her own
arm. Wresting the bracelet from her arm, she throws it into the sea, and
then runs from the deck, unable to bear the sight of it any more" (24 September 1936, 109). Nancy's bracelet forges a connection between her and
the African woman, and it bespeaks doubling, theft, and contamination, simultaneously. This bracelet was "the loveliest of all"—chosen by Nancy as
her prize—but it is now linked to this abject woman. Was Nancy's bracelet
the matching twin, and was it stolen as part of the trade? Was the bracelet given to the female in exchange for some kind of favor or as compensation? Is it a mark of ownership or betrothal? The precise origin of the
bracelet is never revealed, but Nancy has now seen the roots of the wealth
she admired and the jewelry she prized, and her sensation of "sin" has
been confirmed. Nancy may also feel that, with the parallel bracelet, that
she too has been "enslaved"—either by Lovett or by the trade itself, which
has provided the jewelry she loves. Thus, much that she has valued—
beauty, wealth, her husband—is revealed to be an outgrowth of injustice,
of victimhood, and of Africa itself—much as the West Indies is the foundation of Sutpen's wealth. It may also horrify Nancy that the jewelry itself
has been on the arms of this woman, and she has been rendered impure by
its touch, much as Rosa Coldfield is shocked by Clytie's touch in *Absalom,
Absalom!* If Faulkner reddens Nancy's hands at the ship's christening, he
blackens her in this scene with the bracelet.

Faulkner's handling of Nancy as a vessel of guilt and responsibility brings
us back to the question of abstraction and historicity that inheres in the
West Indian sections of *Absalom, Absalom!* Even as both drafts of *The Last
Slaver*—especially the first one—evoke a more complex geography of the
slave trade than in anywhere else in Faulkner, that historical/political recovery is revised for an elemental plot of personal, biblical sin. While the
first version implicitly critiques the operations of power within the U.S.
government for enabling or at least tolerating the trade, the second takes
pains to show that the "system works," even inventing an American naval
base to bring the career of the *Wanderer* to a close. Relocating the guilty
plot into the hands and arms of Nancy is symbolically powerful, but largely
as myth rather than history. In giving her a melodramatic connection to the
ship, Faulkner links the personal to the political, as it were, but this connection vitiates the political history of the trade in an almost irrational way:
in what way is Nancy's christening really a causal link to what ensues? Perhaps Faulkner aims to suggest that even "innocent" women are enablers of
slavery, but it seems odd, perhaps even misogynistic, to devote more text

and scenes to painting Nancy as the wellspring of guilt, when Lovett has plied the trade his entire life.

Mythmaking, as opposed to historicizing, characterizes Faulkner's Caribbean and African passages in *Absalom, Absalom!* and *The Last Slaver*, and the revision history of each text shows the author carefully working to obtain this effect. Faulkner succeeds in exposing deep legacies of guilt in each text, but he is less successful in recalling anything deeply historical. Many of his choices—such as locating Sutpen's West Indian apprenticeship in a historically impossible space in *Absalom, Absalom!*, his elimination of Caribbean routes in *The Last Slaver*, and his dismissal of black bodies and black voices in both texts—suggest that he is actively repressing vital historical connections between the United States and the Black Atlantic. Faulkner's choice of the symbolic over the historical in his vision of the hemisphere is all the more striking given the ferocious intensity with which he revisits U.S. Southern history and origins elsewhere in *Absalom, Absalom!*, *Go Down, Moses*, and the Snopes trilogy. Why would an author so committed to chronicling the most problematic sides of his own regional history, including questions of race, power, and racial violence, avoid a comparably illuminating historical vision when turning to the Caribbean and the Middle Passage? Two pieces of evidence might offer an answer. At the end of *Absalom, Absalom!* Shreve McCannon prophesizes the decline of the West through miscegenation, predicting, in effect, an unstoppable expansion of the Black Atlantic: "I think that in time the Jim Bonds are going to conquer the Western hemisphere. Of course it wont quite be in our time and of course as they spread toward the poles they will bleach out again like the rabbits and the birds do, so they wont show up so sharp against the snow. But it will still be Jim Bond; and so in a few thousand years, I who regard you will also have sprung from the loins of African kings" (378). Shreve offers a vision of racial apocalypse, with debased mixed-descent characters like Jim Bond supplanting the West and lines of blackness and whiteness blurring beyond recognition. This fearsome prediction of expanding black power takes on an even greater resonance when one considers that Faulkner's most urgent historical repressions and revisions in *Absalom, Absalom!* and *The Last Slaver* center on blackness in each text. Faulkner edited out the hints of insurrection and embodiment within the West Indian scenes in *Absalom, Absalom!*, effectively reducing the Haitians from a revolutionary force of blackness to eternal victimhood and powerlessness. In *The Last Slaver* Faulkner and his co-writers eliminated black agency and voice altogether, in some ways taking a step back from King's vision of Africanness, which was hardly progressive.

Although *Absalom, Absalom!* and *The Last Slaver* probe the darkest origins of slavery, neither is really concerned with the Haitians or Africans as persons, or even as bodies, but as the raw material of sin and guilt in the New World. Faulkner's hemispheric vision shows a deep awareness of the origins of the Black Atlantic, but also a fear of it, as evidenced in his tendency to repress black agency or to treat it as a source of contamination. In this respect, Faulkner may evoke an image of the Black Atlantic not to recognize a specific history so much as to exorcise it.

NOTES

1. In referring to the "Black Atlantic," I am invoking Paul Gilroy's refiguration of the hemisphere in *The Black Atlantic: Modernity and Double Consciousness* (Cambridge: Harvard University Press, 1993).

2. Maritza Stanchich, "The Hidden Caribbean 'Other' in William Faulkner's *Absalom, Absalom!*: An Ideological Ancestry of U.S. Imperialism," *Mississippi Quarterly: The Journal of Southern Culture*, 49:3 (June 1996): 9. Subsequent references to this text will be cited parenthetically by page number.

3. John T. Matthews, "Recalling the West Indies: From Yoknapatawpha to Haiti and Back," *American Literary History* 16:2 (Summer 2004): 257. Subsequent references to this text will be cited parenthetically by page number.

4. Indeed, one could argue that the insistent critique of womanhood and virginity with the Haitian passages, along with the anxieties about fertility and sexuality, reflects not so much Sutpen's or Faulkner's vision of the island, but the shaping hand of the Compson men, who return to these themes almost obsessively in *Absalom, Absalom!* and *The Sound and the Fury*.

5. Stanchich, for example, argues that Sutpen "doubles for the American national conscience" (4). Matthews sees the Haitian passages as a source of "potential recognition about the South's obscured origins" (256). Both of these claims, as attractive as they are, make a leap in representation that is not supported by Sutpen's position in the novel as a quitessential outsider—wherever he is.

6. Vera Kutzinski makes a persuasive case that it is Cuba, not Haiti, that is a more probable source of wealth and slaves for someone in Sutpen's position at that time. See Vera Kutzinksi, "Borders and Bodies: The United States, America, and the Caribbean," *CR: The New Centennial Review* 1.2 (2001): 55–88.

7. Gerald Langford, *Faulkner's Revision of "Absalom, Absalom!": A Collation of the Manuscript and the Published Book* (Austin: University of Texas Press, 1971), 255. All of my references to the original manuscript of *Absalom, Absalom!* are taken from Langford's collation. Subsequent references to this text will be cited parenthetically by page number.

8. William Faulkner, *Absalom, Absalom!* (New York: Modern Library, 1936) 247. Subsequent references to this text will be cited parenthetically by page number.

9. Roberto Fernández Retamar observes that such justifying distinctions between Anglo-American colonialism and Latin colonialism (which invariably situate the Anglo-American as more civilized and humane) are foundations of the intellectual tradition of American exceptionalism. He effectively critiques this tendency in "Against the Black Legend," in *Caliban and Other Essays* (Minneapolis: University of Minnesota Press, 1989), 56–73.

10. The film was directed by Tay Garnett and released as *Slave Ship* in 1937. The screenplay drafts retain the original novel title, *The Last Slaver*. Because it is those drafts I am analyzing in this essay, I refer to the project by that title as well.

11. Two sources explain Faulkner's involvement with this project. The first is an archival

letter: Nunnally Johnson to Darryl Zanuck, 24 September 1936. Albert and Shirley Small Special Collections Library, University of Virginia. The second is John T. Matthews's already cited article, 249.

    12. George S. King, *The Last Slaver* (New York: Putnam's, 1933) 21.

    13. William Faulkner, Sam Hellman, and Gladys Lehman, *The Last Slaver*, Ts., 24 September 1936 (Albert and Shirley Small Special Collections Library, University of Virginia), 57. Subsequent references to this text will be cited parenthetically by date and page number.

    14. William Faulkner, Sam Hellman, and Gladys Lehman, *The Last Slaver* Ts, 10 October 1936 (Albert and Shirley Small Special Collections Library, University of Virginia), 98. Subsequent references to this text will be cited parenthetically by date and page number.

Faulkner and Me

TIERNO MONÉNEMBO

The pin-ball machine, the jukebox, the drink machine, the TV, still completely new in this part of Africa, all these machines were for us, the "underdeveloped," like Armstrong's then-recent steps on the moon. The wooden shacks lined up as in a Confederate soldier's camp, everything seemed like in America on this neglected campus stuck between the bypass and the jungle. It was the early 1970s, in Abidjan on the Ivory Coast, at the university residence hall Mermoz when I was like a colleague of Schumann and Burnham, the tragic figures of *Pylon!*

It was at the corner of the drink stand, on a table where the students came to play poker, that I saw the book for the first time. It was missing the cover and perhaps a good dozen pages. A thing without a beginning or an end; the text, in places, nibbled on by termites, and because of that, not one chapter was complete! Borges had not yet written *The Book of Sand*, and I already had in my hands a preview of a top secret novel, impossible to decode because of its condition as well as its author who, more than anyone, endeavored to make literature a labyrinth where one was sure to get lost; a labyrinth where one takes pleasure in getting lost. Édouard Glissant described the work I held in my hand as that of an architect who assembled an entire monument around a hidden secret but who all the while is pointing it out and concealing it at the same time. Stunned by the unfurling of sentences, dazed by the flood of images and adjectives, I did not immediately pay attention to the title and the author's name. Nor did I understand the importance of my discovery when I realized a few days later that it was *The Sound and the Fury*.

I knew very little about American literature. To tell the truth, besides the Black Brothers (Richard Wright, James Baldwin, and Langston Hughes that every kid of African independence owed it to himself to read), my shelf on this subject was limited to a few issues of *Reader's Digest* and one or two books by Pearl S. Buck. Mark Twain and Hemingway, they sounded slightly familiar, but Faulkner—I had never even heard of him.

The object that I had in my hands had therefore no more interest than those James Bond movies or old *Paris Match* magazines that rich families left lying around in their living rooms. Besides, I had only one wish: to put the thing back where I had found it after having flipped through a few pages. I had never read a text as poorly done, a story so unlikely or incredible. I visualized the angry red ink that my professors would have poured out on the margins of my essay if I had had the audacity to present them with such a rag. And it goes without saying that it would have been their right: their role consisted of teaching us literature (good literature!) and helping us master French (good French!). They were paid to punish our errors in taste and our peculiarities of language, to oversee our diction, and our past participle agreement, under the merciless eye of the *Grevisse* and the *Littré*.[1]

"That which one understands well will be clearly stated and the words to say it come easily." Indeed, after a long amnesia from the shock of colonization, in the 1970s, we had just regained consciousness and rediscovered the thread of our memory and our identity. We were Negroes, Africans, Independents, and we proclaimed it all day long with the great sounds of the kora[2] and the balafo[3] on the public squares or on the radio stations. Independents, truly recent Independents! We lived from then on in republics, the African republics, but as for syntax and grammar, we were still under the rule of Mr. Nicolas Boileau, the seventeenth-century French writer and arbiter of style. Fifteen years had not been enough to make us lose all our good habits as little colonials. Despite the euphoria of freedom, certain schools were still organizing "the week of good French," the annual ceremony during which those of us who had not spent our time absorbing Molières language were overloaded with encyclopedias and pens.

Proper usage required speaking in appropriate language and writing in a clear, proper, and clean style. But with Faulkner, there was not one *correct* sentence (read: you must have a subject, a verb, and modifiers)! Was there even one proper, orderly sentence within this gibberish, in which the sentences, instead of stopping, were all tangled up in an extraordinary crash of senses, images, and sounds? I understood perfectly why someone had left this book lying there in the corner of the drink stand where students came to kill time. The poor guy who had bought it had no doubt regretted it immediately, and had taken revenge on it by tearing out a few pages. I sensed in a confused way that this book smelled of sulfur and that it was not to be placed in just anyone's hands. That it was the work of the devil, perhaps. As all true believers will tell you, there is nothing more tempting than the devil.

However wary I tried to be, I could not tear myself away from it. It held onto me with the same malevolent force as those women whose dissoluteness we disapprove of but who bewitch us with their enticing bodices, their eyes burning with desire. I ended up taking the book with me to my room after having assured myself that no one would claim it. And I spent the following months trying to penetrate it with the slowness and profuse sweating of an army of laborers attacking iron-hard soil to dig a tunnel.

That is how for the first time, I found myself facing Faulkner's universe that right away seemed to me like a gigantic and extravagant castle, enveloped in mist. Assuredly, a big piece stood before me: alluring but hard to swallow! Where should I start? Obviously, I had not chosen the easiest. *The Sound and the Fury* remains without doubt the most obscure, the most impenetrable of this gigantic dwelling riddled with mazes and chasms, haunted by simple minds and burned out heads, with old ghosts and dying heroes. It seems to me that this book, more than all of Faulkners others, corresponds to Glissant's definition: "The work of Faulkner always appeared to me thus: a delayed revelation (without having anything to do with the suspense of a mystery novel) which produces its technique not from clarification (neither psychological, nor social nor . . .), but in the end, by combining a mystery with a spell of dizziness—accelerated more so than resolved by this crazy virtue of differentiation and unveiling—around a place which remains to be defined."

OK, meanwhile, for the poor African student that I was, the language tasted like scotch (rough, burning, intoxicating) and through page after page the tale became a true Chinese puzzle. I quickly got lost in the meanderings of this story of castration and stuttering, incest and hate. I understood the Compsons' torment and the slow and inevitable decay of their family, but I could not make out the characters, and above all, I wasn't able to follow their genealogical lines nor understand the violent and troubled feelings that moved them. Too much of Jason and Quentin! And then, Benjy! To choose an idiot as the narrator, what an idea!

I gave up several times, but the obscurity and strangeness of the book pushed me to continue even if, after arriving at the last page, I still hadn't clarified anything. Even today, I strongly doubt that I understand Jason's hate for Caddy, Dilsey's blind devotion to the Compsons, the mysterious links that unite Lester and Benjy, the castration and imprisonment of the latter, etc. Oh well, I tell myself, you don't understand what the Beatles are saying either, but you still spend your time humming "Yesterday": "Forget the story, hang on to the music." What I did was this: I put Mr. Faulkner away next to the Beatles and the Rolling Stones, Otis Redding and James Brown, the superstars of rock and rhythm and blues (the Beethovens of my adolescence), who spoke to me about the demons and the marvels of my era in a language that was foreign to me. In the end, I said to myself that in this novel, the meaning is not found in the chronology of its events but in the importance of their arrangement, exactly like sheets of music in a musical work.

I was comforted by this idea upon my arrival in France in the summer of 1973. There I was able to procure a complete volume of *The Sound and the Fury* with an introduction by Maurice Edgar Coindreau (who first translated Faulkner in France) published in 1937. I was happy to read that the composition of *The Sound and the Fury* is essentially musical. Above all, I was glad to learn that "the entire book vibrates with sound and fury and will seem devoid of meaning to those who believe that a literary man must produce a message or serve some noble cause. Mr. Faulkner is content to open the gates of hell. He forces no one to accompany him, but those who do so will not regret it."

Well, let it happen! I got up my courage in both hands and jumped headfirst into Faulkner's hell without having been invited, and I admit that to this day I have never regretted it. It has now lasted for years. I understood entering into Faulkner's work meant going back to school, lets say, or more so to the very beginning. School is a place for mere formation while initiation is a place of transformation. After a series of tests, the initiate undergoes a metamorphosis on the inside, and his vision of the world changes. He acquires a new state of mind that is more in harmony with the extraordinary complexity of things. This is the experience that I underwent while reading Faulkner. That idiot Benjy taught me that we are all a little lame and necessarily clueless before history's cyclone and the lulls and postponements of life. And perhaps that is literature: an attempt (stammering, stubborn, definitively hopeless) to name and describe the world, to condemn it, to tolerate it (for lack of being able to give it meaning). In the beginning, the word (of God), in the end, the stutter (of Man). To write is to attempt to initiate oneself into creation's mystery! Yes, to read Faulkner is to be initiated, to detach ourselves from the world in which we had lived in order to enter into another world more obscure, more vertiginous, more terrifying. Then, the initiation consists of a series of tests that become more and more arduous, like the steps of a staircase. The initiates advance in silence, step by step, lined up one behind the other: it being impossible to proceed to the next step if we have not yet entirely assimilated the preceding one's lessons.

I therefore continued savoring *The Sound and the Fury* for several years before daring to push farther into my Faulknerian ascension. By chance I stumbled upon *As I Lay Dying*. I found it a bit more accessible even though its structure remained just as Faulknerian, that is to say, conceived outside the model of classic dialogue and chronology. The theme is the same as in *The Sound and the Fury*, and—as I later realized—throughout most of the work: a family (a tribe, I would call it) formerly prosperous, powerful, and united is slowly falling apart following a tragedy (war, accidents, the death of a grandparent or a patriarch). This is the chance for the author to sketch for us the portraits of different members of the clan. In the forest of symbols and signs, behind the fog of confusing words and crazy soliloquies, little by little we can discern their faces and their temperaments. We perceive the subconscious, the naïveté, the childish stubbornness or the peaceful resignation with which they react to each other before destiny's cruelty. With his subtle and suddenly dazzling monologues and flashbacks, Faulkner lays out for us one of his morbid sagas of which only he knows the secret, and within which, with sharp lurches, more flashbacks, fleeting descriptions and insistent repetitions, he continuously questions the extraordinary troubles of human reality. Like a magic paintbrush, the sprawling, gigantic tentacles of meticulous language get into all the nooks and crannies of human existence. This brush restores the most attenuated memories, the most unexpected emotions, and the most hidden feelings. Love and hate, grudges and indulgences, all the ingredients that men have used to love and hate each other. Faulkner has unveiled to us the glimmers of light and the shadowy zones of this weird organ we call the human soul, without ever clothing it in a judge's or moralist's robe. This means that in the end, contrary to what we find in "well-intentioned novels," we never know who is the good or the bad guy, the victim or the executioner. The beings are simply unveiled to us, and we must read their nakedness to try to understand the inexplicable tensions and dark, mysterious, melancholic forces that drive them and bring them to life. Faulkner is not a judge, but a simple physiologist who is satisfied with showing us how the story or the lives function. This is particularly true in *As I Lay Dying*. To me, this novel, with the color of mourning and the feeling of a funeral wake, represents the most complete and successful example of Faulkner's novels. We find there, and in its most developed form, the "things" that make up Faulknerian method: interior monologues, simple people's language, and recollections of the past.

The drama does not unfold with an idea nor an act but in a special atmosphere and perhaps simply in a particular setting. The dramatic tension is not accomplished through the characters, but in what happens around them. It is before the mirror of death (before God's judgment) that man is truly unveiled. This is what I thought I understood in the novel. And it is based on this idea (true or false) that I constructed *Pelourinho*, the novel that I dedicated to Brazil. My intention was to conjure up Salvador de Bahia on the measure of Faulkner. After all, only Faulkner's confused dialogues and elliptical sentences are up to explaining the tangle of races, destinies, and people who shape the world of Christopher Columbus.

Even though two decades passed between my reading *As I Lay Dying* and my trip to Brazil, it is clear that my book owes something to Faulkner's. Seeing for the first time Pelourinho's legendary square, I said to myself that there are places predestined for drama. In essence, squares are theater stages. Both create, in the splendor of their balconies and picturesque terraces, an atmosphere of misunderstanding and sadness. In short, the scene is already set, and all that remains is for the characters to enter and act out the drama. In *As I Lay Dying*, the drama had also been sketched out well before the mother's death. It was already there in the isolation on the farm, in the oppressive atmosphere of prayers and the unspoken words, interrupted by silent meals and hard work in the fields. This mother who is dying, these strikes with a hammer that make her coffin, the appearance of vultures around the wagon, this symphony of somber and shocking monologues as if the characters were speaking under the direction of a virtuoso! Doubt is not permitted: Faulkner is above all a composer, a director, a writer of atmosphere!

But let's not get on the wrong track: let's try to curb reductions above all when it comes to such a star! Faulkner is also a language, a language that attains in *As I Lay Dying* incredible perfection. Ah, these peasant words that have the harshness of truth, the flavor of prose, and the appropriateness of a poem! "William Faulkner knows all the secrets of verbal alchemy. . . . He equally knows the power of the unexplained," rightly said Coindreau. Verbal alchemy, the power of the unexplained! A true delight for the African that I am! Don't forget that I came out of the oral world, that of the unexplained, indeed, and that these are the blood-red currents of the word that are flowing through my veins! I lean toward those writers whose style constantly oscillates between the spoken and the written. My favorite writers are Rabelais, Faulkner, Joyce, Céline (Ahmadou Kourouma is, certainly, a son of the Malinké[4] language, but also a descendant of the latter).

And if it were necessary to choose among this magic quartet, without hesitating, I would choose Faulkner. It is he—oh yes, Mr. Coindreau! —who knows best the mysterious alchemy of words. Working like a goldsmith, he succeeds in uniting the "simple" speech of blacks and poor whites in the Deep South with biblical writing. This, Glissant very well understood: "The usage of these interior monologues that run into each other never abandons the tone of peasant speech, nor the (literary) height of epic questioning." The peasant tone is there to give the characters substance and legitimacy in the tale. And each one of them plays music that is his own: avarice, lunacy, greed, egoism, pain. Never was I so deeply moved by a novel, I mean, physically affected. I had the impression that I was experiencing, in my mind but also my body, the misfortunes of this poor Mississippi family haunted by the combined effects of destitution and malediction.

Here, as in most of his novels, Faulkner is not happy to describe or analyze, he *explains*. He makes us see the story; better yet, he makes us live it. Readers do not read Faulkner with their eyes but with all the pores of their bodies. They are not passive witnesses of the story that is unfolding before their eyes, and the protagonist who is dominating the scene. As a reader you are hungry and hot, and your head or foot aches when his does.

This is particularly true for *Light in August*, the third step in the house of Faulkner where I placed my feet. As a student, I was living in a maid's room[5] that was particularly poorly heated the day I opened this book. And believe it or not, I began sweating profusely when I arrived at the passage where Lena Grove, breathless, struggles to climb up a hill while watching behind her a wagon standing beside the road. Is it the effect of cinema? Faulkner's writing, although very intellectual in its style and subjects of investigation, produces a physical effect on the reader who truly feels the ideas and sensations explained in the book.

I remember the scene in *The Unvanquished* after the South's defeat and abolition, when the whites were hiding in their homes while the large groups of newly freed blacks, like storm clouds, wandered across fields singing gospel hymns. This very biblical scene (often seen in Faulkner) is also very alive. We see distinctly the ancestors of Malcolm X and Martin Luther King, those exhausted silhouettes, peaceful and obstinate, who prevail over weather, rivers, and plains. We distinctly hear them singing "We Shall Overcome."

And since we are speaking about blacks, it is time to look into their relationship with Faulkner. With few exceptions (*As I Lay Dying*, *Wild Palms*, *Pylon*), blacks are very present in his novels. In spite of this fact, I read here and there that Faulkner's feelings for them were ambiguous, almost hostile. Some critics have asserted that the father of the character Christmas looked down on people of color and rejected any notion of intermarriage. Others say that his attitude deep down was only that of a white Southerner at that time period: someone who could not cope with General Lee's defeat and the loss of old privileges and who had a tendency to put the blame on the blacks much more than on the Yankees, for his disappointments in history. A lost soul, in some sort, whose behavior toward African Americans would be more motivated by fear of the future than by hate. Others still affirm without really proving it that Faulkner was antiracist and favored civil rights and the emancipation of blacks. But perhaps, we will never be completely enlightened about our author's true feelings on the question and like many whites who find themselves in the same situation (did he not say, one day, that he had the same anguish as Camus?), he chose to prefer his native home over global racial justice.

It remains that in his books, blacks exist. Their existence is not denied. It is, in itself, if not a reason to exonerate him, at least a serious indication to presume him innocent. Besides, it is a black man, Édouard Glissant, who rushes to his aid each time suspicions arise: "Perhaps he accepted that the Blacks cry of revolt went without saying, but also decided that it was not up to him to take up the struggle. . . . Faulkner is not a soldier in the war for Civil Rights or a reformer of society. . . . Writing does not leave very much space for social reform."

The white "plantation" writers, to speak like Glissant, have thoroughly spoken to us about the place where they were born. But they are not numerous, those whose attention lingered on their human environment, the shapeless and peripheral mass of the natives. The natives of the West Indies are insignificant if not absent in the works of Saint John Perse. The Arabs are only shadows in Camus. One could transplant the décor of *The Stranger* to Antibes or Sète[6] without at all changing the sense and the subject of the book. One remembers that in 1964 the Algerian writer Mourad Bourboune criticized the author of *Exile and the Kingdom* of writing as if he had never met an Arab.

In Faulkner's writings, on the contrary, black characters abound, and if they are not at the heart of the work, they are often the essential links in the evolution of the drama. They are secondary characters, it's true, but they are deciding factors in the configuration of white characters and in the unfolding of the story. They wonderfully support with their accent and language the rhythm of the narration! They are often at the origin of these sudden, dazzling resurgences (a resurgence of intrigue and style), to which Faulkner has the secret. Dilsey is not equal to Caroline or Caddy, and Lester does not attain the symbolic and emotional value of Benjy, but none of them is superficial or caricatured. They are described truthfully "with the simple and deep joy of people of [their] race." One presents them to us as they are: in their deplorable condition and with all the spontaneity of their being.

Without blacks, Faulkner's work would not be the same. "The Blacks are the background, the witnesses without the extravagances of the Whites," affirms the great connoisseur Coindreau. They color the scene; they accompany the often chaotic destiny of their white masters. They symbolize passiveness but perhaps also a lasting quality. In these gloomy sagas where, with each page, the winds of madness and malediction blow, it is they who maintain reason and hope. It is in the hands of old Dilsey that in the end lies, "the ship gone adrift that is the Compson house." In a universe that is always crashing down, they are the only ones who remain constant. They do not get promoted or lose their rank. These are unchanging figures definitively etched in time. Between wisdom and powerlessness, they are participants, impassive to the hopeless agitation and the childlike steps of history. They represent the concrete and wise aspect of existence.(Glissant has remarked that when speaking of them, Faulkner always employs an objective narration, never subjective narration, never an interior monologue.) If they never leave their servile condition, they are the only ones, at the end of the tale, to escape annihilation.

They are the figures of passive resistance and therefore of continuity in the universe, where, sooner or later, everything will end by breaking down and crumbling. Alain Desvergnes, who attempted in his photographs to recreate the imaginary Yoknapatawpha County, describes the Faulknerian universe as the tragedy of descendants. The only ones who survive are those who have the capacity to adapt and the voracity of insects and rats (the Snopeses, for example) or those for whom the duration, wait or survival have become, by the force of things, second nature (the descendants of slaves, those who "endured.")

The tragedy of the descendants is truly a constant in the Faulknerian approach, but in my opinion, one must research the early stages where the books finds their source. The source of these curses dates back further than the Civil War or the death of the patriarch. The trouble comes from the rupture in the genealogical lines. I believe that it is Sartoris for whom Faulkner writes: "We all come from the Old Bailey." Otherwise stated, the tragedy of the descendants dates back much earlier than the decline and later death of Jason Compson, or the brutal death of John Sartoris. They arrive in America with tragedy. The curse begins with the distancing from the ancestors. As in the Bible, sin was committed in the beginning. This means that for whites and blacks, people are not really born: they come into the world to atone for their sin.

Until I read Faulkner, I thought that this curse, born out of the rupture in the genealogical lines, only concerned the descendants of slaves. The slow and sure action of his poison was only found in the works of Richard Wright, Joseph Zobel, Bertrand Jemener, or Simone Schwartz-Bart. Now I know that this maddening distortion of history goes beyond the blacks (whether they be from Mississippi or the Caribbean) to encompass all the Americas. In essence, it is the break in the genealogical line that is at the origin of the tumultuous saga of the Americas. It is the fundamental material of its literature.

But perhaps I am rambling by saying this, and it would be better if I arrived at the question that has been burning inside me since the beginning: why are the writers of the Third World so fascinated with Faulkner? We know that his influence is evident in the works of Mario Vargas Llosa, Gabriel García-Márquez, Frank Etienne, or Édouard Glissant. To this question, one is tempted to respond by imitating Glissant: "Needless to say, because he is a plantation writer!" Only his instructing shadow watching over us is not restricted to the Caribbean and Mississippi. His shadow stretches to the deserts and forests of Africa. The Algerian Kateb Yacine identified with Faulkner, the same as the Ivorian Ahmadou Kourouma or the Malian Yambo Ouologuem. Actually, it is because he tackles the two primordial questions of the literature of young nations: language and the relationship with history.

Faulkner is not an easy writer or a master of convenient thought. His language is hermetic, his message too obscure, too elliptical to be understood by common mortals. The stories that he tells, too far from my own realities! Why then has he succeeded in holding onto me, in casting a spell on me? Why has he fascinated us and continues to fascinate us so? For one very simple reason: because he deals with the two big questions that haunt African literature: language and history.

Born in an African language and in a cradle shaped by the soft material of oral tradition, educated in a European language and according to the canons of writing, the problem of language arises as soon as the African picks up a pen. Is it necessary to write in Fulani[7] or in French? And if in French, then in the style of Balzac, Chateaubriand, or in one's own style, that is to say, subjecting the words that came to us from France to the canons of African syntax, making the French language wear a boubou[8] like Ahmadou Kourouma advocated? It is for all of these reasons and still many others that the famous Faulknerian "verbal alchemy" interests us so.

The second question is one of history. For the Compson and Sartoris families, as with all the defeated, the story is not a long and calm river but more of a source of eternal remorse and torment. After the roar of battles and confrontations comes the long rumination of defeat. While the winners sport their medals and laurels, the defeated start the long ordeal of questioning and mourning.

The question, the art of questioning! That is what dazzles us in Faulkner!

With unequalled obstinacy, Faulkner interrogates history and succeeds, with the angle of literature, in making it admit what no other discipline could. In reading Faulkner, I say to myself that this literary questioning makes it more possible to exorcise the old demon than ideological demonstrations. To tame these monsters, there is nothing better than to invite them into your living room. Is that not what Freud did in bringing out the madness of the logic behind electroshocks to submit it to psychoanalysis?

Faulkner, who read the Bible, gets past these circumstances to bring the world back to what it was in the beginning (at this terrible start where there was only the word): a question. A question full of sound and fury without any response.

In essence, he imitates God like all the great creators. In saying this, I realize how much that exonerates me from not having understood much in *Sartoris* or *Absalom, Absalom!* Just the same, I knew it from the beginning: Faulkner is neither an easy writer nor a master of convenient thought. His language is hermetic, his message too obscure, too elliptical to be understood.

His books remind me of the phenomena of creation: nature, the cosmos, the seas. One cannot understand them. It is enough to simply contemplate their pure beauty and experience their impenetrable mystery.

NOTES

Lydia Hailman King translated Tierno Monénembo's essay from the French. King received her MA in French at the University of Mississippi and has also studied at the Université Paul Valery and Université de Lausanne. She has taught French at the University of Mississippi and is currently a First Amendment Center Online intern in Washington, D.C.

1. Reference books on the correct use of the French language
2. 21-stringed West African musical instrument resembling a harp or lute
3. wooden xylophone
4. African language in the Mande family, spoken in Mali and Guinea.
5. *Chambre de bonne*: attic room often rented to a student
6. Cities in southern coastal France
7. West African language
8. Flowing, wide-sleeved robe worn in Africa

Contributors

Melanie R. Benson is assistant professor of English and director of American Studies at the University of Hartford, Hillyer College. She is author of essays on Barry Hannah and Louis Owens and *Disturbing Calculations: The Economies of Southern Identity in Postcolonial Southern Literature, 1912–2002*, a volume on the University of Georgia's New Southern Studies series.

Manuel Broncano is associate professor of American Literature at the University of León, Spain. He has published several books in Spanish on American literature, including *Brief Worlds, Infinite Worlds: Flannery O'Connor and the American Short Story*, *The Frontier: Myth and Reality of the New World*, and a forthcoming volume, "Multicultural Societies: Artistic Discourse and Identity." He is currently working on a book-length project, provisionally entitled "South by Southwest: Magical Grotesque and Border Culture in Southern Fiction."

Keith Cartwright, assistant professor of English at the University of North Florida, has published on African and Caribbean literature, most notably his volume *Reading Africa into American Literature: Epics, Fables, Gothic Tales*, selected as a *Choice* Best Academic Title for 2003. He is currently working on a book-length project on crosscurrents of Caribbean/coastal Deep South rites and writings.

Leigh Anne Duck is associate professor of English at the University of Memphis. She is the author of *The Nation's Region: Southern Modernism, Segregation, and U.S. Nationalism* and essays on Faulkner, Zora Neale Hurston, and V. S. Naipaul.

George B. Handley, professor of humanities at Brigham Young University, has written extensively on the Caribbean and Latin America and their relationship to the South. He is the author of *Postslavery Literatures in the Americas: Family Portraits in Black and White*, selected as a Choice Outstanding Academic Title for 2001, and *New World Poetics: Nature and the Adamic Imagination of Walt Whitman, Pablo Neruda, and Derek Walcott*. He is coeditor of *Caribbean Literature and the Environment: Between Culture and Nature*.

Jeff Karem is associate professor of English at Cleveland State University. He is the author of *The Romance of Authenticity: The Cultural Politics of Regional and Ethnic Literatures*, as well as essays on postcolonial theory, Richard Wright, and Leslie Marmon Silko.

Mario Materassi is professor of American Literature at the University of Florence, Italy. He has published extensively on Faulkner, including two books in Italian, *Faulkner's Novels* and *Faulkner, Again*, as well as translations of *Soldiers' Pay*, *As I Lay Dying*, *Privacy: The American Dream: What Happened to It?*, and a forthcoming volume, *Sanctuary*.

John T. Matthews, professor of English at Boston University, is the author of *The Play of Faulkner's Language* and *"The Sound and the Fury": Faulkner and the Lost Cause*, as well as numerous essays on Faulkner, literary theory, and cultural studies. He is currently working on two books: *Look Away, Look Away: The Problem of the South in Modern Culture* and *Faulkner: A Short Introduction: Seeing through the South*.

Tierno Monénembo is the pen name of Thierno Diallo, a native of Guinea in West Africa, and now living in France. He is the author of eight novels, the most recent being *The Oldest Orphan*, based on the Rawanda genocide. He holds a doctorate in biochemistry and has studied and taught in Senegal, the Ivory Coast, Brazil, Algeria, Morocco, and France. An earlier novel, *Les ecailles du ciel* (The Shells of the Sky) was awarded the Grand Prix de l'Afrique Noire.

Elizabeth Steeby, a graduate of the Sally McDonnell Barksdale Honors College at the University of Mississippi, is a student in the Ph.D. program in literature at the University of California at San Diego. She is completing her dissertation "Plantation States," about plantation structures and culture in the post–Reconstruction U.S. South and Caribbean.

Takako Tanaka is professor of English at Nagoya City University, Japan. She has written twenty essays on Faulkner, and a volume in Japanese, *A Study of Faulkner's Fiction 1919–1931: Body and Language* (2002), as well as essays on Arthur Miller, Tennessee Williams, Henry James, and F. Scott Fitzgerald.

Annette Trefzer is associate professor of English at the University of Mississippi. She is the author of *Disturbing Indians: The Archaeology of*

Southern Fiction and the forthcoming *Transculturations: Ethnographic Fictions in the Global South*. She is coeditor of *Reclaiming Native American Identities* and "Global Contexts, Local Literatures: The New Southern Studies," a special issue of *American Literature*.

Index

www.ingramcontent.com/pod-product-compliance
Lightning Source LLC
Chambersburg PA
CBHW030308060726
47498CB00002BB/549